HOW TO WIN

Rugby and Leadership from Twickenham to Tokyo

CLIVE WOODWARD

HOW TO WIN

Rugby and Leadership from Twickenham to Tokyo

HODDER

First published in Great Britain in 2019 by Hodder & Stoughton
An Hachette UK company

This paperback edition published in 2020

1

A CIP catalogue record for this title is available from the British Library

Paperback ISBN 9781529339413
eBook ISBN 9781529339406

Typeset in Fresco by Palimpsest Book Production Limited,
Falkirk, Stirlingshire

Printed and bound in Great Britain by Clays Ltd, Elcograf S.p.A.

Hodder & Stoughton policy is to use papers that are natural, renewable
and recyclable products and made from wood grown in sustainable forests.
The logging and manufacturing processes are expected to conform to the
environmental regulations of the country of origin.

Hodder & Stoughton Ltd
Carmelite House
50 Victoria Embankment
London EC4Y 0DZ

www.hodder.co.uk

CONTENTS

I   **The Rugby World Cup**   1
     The history of a tournament

II   **2003 Revisited**   21
     The story of the day . . .

III **Introduction to Teamship**   33
     Leading the culture of a winning team

IV   **A guide to my coaching terminology**   45

V   **Full-back** (15)   49
     Talent alone is not enough: DNA of a Champion

VI   **Right winger** (14)   63
     Speaking one language

VII **Outside centre** (13)   83
     How to build a winning culture:
     the mindset of a high-performance team

VIII **Inside centre** (12)   111
     Performance behaviours: 3D Learning

IX   **Left winger** (11)   131
     Transparency, innovation and room for the rookie

X   **Fly-half** (10)   153
     How do you want to be remembered?

XI **Scrum-half** (9)   165
    Never stop asking why

XII **No 8** (8)   181
     Thinking correctly under pressure

XIII **Openside flanker** (7)   199
      How do we do it better than anybody else?

XIV **Blindside flanker** (6)   217
     Learning the value of self-control:
     dislocated expectations

XV **Second row** (5)   237
    What makes a great individual?

XVI **Second row** (4)   247
     The Hive Learning model: digitising the process

XVII **Tighthead prop** (3)   265
      The power of sponges and rocks

XVIII **Hooker** (2)   277
       Operational culture: checklists not to-do lists

XIX **Loosehead prop** (1)   289
     Moving beyond number one

XX **Japan Rugby World Cup 2019**   299
    How the World Cup was won

XXI **Japan Rugby World Cup 2019**   325
     The story of the World Cup final

     Acknowledgements   339
     Picture Acknowledgements   341

For Zephie, our first grandchild

CHAPTER I

THE RUGBY WORLD CUP
The history of a tournament

Rugby is a game of contradictions. It is a game that requires power and strength, but is controlled by a web of laws that can bewilder new players. It is a game that finds room for every size and shape, despite ever-increasing collisions and bulking frames. It is a game that demands a complete set of handling skills and footwork, but in which the most valuable player may not even touch the ball. It can necessitate a sledgehammer or a paintbrush. It can be won by the collective muscle of a forty-yard driving maul, or the wizardry of one magic individual. It is, after all, that 'game for thugs played by gentlemen': a sentiment which captures rugby's punishing physicality yet acknowledges the profound respect that binds its players together.

For many, rugby has such an intoxicating appeal that the regular cycle of fixtures punctuates the annual calendar. The Six Nations introduces the arrival of spring. The turning of the autumn leaves means the November Tests are fast approaching. For players, the four-year cycle of a single World Cup tournament can become the defining landmark around which life is navigated. For a few, a single match can transcend the scoreboard and help write the story of their life in a way that could never be predicted.

And so, time and again, the Rugby World Cup has proved for me.

It is a unique and glorious competition that, with each four-year iteration, is proving more intoxicating in its drama, more global in its reach and more compelling in its storylines. If you know anyone involved in the professional game, you will know that life is lived in four-year chapters.

It is this tournament that drives the ebb and flow of the sport itself: the cycle of coaches, the retirement of players, the founding of fresh principles and playing strategy, the changing of laws and tactics, the building of new cultures and the recalibration of any country's ambition. There is no equivalent sporting tournament that is as physically gladiatorial in its combat or in which its players are willing to put so much on the line for victory.

The narrative around sport is riddled with cliché, but rugby is one game that truly earns the language and lexicon of battle. For the winning team, it is seven weeks of high-pressure endurance after years of preparation: an extraordinary assessment of physical resilience and mental aptitude. The ultimate test of leadership.

And yet, the Rugby World Cup remains a tournament in its infancy. The game turned professional in the summer of 1995 and so we have only really witnessed six professional tournaments. The three tournaments from 1987 to 1995 were amateur in name and embryonic in their structure. Since the idea of a World Cup was first put forward, the game has evolved in so many exciting and innovative ways. Each tournament has marked the game's tactical expansion and seen the emergence of new audiences. While the Olympic Games is built on a foundation of celebrated ancient history and a recognised global tradition, the Rugby World Cup has established itself only very recently as one of the world's leading sports tournaments.

I believe, and very much hope, it will grow further still.

The beginnings

The game was never going to be able to compete as a truly international spectacle – commercially or otherwise – without a stellar competition. Even though the Six Nations Championship was born in 1883, albeit in a very different format, it was almost a century before a global rugby competition was established. There were still political rumblings prior to the crucial IRB meeting in 1985, and it was South Africa's decision to support the idea (despite knowing they could not compete for political reasons) that finally tipped the balance.

It is a tournament that has trod a familiar path around the world and has only recently established itself on new shores. The Japan tournament could – and should – catalyse the game to new levels. With greater attention from Asia and America, and more infrastructure for the talented but largely ignored Pacific Island nations, the commercial pull of rugby will surely result in still better players, better competition and better tournaments.

The amateur tournament in 1987 was a very different occasion from the vibrant neon drama of the Japan World Cup thirty-two years later. For starters, there was no qualification process. Instead, the sixteen teams were made up of the seven nations of the International Rugby Board (what has since been renamed World Rugby) and the remaining slots were arranged by invitation only.

That first World Cup boasted a cumulative worldwide audience of 300 million television viewers. It is evidence of the explosion of the game in the professional era that the modern World Cups now comfortably surpass global viewing figures of 4 billion, with more than 60 million people in Japan (half the country's population) tuning in for their quarter-final defeat by South Africa. With gate receipts, broadcasting rights and sponsorship, the sport is reaching new levels and new audiences – something it will have to continue to do if it seeks to cement itself as a truly global sport.

Reflecting now on that 1987 tournament, you get a sense of just how quickly the game has progressed in the subsequent decades. Physically, the players then bear little resemblance to the gargantuan specimens that squeeze into quick-dry Lycra shirts today. Yes, they were athletic, fit and supremely talented sportsmen, but the collisions and impacts, in both the tackle and the breakdown, did not generate the same force. The average rugby player in Japan was two stone heavier than their opposite man would have been in 1987. The games were less structured, and without the Television Match Official – such a familiar accompaniment to matches in the 2019 tournament – the players were less scrupulous when it came to tackle technique and rucking etiquette.

That opening tournament featured many one-sided thrashings and it is in the game's best interests that such imbalanced match-ups are diminishing every four years – even if there is still a disparity of resource and support that World Rugby needs to fix for the good of the game. Similarly, in an era before the rewarding of bonus points for close defeats (fewer than eight points) and prolific attacks (four or more tries scored), there was also less incentive for losing teams to keep fighting in scrappy fixtures.

These were cherished occasions for those players involved, many of whom had to forfeit a mortgage payment just to make an appearance at the tournament or to pay for the flight and accommodation. If you needed an extension built, a new filling or help with a legal dispute, you just had to ask a team-mate! This was a time when players stayed on the field at half-time, with access only to water and oranges, and not even the captain was allowed to speak to the coach during a match.

But the path was soon laid for the global explosion of the modern game.

1987

Hosts: New Zealand and Australia
Winners: New Zealand

I have never been the kind of person who worries about fate or destiny, but the Rugby World Cup has conjured up some unexpected symmetry in my life.

In 1987, I was living in Manly, Sydney, and enjoying the Australian lifestyle when the inaugural Rugby World Cup tournament was launched. As I sat in the stands of the Concord

Oval, watching England play their first ever World Cup fixture, I could never have predicted that I would return to those Antipodean shores exactly sixteen years later in charge of the England team and hell-bent on winning the trophy.

The opponents that day in 1987 were Australia. The tournament came two years after my last game in the England team and I was now a local Sydney resident and playing for Manly Rugby Club. The match was being played in a small 20,000-seater stadium and, bearing in mind this was also the opening match for one of the host nations, I can remember feeling perplexed and infuriated that the stadium was not even full. The sport had not begun to recognise its own potential. For England's second fixture, only 5,000 supporters attended, and the Japanese opposition that day were skilful – showing flashes of ambitious rugby – but unused to such powerful opposition. It is a sign of the game's progress that such an unestablished rugby nation has now hosted a riveting World Cup tournament and become everyone's second-favourite team.

From each World Cup, I have learned valuable lessons that have shaped my understanding of leadership.

Ahead of that first World Cup, I was in a position to offer insight and assistance. It surprised me that I did not hear from anyone involved in the coaching and playing team. By 1987, I had played for England more than twenty times, and been on two Lions tours as a player, but ahead of this first global tournament, nobody thought about asking me for information on opponents, tactics, logistics, accommodation – anything. I was only too willing to help.

At the time, I was captaining Manly and playing against the

likes of Eddie Jones and Michael Cheika at Randwick, who were as fierce and as uncompromising an opposition as you can probably imagine them to be. My club team-mates were in the Australian squad, yet nobody from the England set-up ever approached me. From a coaching perspective, it served as a valuable lesson to me about tapping into the insight available to you; about identifying the knowledge that is of most value and working out how to find it.

In fact, in the end it was the Australians who tried to use me. Alan Jones, the Australia head coach, tried to persuade me to play for the Wallabies! I was playing some of my best rugby for Manly, because we played a quick, expansive, high-tempo brand of the game that suited both my ambition and strengths as a player. A few years earlier, Jones had watched me play a few games for the club and went home to check over the regulations to see if I could qualify for Australia on residency grounds. I ended up going to an Australia training session in Sydney. It was a bizarre feeling. It is not often that an Australian sportsman is rendered mute, but the sight of me warming up alongside the likes of Nick Farr-Jones, Michael Lynagh and David Campese was enough to silence the lot of them.

My other striking memory of that tournament is the celebrated Serge Blanco try against Australia in the semi-finals. I was sitting low down in the corner of the stands with Blanco running right at me and I was within diving distance of the mud where he finally touched down. It was an extraordinary run of play, distinguished by frenetic but skilful French passing, with running lines in every direction and no structure behind the attack. I think just about every player in the team must have passed, popped or offloaded the ball at one point in that attack. It was a magnificent try to watch at first hand, and so typically French in its chaotic beauty. Nobody knew what was going to happen next, certainly not the French players!

But it was ultimately no surprise when New Zealand won that inaugural World Cup. The team of that era included legendary players of the 1980s, led nominally by captain David Kirk, but in a side consisting of the likes of Sean Fitzpatrick, John Kirwan, Grant Fox and Michael Jones. It would lay the foundation for New Zealand's dominance of the modern game and a remarkable run of success.

From that team I learned that World Cup champions need to possess a range of attacking weapons: to be able to choke an opponent out of a game with set-piece dominance and pressure, but strike with skill and precision when the time is right.

1991

Hosts: Home Nations and France
Winners: Australia

Four years later, I learned another important lesson from the 1991 Rugby World Cup. There are England players still haunted by that tournament. The memory can still reduce them to tears.

The pool matches had been defined by England's dominant pack up front, and they had utilised that advantage right up until the final, muscling their way past France and then Scotland in the knockout stages. England were too big and too powerful for any other side. The forward pack was amazing, not only dominant in the set piece, but a real engine around the pitch, supported by good kicking half-backs who could control a game comfortably, especially in terms of territory.

But then – to their infamous cost – they responded to David Campese's teasing mockery.

Campese was a mercurial, maverick player who could ghost a defence with a step and a turn of pace – but he was just as quick with his tongue. In the week before the final, he gave an interview in which, among plenty of other things, he said: 'I wouldn't play for England even if you paid me. Playing that sort of boring stuff is a good way to destroy the image of the game. They're all so scared of losing over here, they won't try anything.'

His words hit home. England came out for the final and tried to play like Australia; Australia came out and played like England. The team had allowed Campese's acerbic soundbites to shift both their mindset and their game plan. They decided to go out and show the world that they could play a fifteen-man game and take on all-singing, all-dancing Australia.

It was a huge lesson for me from a coaching point of view: a lesson in ignoring the soundbites amplified by the media (which is only more relevant in modern World Cups with social media and 24/7 online news); a lesson in staying true to your established playing principles; a lesson in obeying reason not emotion, recognising whose opinions to value and whose to ignore.

Watching that final, I could not believe my eyes. You play to your strengths. You don't get wound up by nonsense.

1995

Hosts: South Africa
Winners: South Africa

On rare occasions, we are privileged enough to witness first-hand sport's capacity to act as an agent for change and the 1995 World Cup will forever be remembered – and cherished – as the tournament that offered some healing and unity to what was a fractured Rainbow Nation.

The Springbok logo had long been viewed as a badge of segregation, but South Africa's task was to find unity among division, regardless of colour, creed and politics. Up until that tournament, South Africa had never played a minute of World Cup rugby because of the ban imposed on them during the apartheid era. While I am usually nervous about mixing sport with politics, here was a tournament that genuinely acted as a force for good.

The unforgettable images of Nelson Mandela climbing the stage in a Springbok jersey and presenting Francois Pienaar with the Webb Ellis trophy is one of the iconic sporting images of the twentieth century, capturing the power of sport to unite. It was a handshake that reverberated around the world, seen by millions who had never watched a game of rugby in their lives, as a political statement of solidarity.

Interestingly, during the tournament, Pienaar and his side remained relatively oblivious to the political weight the tournament was carrying for the nation. He even said that he questions how the team would have coped if they had known what was happening at the time. That was a lesson for me, albeit in a very different context. Managing pressure was to become a core component of my leadership philosophies. In fact, I wanted to find ways not only to cope with pressure, but to thrive under pressure.

This was also the tournament that saw the emergence of Jonah Lomu as the first of a new breed of player, especially in the backline. He possessed a monstrous, hulking physique but had a turn of pace that put the fear of God into opponents (including England!). It is remarkable to think he had only just turned twenty-one (and an impressive 18 st 8 lb). In many respects, his impact on the game brought a revised focus on muscle bulk and explosive power. He scored four tries against England in the semi-final, his first after just seventy seconds, and his infamous wrecking-ball bulldozing of England's defence was eye-watering to watch.

From a coaching perspective, Lomu's performances forced a rethink in tackle technique and defensive strategy. As more and more players took to the field boasting similar physiques over the next decade and beyond – 6 ft 5 in plus and more than 110 kg became normal for back-row players, and then normal for centres, too – the emergence of double-tackling as a whole-team defensive strategy became necessary. The two-man tackle would generally mean the inside man 'chopping' at the ankles of the ball-carrier, and the outside man hitting hard at ball height to arrest momentum and then compete for possession of the ball at the breakdown. England were caught trying to stop Lomu individually and . . . well, you've seen the footage.

Rugby was also on the precipice of professionalism. You knew the game was never going to be the same again.

1999

Hosts: Wales

Winners: Australia

The 1999 World Cup was my first as England coach, but despite working as hard as we could to put ourselves in a strong position, the infrastructure of the RFU meant we took a 'fingers crossed' approach to the tournament. I had been England's first professional head coach for two years, but I was not yet working in a professional environment.

Selection is one of the essential responsibilities for the head coach, and for England's defining pool match against New Zealand, I got it wrong. Jonny Wilkinson was already on the way to becoming one of the best players of a generation, but he had only just turned twenty and had played most of the season at centre. On reflection, selecting Paul Grayson at fly-half, and picking Wilkinson with Jeremy Guscott at the centre, would have given us the right blend of experience, stability and guile. It was a vital lesson for me to learn. World Cups are not a time for experimenting or developing players – as Australia and France learned in Japan – nor are they a time for sentiment.

I remember also that we matched New Zealand physically, but that we had so much to learn about establishing the right mindset. I then over-corrected my mistake by selecting Grayson at fly-half for the quarter-final but not picking Wilkinson at centre. It was another valuable lesson: how often in a Test match do you see a team compound an error by immediately making a second error, trying to 'force a play' or 'fix the outcome' rather than working through a process?

The quarter-final defeat by South Africa was brutal, but the mitigating circumstances made me furious. South Africa had been waiting for us for nine days, while we had a single day to prepare after attritional, violent encounters with Tonga and Fiji. A Test match is a bruising occasion and players need appropriate – and equal – recovery time. This is something that World Rugby organised more fairly in 2019 (arguably one reason why so-called 'tier-two' nations enjoyed their most successful World Cup, with more victories, smaller losing margins and an Asian representative in the quarter-finals).

In that 1999 quarter-final, South Africa fly-half Jannie de Beer kicked five drop goals against us in one game. It certainly ensured we recognised the value of that tactic in keeping the scoreboard ticking over and tightening a grip to control a close match. I would remember that lesson, too . . .

Australia would, of course, go on to win the tournament. Their captain, John Eales, offered a masterclass in communication with the referee during the final, making clear to Andre Watson that he was genuinely worried for the safety of his players because of gouging by the French opposition and that he was willing to walk them off if he felt they were not being protected. By 2003, when Watson would once again referee the World Cup final, our strategy was that Martin Johnson would not speak to the referee at all. Watson was an authoritarian figure who did not like bigger players standing over him, so we used Matt Dawson, masterful communicator that he was, to manage much of that referee dialogue and he did it brilliantly.

My final lesson from that tournament concerned strength and conditioning. We were blown away by New Zealand and South Africa because they were physically better prepared: more powerful and more athletic, especially in the last twenty minutes of matches. I knew we had to match their size and power, but to do so in a way that would never jeopardise our mobility as a team. I wanted power players who were aerobically fitter than any other team on the planet.

I knew I had approximately fifty matches between World Cup cycles to get things right next time.

2003

Hosts: Australia
Winners: England

Flying to Perth on 2 October 2003, everyone on the plane knew that this was a very different World Cup. In fact, it was a unique World Cup for an English sports team: we were number one in the world rankings and favourites with the bookmakers. Such acclaim brings a different set of pressures. But, as the next chapter will tell, we had prepared for this, all the way up to a right-footed drop goal by a left-footed fly-half in the dying seconds of the final . . .

2007

Hosts: France
Winners: South Africa

England were beaten 36-0 in their pool match against South Africa – and then narrowly lost to the same opponents in the final six weeks later. It was not a pretty World Cup campaign, but an impressive one in terms of siege mentality. At times it felt like sheer bloody-mindedness – the collective will of players like Lawrence Dallaglio, Phil Vickery, Jonny Wilkinson and Josh Lewsey – driving them to the final. Their mindset on match day was simply to front up and wrestle victory.

England's set piece was phenomenal, especially their bludgeoning scrum, and the game was being refereed at this World Cup in a way that favoured strong set-piece dominance. It was difficult to compete for turnover ball, and so a reliable set piece brought security of possession.

It is the aftermath of the 2007 World Cup, however, that offers the most significant lesson in terms of leadership and building a winning culture.

The other story of the tournament was the unpredictable French team stunning the All Blacks for a second time in a World Cup. They were 13-3 down in the quarter-final, but they came back to win 20-18 – including 'that' forward pass, which became a source of national mourning in New Zealand. Exiting at the quarter-final stage is unacceptable for the All Blacks and it remains their worst ever showing at a World Cup tournament.

Worse still, having won the inaugural tournament, they had not lifted the trophy for twenty years.

But what they did next transformed New Zealand rugby in the modern era and re-established their sustained dominance in the game (as well as their World Cup record). They launched an uncompromising review of their entire structure and culture as an organisation. It was forthright and unapologetic and it rooted out the issues that had seeped into their high-performance culture: complacency, arrogance, laziness. In light of its findings, they rewrote their standards and expectations at every echelon of the game, from backroom support staff to player behaviour, and they transformed their performances on and off the pitch.

The rules they wrote were accountable and binding, and they started to win World Cups again . . .

2011

Hosts: New Zealand
Winners: New Zealand

From a New Zealand perspective, this victorious tournament in front of adoring home support embodied their rebirth after the inquisition of 2007, and the unfortunate habit they seemed to have developed of peaking between World Cup tournaments, rather than for them. Their re-emergence to dominate the global game came because they modified their culture and set new standards of performance behaviours. The strength of this culture was evidenced by the way they lost Dan Carter - the poster boy of the tournament and one of the most gifted players of his generation – yet the team's record remained unblemished.

Ireland's 'choke' tackle – in which a defender would surround and suffocate an attacker, keeping them on their feet and enforcing a maul and, ultimately, a turnover – became the defensive innovation of the tournament, while Wales lost their semi-final against France by a single point after Sam Warburton's sending-off for a tip-tackle. History was rewritten in 2019, when France had Sébastien Vahaamahina sent off for a maddeningly self-defeating violent elbow on the chin of back row Aaron Wainwright, and it was Wales who won the knockout game by a point.

From an England perspective, it was a dreadful tournament and, from a personal perspective, it was a source of great pain watching it all happen to Martin Johnson. He remains one of the most revered and respected players in the history of the game – let alone English rugby – but he endured a torrid tournament as head coach. He was not given the chance to build sufficient experience – nor did he have the support – to manage an extremely challenging set of circumstances.

Johnson was a dream to coach: he trained hard, then went to bed, on repeat. He was so meticulously brilliant in his attitude and preparation, his only mistake was assuming that everyone else around him would do the same.

2015

Hosts: England
Winners: New Zealand

After six years of working with the British Olympic Association and Team GB in the build-up to the London Olympics of 2012, I knew full well the pressures that a home tournament can bring. While home support can help carry a nation – as we saw so spectacularly in Japan – it can also suffocate. Sadly, at this tournament, England earned a unique record in World Cup history, becoming the only host nation to fail to qualify from their pool.

The England team of 2015 possessed some seriously talented players who would go on to demonstrate in Japan the quality of rugby they were capable of producing. But the whole set-up in 2015 seemed too conservative and inflexible. Without adapting to their opponent, they appeared to use the same tactical blueprint for every game. Flexibility is key and England lacked this vital asset.

But it was not just a poor World Cup from England's perspective: not a single northern-hemisphere team were left in the tournament after the quarter-finals. Thankfully, we were to see a better showing in 2019.

The most treasured moment from the 2015 World Cup was Japan's 'rope-a-dope' 34–32 victory over South Africa, since branded 'The Miracle of Brighton' and turned into a movie. It was one of the great tournament upsets, as unexpected as Western Samoa's 16–13 victory over Wales – in Wales – in 1991, but much more spectacular in its dramatic conclusion. Karne Hesketh crossed in the final seconds of the game against the two-time champions to register Japan's first World Cup victory for twenty-four years. They played such a fast and ferocious brand of rugby, showing the world the dynamic, expansive, eye-catching team that Eddie Jones had helped them become before Jamie Joseph would develop them further still for the next World Cup.

And then, of course, there was that tournament in Japan . . .

CHAPTER II
2003 REVISITED
The story of the day . . .

On arrival in Australia, I reflected on what I had learned from all those previous World Cup tournaments, both as a supporter and as head coach. For starters, the local media were more intent on winding us up than watching us play, but I remembered Campese's words in 1991 and laughed it off as distracting noise.

There was a wonderful mocking front page, published midway through the tournament by the *Sydney Morning Herald*, showing Wilkinson in his familiar pre-kick crouch, going through his focused process, tauntingly captioned 'Is This All You've Got?' Australians are fierce competitors, but from my time at Manly I also know they can be honourable, magnanimous losers, and, after the World Cup final, the same newspaper's front-page apology was both amusing and dignified.

Obviously, the tournament was not only a story about England. It was a tournament in which the Pacific Island nations truly showed flashes of their extraordinary potential to over-achieve with their trademark blend of bulldozing power and deft skill. I also remember the Samoan and South African teams kneeling together in prayer in a symbol of absolute mutual respect after a physical encounter.

But inside the England camp, we were really only worried about one thing: winning.

A World Cup tournament is a long seven weeks after four years of preparation. Time can pass slowly and I knew it was important to stay relaxed and confident. As meticulous as our preparation was – and it really was as professional and method-ical an operation as I have been involved in – there are some things for which you cannot prepare, things that will test your ability to stay rational and focused when the unforeseeable rears its head.

For example: when the world's press swooped in on our final training session ahead of our South African pool match – including TV helicopters and satellite trucks – because of rumours Prince Harry was joining us for a training session; when we found ourselves in a court room in Sydney in front of a discipli-nary committee for accidentally (and very briefly) fielding sixteen men on the pitch against Samoa, at risk of being ejected from the tournament; when opposing teams tried to get the media to bite on ridiculous stories about certain players being too old or too slow; when it transpired that the English media and press journalists had been booked into the same hotel as us in Queensland during a few 'off' days of rest; when we found ourselves being kept awake all night by Australian fans driving past the team hotel and honking their horns – along with the fleet of the Manly Fire Brigade – in an attempt to disrupt our rest. We were certainly tested.

In each of those contexts you rely upon the culture you have established as a group: one based on trust and focused on process. You cannot predict each of these contingencies, but you can plan precisely the methods you will use to counter them. Yes, we knew we were up against one of the tournament's best lineout defences in South Africa, but we backed our system. Yes, we had to employ our resident QC, Richard Smith, but I had already ensured we had his services ahead of the tournament. Yes, we had to take all manner of competitive 'banter' from local fans and oppositions – but none of this was allowed to disrupt our tournament, because we had our own established rules of operation in place. In Perth, Melbourne and – ultimately – Manly in Sydney, I had ensured we had stayed in each of these team hotels on our summer tour, so that everything was familiar and the environment was entirely comfortable for the players to prepare perfectly and excel on the pitch. We knew we had built the platform for a winning campaign.

Our preparation had been focused on the idea of 'head space', about getting your mindset right so that no distractions could cloud your judgement. A small moment that captured that mindset for me was the reaction of our players at the final whistle of the semi-final. It had been a bruising, physical encounter with an undisciplined French team clearly targeting Jonny Wilkinson and trying to intimidate our key playmakers. But at the end of a hard-fought win, and having secured a first World Cup final of the professional era, our players just shook a few French hands and walked straight off the pitch. There were no celebrations in the changing room, either.

Meanwhile, at the end of the other semi-final, Australia did a triumphant lap of honour after beating the All Blacks. I watched that closely and wondered if it offered a clue about their mindset.

And then came the final itself . . .

The calm before the storm

I can tell you very precisely the quietest changing room I have ever been in, even the specific moment. It was at 7.45 p.m. on 22 November 2003 in Sydney's Telstra Stadium: the England changing room fifteen minutes before the kick-off of our World Cup final. There was no need for music or rhetoric, and there was no need for new instruction. The warm-up was over and the only sound was the occasional stud scratching the hard floor. Every man knew exactly what he had to do.

Reflecting now on the day itself, I think it encapsulates the Teamship model of a winning culture. We were a team who knew the intricacies of every process and had every confidence in our preparation.

The day of the World Cup final was just about the longest of my life. I could not sleep with the adrenaline and found myself walking up and down Manly Beach just after sunrise, pondering the day ahead – like so many years before when I first arrived in Sydney back in the 1980s. Early morning is the best time to be on Manly Beach. It is the stillest time, before the wind picks up, the clean waves disappear and the surfers colonise the sand. Only this morning was different because I was mentally rehearsing all the possible scenarios we might encounter over the next fifteen hours, all the obstacles that might obstruct our path to

World Cup Victory – including our last-minute drop-goal routine.

Our first meeting was at 11 a.m. I wanted the players to get as much rest as they could in the circumstances, then eat breakfast in their own time. This was our usual routine, and the last thing you want to do is to disrupt that process. To minimise travel and to preserve energy, we drilled a few lineouts on the pavement outside the hotel, right next to the beach. It caused a bit of a stir with the fans, drawing an excitable crowd, but it was certainly worth the hassle.

The players went off to have some lunch and another rest, but I was wired and, knowing Manly well from my time there in the late 1980s, I decided to go out for lunch. This was a special day and I wanted to feel the atmosphere. I did not want to sit in a dark corner by myself, but to be with family and friends, largely because they would know how to be with me on such a significant occasion. I met them in a café and it was absolutely packed. By this stage of the tournament, Manly had been overrun by England supporters who had travelled a long way from home to support us. As I walked in I was warmly greeted, quickly followed by some confused whispers: 'Why is he here?' 'Shouldn't he be preparing with the team?'

I could answer those questions with two of my own: *Where else would I be? And doing what exactly?*

We were ready for battle. It was still seven hours before kick-off and all I needed to do at this point was keep everyone calm. I still remember that very special hour, the quiet calm in the eye of the storm as we sat on the cusp of achieving everything we had dedicated our lives towards. I had a ham sandwich and a cup of tea with Jayne, Jess, Joe and a few close friends. It was a magic moment, the best way to keep myself calm and focus on methodology.

Again, I knew the i's were dotted and the t's were crossed on the entire operation. There was no point fretting in the team room with no purpose, and I knew that lurking around the hotel and double-checking on management and players, who I knew were doing their jobs, would have been counterproductive and intrusive.

If the only possible net gain in any action is loss-making, then sit still and do not do anything.

The match

Everything ran like clockwork because we had planned it down to the final detail. We had even timed what video footage and what music would be playing on the team coach as we turned into the approach to the stadium for the final two minutes of the ride.

The warm-up was a checklist exercise of meticulous detail and we were raring to go – in absolute silence.

Typically, just before a game, Martin Johnson would lead the team up the tunnel, then stop near the mouth before the players reached the pitch. He would turn around to offer one final emotional appeal or to revise a key message, then the team would run out to the roar of the crowd.

Not this time. This time he stopped, turned around and had nothing to say. He just shook his head. No words would do justice to this moment. This was it. His furrowed brow said it all. Let's just get on with it. It was at times like that when I knew the culture was right. The accuracy of our decision-making, the communication, the composure, the planning – everything had been building to these moments of understated professionalism. The captain was not going to speak for the sake of speaking.

Better was to come at half-time. Our half-time drill was precisely structured and there was space for the captain to speak. On the way back out for the second half, I remember he turned to the room and said: 'We're winning. If everyone does their job properly, we win the second half and we win this game.'

It was a simple message and all that was needed. At moments like that you have to ignore the wider context and reduce the game to its simplest processes, focus on what you have prepared for.

Extra time

When the whistle blew for full time, and we had another twenty minutes to settle this most epic of World Cup finals, I found myself sprinting down to the pitch, racing Australia coach Eddie Jones, who was doing precisely the same thing.

There was one person I wanted to speak to before extra time started, and that was Jonny Wilkinson. He started to head towards the huddle, but decided halfway that he would be better off spending his time keeping his feet moving and practising his penalties. It was entirely his decision to make in the circum-stances – and most certainly the right one – but it just so happened that there was one urgent message I was determined to give him before we kicked off again. I broke from the huddle and made my way over to him.

'Jonny, keep moving but listen up for a second. Now we've brought on Catty [Mike Catt] for Tinds [Mike Tindall], we need to tweak our game plan slightly and begin to play to the corners. We have two kickers.'

He looked at me for a second, and for the first and only time in his entire life, he swore at me.

'No shit, Clive!'

As it turned out, the first penalty we were awarded in extra time, in the 82nd minute, was within a few feet of where Jonny had been practising (and swearing at me!) in the break.

A culture embodied in a winning moment

The lineout at the end of the game remains one of the gutsiest throws – and calls – I have ever seen. It again embodied our Teamship principles, both in terms of Ben Kay's decision (his empowerment and wherewithal to make that call) and Steve Thompson's execution (the precision to throw so accurately under the highest conceivable pressure the sport could create). The easy, expected throw was to Martin Johnson at the front, but Ben saw Lewis Moody unmarked at the back of the lineout. We trusted ourselves because of the Teamship culture that had been nurtured over the past four and more years. In fact, when Ben made the call, you could see Steve's body language say it all: *Thanks for that, mate!*

We called a simple strategy off the lineout: alternate left and right attacks around the fringe of the breakdown that meant we could score a try under the posts – always our primary ambition – or at least maximise the target for any drop-goal attempt by staying in the middle of the pitch. Because the Australian players were intent on charging down any kick by Jonny Wilkinson (understandably, it turns out!), their defence was spread wide and Matt Dawson spotted a pocket of space around the fringe of the breakdown. That extra twenty yards got us within range. In fact, it got us in the perfect position. Next moment, Neil Back was standing at first receiver and communicating to Martin Johnson to carry the ball for another rumble so that Jonny could get set up properly. Everyone was doing their job and everyone was making the same decisions they would on the training paddock at Pennyhill Park and executing with the same accuracy, as if nothing additional was at stake. At the bottom of the ruck, Jason Leonard was sitting on Matt Dunning to stop him getting up to charge down Jonny's kick. Every man was doing his job. Nobody was flustered by the occasion.

Because of the angle, the pass went to Jonny's wrong side, so he had to make the drop goal with his wrong foot, and, as the ball sailed over, my only thought was the next phase and getting an answer from somebody around me: 'How long left? How long left?'

We had spent years with that team working on a framework to manufacture three points when needed. The culture demanded that people should know their roles and also everyone else's roles, so that it was as professional and ruthless a manoeuvre as it could possibly be. Under the ultimate pressure, everybody carried out their roles impeccably. All that hard work, diligence and obsession over the years manifested in a single moment in which we were obliged to put into practice in one passage of play a perfect execution of our drop-goal routine. It was our time.

Taking it all in

After the euphoric celebrations on the pitch, I remember taking a moment of reflection for myself. I was sitting on the floor of the coaches' room in the bowels of the stadium, trying to drink it all in and feeling enormous gratitude towards the players and the coaches around me for the commitment, passion and drive they had consistently demonstrated over the past four years in order to achieve this feat. This moment was the culmination of all our work, on and off the pitch, coming to fruition in perfect synergy.

Interestingly, none of the players or coaches involved in that evening have ever rewatched that final, myself included. For us it remains a first-person experience, wrapped up in the sights, sounds and smells of that stadium on that historic night. Watching it back would bring a sense of detachment. Funnily enough, by never rewatching it, the memories are preserved in crystal clarity, untarnished and uncorrupted by different perspectives and the washing-out of time.

2003 World Cup final team sheet

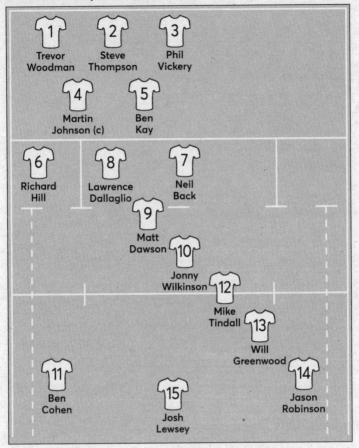

1 Trevor Woodman
2 Steve Thompson
3 Phil Vickery
4 Martin Johnson (c)
5 Ben Kay
6 Richard Hill
8 Lawrence Dallaglio
7 Neil Back
9 Matt Dawson
10 Jonny Wilkinson
12 Mike Tindall
13 Will Greenwood
11 Ben Cohen
15 Josh Lewsey
14 Jason Robinson

Replacements:

16 Dorian West
17 Jason Leonard
    (for Vickery, 80 mins)
18 Martin Corry
19 Lewis Moody
    (for Hill, 93 mins)
20 Kyran Bracken
21 Mike Catt
    (for Tindall, 78 mins)
22 Iain Balshaw
    (for Lewsey, 85 mins)

Squad members (whose attitude and professionalism was an integral component to this victory):

Stuart Abbott

Andy Gomarsall

Paul Grayson

Danny Grewcock

Dan Luger

Mark Regan

Simon Shaw* *(not in original squad but injury replacement for Grewcock)*

Julian White

Joe Worsley

CHAPTER III

INTRODUCTION TO TEAMSHIP

Leading the culture of a winning team

Sport and business have more things in common than you might think. Put aside the operational details of your working life – the specific mechanics of the day-to-day – and you would be surprised at the lack of distinction among high-performing environments. You might imagine an England strength-and-conditioning dead-lift session is markedly different from your 10 a.m. strategy meeting, and of course in the most concrete respects you are right (unless your company operates an unusual meeting protocol). But commerce and sport are essentially about managing outcomes, often in the face of unpredictable competition and market forces, and about taking the necessary steps, through directed strategy and action, to control results. I imagine this part, no matter your expertise or profession, sounds more familiar.

In both contexts, sport and business, bad practice is equally harmful and self-defeating and – much to my continued bewilderment – equally prevalent. One of the ambitions of this book is to provide the necessary guidance to combat this.

Sports fans are a disparate but passionate bunch of people. Professional sport is a broad church whose supporters span a diverse range of cultures, creeds and opinions across the globe. Yet almost all supporters share one trait: they are readily swept up in, and utterly absorbed by, the drama of sporting occasions. Often that narrative serves as an escape from professional pressures closer to home – the boss, the profit margin, the Monday morning briefing, the looming deadline, another all-nighter. But for those on the inside, for 'the man in the arena', to quote Theodore Roosevelt's famous speech, those few men and women responsible for the perfect execution of that performance on match day, winning is not a distraction or a social activity or a leisure pursuit: it is the only acceptable outcome of a lifetime of devotion and investment.

We are not here for the drama. We are here to win.

Sport is business in every sense of the word. And to that end, I believe I was one of the first professional sports coaches to use a business model in my search for excellence – and I believe this underpins the ultimate successes. I worked in business for sixteen years before I became England's first professional rugby coach, and it was what I had learned in that business context that defined my approach to professional sport. For me, circumstances conspired to provide a unique context at the dawn of professionalism in rugby, but there are countless other examples. Maurizio Sarri started coaching in Italy's lower football leagues in his spare time while studying economics and working in a bank. He used his experience in the sector to inform his management of both people and strategy. In his one season at Chelsea, the team finished third in the Premier League and won a European trophy.

The Black Book

The England Squad Handbook soon became known by everyone on the inside simply as the '**Black Book**'. It was produced for every member of the playing and management team, collected in the team room on arrival and returned on departure. By the time of the 2003 World Cup, it had expanded to include seven distinct categories, thirty-five sections, 240 '**Teamship rules**' and more than 10,000 words of text. It was a living document that embodied our professionalism and loyalty, and it served as our guide for every facet of our high-performance operation.

> **Teamship rules:** A set of winning behaviours, rules or principles created, and agreed to, by every member of a team or organisation.

The opening page was written by me and set out the plans for our preparation and principles of coaching leading up to, and during, the 2003 World Cup. As it was a working document, I expected players to have it with them at all times. In it, I made it clear that we were a very good team, but that I wanted us to become a great team.

The opening address outlined the key divisions of the Black Book – Players/Management; Coaching; One Team; Medical/Fitness/ Nutrition; Personal Preparation; Admin/IT – and explained how we had to become specialists in each of these disciplines. In the two years before the tournament, we had instilled the phrase 'Beyond Number One', and it was our goal to be better than any high-performing rival in every key area. Although this would be no guarantee of success, it was a clear statement of what we were about.

But the end of my opening statement had another key message: enjoy.

I wanted the players, and everyone involved in the operation, to recognise the privilege of being a part of this experience. Representing your country – and arriving at a World Cup as favourites – happens only to a select few. This was an incredible opportunity in our chosen profession, and it was an opportunity to enjoy.

This book is an evolution of that opening page: a blueprint for businesses or sports teams to generate their own Black Book and to thrive in their own **winning culture**. The following fifteen chapters constitute the collected philosophy and principles of leadership I have developed during a lifetime working at the heart of elite environments, from the rugby field to the boardroom, and I hope it can serve as an operational manual.

Ultimately, a winning team needs to generate one Black Book for the team and one Black Book for each individual. A rugby team works as a perfect analogy for a business in this way, as each position requires a specific collection of assets necessary for the success of the whole.

A range and diversity of experience

The model of operating that I call '**Teamship**' began decades ago and continues to evolve today among the teams with whom I work in the sports and corporate world. Just as England's Black Book was a living, breathing manual that was always under review and scrutiny, so my attitude to success in business and sport is always developing. My experiences have taken me to two Rugby World

Cups with England. I have led the British and Irish Lions to New Zealand and acted as director of sport at three Olympic Games, culminating in London 2012. I have also run multiple businesses on the threshold of technological innovation, from modernising the professional culture of Xerox in Sydney in the mid-1980s, when social media and fibre-optic broadband was a pipe dream, to digitising communications and operations in a contemporary working context with emerging technologies. I have worked in a multinational corporation, and I run my own businesses today. I list this range of experiences for one very important reason. Each of these environments presented its own unique set of challenges, but I learned from each one and emerged more informed and more committed to the very simple idea upon which this book is based: it is culture that lies at the very heart of success.

Like a rugby team, which can only perform to the level of its constituent parts working as one cohesive unit, this book offers a holistic model of building a winning culture. Once the operation becomes fragmented and individualised, you give your opponents the edge.

I have always striven to excel in worlds where results are everything. I would not champion this model unless I knew it won more rugby games or brought more bottom-line profit. I have never worked in an environment in which establishing and protecting this culture has not brought its own rich rewards, internally and on the global stage.

I should offer a word of warning: success is never an unbroken series of victories. Winning does not happen in straight lines. I have made plenty of mistakes (in my experience, anyone who claims otherwise is being dishonest). I was appointed as the first full-time professional coach of the England rugby team in 1997 and arrived at Twickenham on my first day in the job to find no desk and no office. England were at number six in the IRB World Rankings and had never been ranked higher, nor had they ever beaten a southern-hemisphere side more than twice in a row. I did not inherit a culture geared towards any consistent success – in fact, it was more reliant upon an unpredictable talent pool and a lot of good luck. But I soon learned that if you can get a team of people to commit to a certain set of non-negotiable standards – or **winning behaviours** – then you lay the foundations for success.

Winning cultures in sport and business rely on one and the same question: how do you get people to work collectively together to be as effective as possible?

What is leadership?

According to the Harvard Business School, around 3,500 books on leadership are published every year. I cannot claim to have read every one, but I can say that I have never read a book on the subject that is concerned with the style of leadership I have tried to develop over the past three decades. These conventional books always seem to focus on the leader as the arbiter – and measure – of success. They are inward-looking and, by definition, self-limiting. A real leader looks outwards, to their team and to harnessing the collective potential of their talent pool. This is the first necessity. It is collaborative leadership in its purest form.

The second necessity is passion. I have moved across both sports and businesses and the evidence is overwhelming: the key to driving a winning culture is having an affinity with your product. Whether you are in real estate, Premier League football or microchip technology, whether you are the CFO of a financial conglomerate or you sell forklift trucks, if you have a passion for the subject and an understanding of management, you can lead.

The third necessity is to move beyond tired clichés about leadership. We have long been fascinated by the ideals of leadership. Historical figures from Julius Caesar to Napoleon Bonaparte have been revered and vilified in equal measure. If history really is 'written by the victors', then it is, furthermore, so often written *about* the leaders. Literature, too, seeks to capture the idiosyncrasies of leaders who pursue power in such different (and calamitous) ways. I remember studying Machiavelli's *The Prince* while stuck within the claustrophobic rules of a naval boarding school and, even then, I was convinced there were better, fairer and more effective ways to lead. Some of our most celebrated literature is centred around power-hungry leadership. Consider just the tragedies of Shakespeare and you jump from the paranoid violence of Macbeth to the suffocating jealousy of Othello, from the egotism of Caesar to the lunacy of Lear. They continue to appeal to audiences because they explore power, scheming, in-fighting, control, suspicion, disloyalty – and their leaders are models of what not to do.

Here I seek to offer a different style of leadership for the modern world, one that moves beyond this tired and conventional model of power-hungry despots leading a regime. This is a leadership model that does not undermine the authority of the person in charge but does look to harness the collective investment of every member of the team. Crucially, the style of leader I will propose in this book is not someone who defers power or exposes an organisation to an absence of hierarchy. Instead, a real leader utilises the talents of a company or team in a mutually beneficial way and harnesses their exponential potential. This model does not result in a lack of accountability, nor does it introduce a vacuum of authority. It creates a thriving team that surpasses its potential through its sense of collective control.

Total Business and the Teamship model

I was frustrated as a rugby player. The style of rugby played at the time was very different from how I wanted to play. This was especially true at international level, where England seemed more committed to conservative, tight-five-focused drudgery than any exciting, dynamic, fluid game. Given my experiences, I certainly never envisaged becoming a coach.

But I was inspired to begin coaching rugby by Jim Greenwood's iconic coaching manual, *Total Rugby*, and I was lucky enough to play under him for four years, at Loughborough University, and experience his philosophy at first hand. It remains an amazingly prescient and progressive take on the sport, still applicable in the modern, professional era, and it espouses a dynamic, high-speed, high-octane approach that instantly appealed to me. I had found a book that articulated everything I felt about the game but nobody in England seemed to be interested in at the time, especially its mantra of well-judged risk-taking. The book is now in its sixth edition (I should know – I wrote the foreword to the most recent one!). I still remember the opening sentences:

> The rugby I'm concerned with as a coach is rugby at its most exciting – the fifteen-man handling game, in which every player is equipped to play an active role as attacker, defender, and supporting player, and in which the overall style of play gives him a chance to do so . . . It's where the game's most memorable expression has been found in the past, and where – because of its wide appeal – its future should lie.

In some respects, this book is my own manifesto on 'Total Business': improving individual and team performance to reach the pinnacle. Why not aspire to run a business in a thrilling way in which employees are equipped to play an active role in so many of the company's ventures? The history of successful companies – especially in the digital era – is rife with examples of Greenwood's 'well-judged risk-taking'.

Different positions in a winning culture

Rugby has long been championed as a democratising force in sport because it is 'the game for all shapes and sizes'. Every individual position requires a unique set of skills, knowledge and expertise that collectively help to form a balanced team; the same is true in any successful organisation. This book sets out the attributes necessary for each position on the rugby field and uses these disparate and varied defining traits to explain the relevant Teamship principle embodied by that position.

The following pages, therefore, lay out the inception and development of my Teamship principles and sum up the symbiotic philosophies of a winning culture. While any given company will not be formed of fifteen people, in any great team all these skills need to be covered. The fifteen principles of Teamship that are explored in the following chapters will, I hope, help you to lead the culture of a winning team in any context. In the words of fabled American football coach Vince Lombardi, whose values came to embody something important to the England rugby team: 'Running a football team is no different than running any other kind of organisation – an army, a political party or a business. The principles are the same. The object is to win – to beat the other guy. Maybe that sounds hard or cruel. I don't think it is.' Nor do I.

Motivation and emotion

I will offer one important caveat here: motivation is a fundamental non-negotiable. I have been privileged to work in environments in which I have never had to challenge the motivation of those around me. In this respect, high-performing sports people operate in the same manner as high-performing business people – they are some of the most competitive and driven specimens on the planet. Furthermore, such people tend to exist in a self-selecting, Darwinian environment that will sniff out weakness soon enough. God help an England player who skipped a gym session on Martin Johnson's watch.

But in the changing room before a Test match, I was one of the calmest heads in the room. It was a conscious leadership behaviour and I prided myself on that composure. Quite frankly, if you need a rousing, Churchillian speech to get you in the right frame of mind to face the All Blacks on the hallowed turf of Twickenham – let alone before facing the theatrical wonder of the haka – then you are in the wrong place. In many respects, my job in those moments was to defuse the emotion, to unwind the players, to focus solely on the practical responsibilities of every member of the team: kick-off, position, first job. I would simply talk through the processes of the first five minutes of the game in terms of concrete actions only.

The cost of culture

A final point about finance: a winning culture costs you nothing, but getting it wrong is the most expensive mistake in business.

In 2003, people used to talk about how much money England had compared with other nations. It was nonsense. The thought process, the environment, the innovation, the planning, the culture, Teamship – those things cost you nothing.

And they are priceless.

CHAPTER IV

A GUIDE TO MY COACHING TERMINOLOGY

Throughout this book, you will come across words and sayings I have collected and developed throughout my career. I thought it might be helpful to put them here as a place of reference. I would like, however, to make a few points clear.

First, I don't always get things right. It has taken a lifetime of learning, discovery and endeavour to put together the content that follows, and I hope it will be of some value to you as an 'operational manual' for how to lead and manage a team successfully.

Second, I begin here with a few key terms that you might find useful as you go through the book. They are fundamental pieces of terminology, accrued over decades and across a range of experiences, that have proved invaluable to me in shaping my leadership and management strategies. If you can pick anything out of this book, and even learn from my mistakes, then you may find value in employing this vocabulary and applying it to your own immediate context.

Third, I am not setting out simply to share the details of my rugby-related coaching knowledge, but to focus on how to lead and manage teams in an environment that engenders success. In that way, my ambition is that the lessons learned along the way should be adaptable and relevant to you, whether you work in sport or in business.

Assume nothing: Question everything and operate on the assumption that nothing is too obvious to be forgotten.

Basics: The things you have to get absolutely right in order to be successful.

Beyond number one: Never settling for being the best but always striving to find ways to improve at what you do and set new standards.

Change Thinking!: Taking a different, innovative approach to old problems often assumed to be the way things are.

Copy culture: A culture concerned with imitation over innovation that will consequently always come second.

Critical non-essentials: The components that are not strictly necessary but differentiate you from your competitors and give you the winning edge.

Dislocated expectations: Constantly changing and challenging the way you think and train so that you are prepared for the unexpected.

DNA of a Champion: The key attributes and strengths necessary for maximising talent to its absolute potential in any individual.

'No if only' culture: An organisation that is meticulous in its preparation to ensure there is no possibility of looking back and thinking 'if only'.

One per-centers: Identifying small shifts in behaviour that collectively have a profound impact on performance.

One Team: A unified commitment to the shared goals of a team or organisation ahead of individual ambition or preferences.

Pressure with pressure: Transforming a moment of perceived weakness or vulnerability into an opportunity to attack.

Rocks: People reluctant to absorb new information or learn new skills.

Silo culture: An organisation operating in separate cut-off groups and not unified by communicating or sharing best practice.

Sponges: People always willing to absorb new information and learn new skills.

Success from Setbacks: Using the most challenging or difficult experiences as learning opportunities to inform future success.

Teachability: Your ability to take on knowledge and your passion for what you do.

Teamship rules: A set of winning behaviours, rules or principles created, and agreed to, by every member of a team or organisation.

T-CUP: Thinking correctly under pressure, ensuring that the stakes in any given situation do not affect the quality of performance.

War room: A meeting room designated as the key place in which the most crucial conversations are had and collaborative decisions are made.

Windows and mirrors: Leaders look through the window and praise the team when things go well, but look in the mirror and take the blame when things go badly.

CHAPTER V

FULL-BACK

Talent alone is not enough: DNA of a Champion

'Leadership and learning are indispensable to each other.'

John F. Kennedy

Winning behaviours: The full-back is the ultimate team player: the last line of defence when under greatest pressure, and dynamite in attack when it is time to strike. Whether you are a CEO or a head coach, this is the one player in whom you must have absolute trust. In rugby, the full-back is often physically placed on the pitch behind the line of attack or defence. He or she must have the vision and imagination to use that perspective to inform decision-making and communicate that precisely to those who need to know, with urgency and clarity. Just as the speed of business has been transformed in the digital age, so the necessary skill set of the full-back has evolved in the professional era – as additional creative playmaker, master tactician, flawless kicker and unbreakable defender. He or she is a true champion and recognises that talent only goes as far as the winning behaviours that carry it.

I stood up confidently and headed to the front of the meeting room. One day soon, I would brand this our '**war room**' in the England camp, but these were early days and I was still learning. I looked around the room at relative strangers. They did not know me and I did not yet know them. It was 1997 and I was new in the England job. I had been given an amazing opportunity and I was determined to go for it. Honesty and integrity are essential qualities for any leader and there was nothing I would say behind the back of anyone in this room that I would not be prepared to tell them one-on-one.

War room: A meeting room designated as the key place in which the most crucial conversations are had and collaborative decisions are made.

'We have a lot of talent in this room,' I began. 'Look around for a second. You are the thirty best rugby players in England right now.'

So far, so good. The players visibly relaxed. It was perhaps the comforting complacency they were used to in the England camp at the dawn of the professional era.

'But let me start with some facts,' I continued. 'We have all this talent, all these resources, but what have we actually achieved?'

There was a silence as thick as syrup. I saw two players at the back of the room catch each other's eye. If they cannot deal with facts, how will they deal with criticism?

'We have only beaten the All Blacks once in our history, and do they have more talent than us? We have only beaten South Africa twice in our history, and never on their soil. Do they have more talent than us? We have never beaten Australia on their soil. Do they have more talent than us?

'You have got to have the talent. It is a fundamental requisite. But talent alone is not enough.'

The final sentiment of that speech – 'talent alone is not enough' – is a phrase that came to define and drive so much of my coaching philosophy. What the players needed to recognise – and what any successful team must recognise – is a particular mindset regarding talent. Talent is sitting in every changing room in Test match rugby, in every boardroom in a competitive company. You must have a certain level of talent before you can get through the door. But success comes down to what you do with it: finding the ways to maximise that talent makes the difference for a winning team.

Getting the right talent is your starting position, not your finishing position. Of course you need talent as the raw material, the petrol in the engine, but I see so many sports teams and corporate businesses hire or buy the right people and think their job is done. It is a damaging assumption, one that is guaranteed to turn an expensive risk into a costly mistake. Modern football can offer countless examples of clubs – or at least chief executives – with deep pockets and short-sighted ideas, who splash big money on buying talent and then assume they can just sit back and reap the rewards.

As a leader, I was haunted by these questions: *How do I leverage talent? How do I leverage the individual talent of every member of my team and take them to a new level? How can individuals – and*

51

consequently the teams in which they operate – transform themselves into winners, capable of achieving the extraordinary?

I have spent years pursuing the answer and have come up with the following model: the DNA of a Champion.

I ran the England team by what I learned in business and I have since run businesses by what I learned running the England team. That continual cycle of critical self-reflection and an attitude of relentless learning are just two crucial components of the DNA of anyone who wants to be a champion.

The DNA of a Champion

Champions require a perfect combination of the right attributes: a balanced blend of innate personality traits and behaviours that can be coached to maximise potential.

> **DNA of a Champion:** The key attributes and strengths necessary for maximising talent to its absolute potential in any individual.

Pick a role within your organisation and draw up a detailed list of the necessary skill set. There will be overlap between roles, but in a well-structured organisation no two positions should have equal application.

In the context of modern rugby, an outside centre and an openside flanker are going to share a large range of skills – such as their athleticism and strength as first or second man at the breakdown, either competing for or protecting the ball; or in their dynamic impact as close-contact gain-line ball-carriers – and yet in terms of anatomical strengths and kicking skills, there will be some profound distinctions.

But building champions is a step-by-step process reliant on the application of both the individual and the coach. So how can you build champions in every position?

The first step: Talent

The first level of attainment is Talent. There are certain basic requirements for a champion athlete or business leader. No coach in the world can make an Olympic rowing champion of someone who is less than five feet tall (unless it's the cox!) or, to get technical, with a VO2 max score in the bottom quartile. Without certain essential physiological, muscular and intellectual capabilities, there can be no success at the highest level. As it happens, Sir Steve Redgrave was selected to row by his PE teacher because of the size of his shoes. But so were thousands of others over the years – and none of them won five gold medals at consecutive Olympic Games. Redgrave possessed something else as well: the DNA of a Champion.

In any given organisation or team, talent will already exist. That is a given and it is your starting point. The teams and businesses against which you go head-to-head in competition

DNA OF A CHAMPION

CHARACTER	CRITERIA	COACHING
TALENTED	**TALENT**	SKILL

TALENT ALONE IS NOT ENOUGH

will be full of talented individuals. To achieve real success, you need to reach above the talent line and do more with the ability you have, to detach yourself from those who believe that talent is all that is required. How do you achieve this? By stepping up the ladder and by becoming a Student.

The second step: Student

You need to learn. You need to become a 'sponge', always absorbing information, rather than a 'rock', rooted in the belief that natural

Teachability: Your ability to take on knowledge and your passion for what you do.

ability is sufficient and there is no need for anything else. You have to be able to grow and develop and learn. 'Teachability' is critical in the DNA of a Champion. This is your ability to take on knowledge, prompted by an intrinsic, insatiable passion for what you do. Sir Chris Hoy, Sir Steve Redgrave and Paula Radcliffe arguably knew more about their sport than those who coached them and that is the greatest accolade that you can offer a manager or coach – that they had the ability to pass on knowledge.

DNA OF A CHAMPION		
CHARACTER	CRITERIA	COACHING
STUDENT	**LEARNING**	SPONGE
TALENTED	**TALENT**	SKILL
TALENT ALONE IS NOT ENOUGH		

In effect, each individual has to operate as if they have their own R&D department, and as the coach or manager, your job is to facilitate this. Organisations who do not make learning a fundamental part of their daily habit will not thrive and, in the long term, possibly not survive at all. Businesses who fail to adapt to changing technologies get left behind and face financial ruin. The creative industries, particularly print journalism, continue to reel from the invasive effects of technology on established models of operation that had worked perfectly well until the landscape shifted.

If you are involved in the hiring process in your business, ask yourself this question: *When you hire staff, do you consider the teachability of the applicant?* The Royal Marines have an informal discussion with each group of soldiers before heading out for any combat situation. Their ethos is that every soldier must be able to board a helicopter in complete knowledge that every other soldier within that command has their back. What I learned from the time England spent training with the Marines is that we too were going to war, in a different way. I needed to be as certain of my players and my coaching team as a soldier. We all needed to 'board that helicopter' confident in the knowledge that everyone in the team was the right man for the job. That Marine mindset ensured that nobody in the England squad lacked the attitude, the intellectual curiosity or the desire to maximise their potential.

There is a skill to hiring the right people with the right talent. The American shoe company Zappos introduced two brilliant initiatives to their employment process. The first is that they under-take a cultural-fit interview for prospective employees which carries the same weight as the more typical skills interview.

Secondly, new employees are offered $2,000 tax-free cash-in-hand after their first week of training if they feel that the job is not for them. With such progressive employment initiatives and such an emphasis on building a cohesive culture, and insisting new employees fit into it, it does not surprise me that the company went from single-site start-up to a $1.2 billion sale in a ten-year period.

A taste of true passion

One great privilege of my role at the British Olympic Association (BOA) was the access and insight it gave me into twenty-six separate sporting operations, nearly thirty cultures of elite performance. One sport I have always particularly loved is boxing. The ring offers a raw, claustrophobic, unforgiving assessment of athletic ability in fierce combat. In this regard, it is one of the purest sports in existence, and one of the oldest.

Within the boxing world, Great Britain is known and respected as a country that can produce seriously tough young men and women. On one of my first visits to review and observe Team GB's boxing operation, I vividly remember sitting down with two young men after a sweaty, tempestuous sparring session in which tempers had flared. They were from travelling communities and had not been blessed with the easiest life, but as they unwound the bindings on their wrists and knuckles they transformed from being predatory competitors straight back into having a laugh with each other. They were clearly close friends who trained with the competitive edge of champions. This chameleonic shape-shifting intrigued me, and I was determined to uncover more about them.

I asked them a little about themselves, who they were and where they were from. I didn't get very far. They weren't ready for small talk. But then the subject turned to boxing and they each grew six feet tall. It really was as if I had lit a fuse somewhere inside each of them. I could not stop them talking. Their passion for their discipline, their knowledge of training, fighting techniques, combinations, fights from history – it was all remarkable, genuinely inspiring. The root of the verb 'inspire' is a Latin word meaning to 'breathe or blow into'. The word was originally used of a divine or supernatural being, in the sense of conveying a truth or idea to someone and of breathing life into them. That has never made more sense to me than sitting down with those two lads, feeling inflated by their passion and by their knowledge of the sport that had given them ownership of their lives. I have never forgotten that conversation. They were not students in the traditional sense of that word – and they may not have thrived in a conventional school setting – but within the school of becoming champions, they were stars in the making. They embodied the Student model in the DNA of a Champion.

Cycle of learning

It is important to acknowledge that learning is a constant cycle and process, always in a state of flux: learning, unlearning and relearning. A know-it-all in any organisation can be just as corrosive as a rock. Anyone who assumes they do not need to learn has no place in a winning environment.

The third step: Warrior

The third level of attainment of the DNA of a Champion is the Warrior instinct. Understanding what you are doing and having a passion to do it better is not sufficient. Simply put, the Warrior instinct is the ability to perform at your best when the pressure is at its greatest – Thinking Correctly Under Pressure, T-CUP: an acronym I will explore further in a later chapter.

This again is not something that is merely hardwired. An individual can learn how to deal with pressure – I have seen it and coached it – and a manager's job is to identify those within their organisation who are open to that idea of thriving under pressure. 'I just can't do it' is a defeatist attitude that has no place in a high-performing environment.

I used to call players like Lawrence Dallaglio 'Test-match animals', and it was meant as a huge compliment – he possessed the kind of Warrior instinct that shone when the stakes were highest. It is the same quality that enables an Olympic athlete to perform at their very best when pressure is at its greatest.

DNA OF A CHAMPION		
CHARACTER	CRITERIA	COACHING
WARRIOR	**THINKING**	TCUP
STUDENT	**LEARNING**	SPONGE
TALENTED	**TALENT**	SKILL
TALENT ALONE IS NOT ENOUGH		

The fourth step: Champion

Finally, you have to develop the mindset of a Champion. This requires numerous attributes, including obsession, responsibility, engagement, punctuality, trust, enjoyment, collaboration. You can sit complex psychometric tests to measure these. Consider what a Champion looks like in your environment, whether that's a workplace or a high-performance sports team. The chances are there are a number of core traits shared by all Champions, such as sacrifice, a competitive drive, perseverance in the face of seemingly insurmountable challenges. What is critical is that you understand and work on your own attitude and that of the members of your team. Ben Ryan, a very talented rugby coach that the Rugby Football Union (RFU) could better utilise, became the Fiji sevens coach ahead of the 2016 Olympic Games in Rio de Janeiro. He took a team who were furiously talented but chaotic and inconsistent – and made them Olympic champions. The team mantra is emblematic of the Champion mindset: *The standard you walk past is the standard you become.*

DNA OF A CHAMPION		
CHARACTER	CRITERIA	COACHING
CHAMPION	**HARDWORK**	ATTITUDE
WARRIOR	**THINKING**	TCUP
STUDENT	**LEARNING**	SPONGE
TALENTED	**TALENT**	SKILL
TALENT ALONE IS NOT ENOUGH		

Retaining your Champions

There is one simple way to evaluate the quality and calibre of individuals within your team: if somebody came to you today and said that they were leaving, how would you feel?

You have to look after your best people and ensure they are challenged and want to stay.

Lesson from Japan: Champions of the tournament

Owen Farrell, *fly-half (England)*

If anyone summed up England's approach to the Rugby World Cup, it was their captain. Regardless of the number on his back in Japan, Farrell led his team by example: uncompromisingly physical, tactically flexible, setting relentless standards in every facet of play, refusing to take a step backwards. His younger self had the same level of aggression without the control, but he has matured into a fierce but disciplined competitor, capable of an imposing tackle or a defence-splitting miss-pass on the gain line. The manner in which he shifted positions during the tournament, and the new discipline in his defensive technique, shows his intelligence as a true, obsessive student of the game.

Alun Wyn Jones, *second row (Wales)*

The seasoned veteran did not have a consistently eye-catching tournament in terms of individual performance, but his leadership was exemplary. He is an athlete whose sustained commitment and professionalism has protected the longevity of his career at the highest level. The role he plays for the Wales team is similar to the one played by Martin Johnson in 2003 – a body-on-the-line, do-as-I-do captain. After Sam Warburton's premature retirement, Jones has become the ultimate on-field general for Warren Gatland's gain line-focused, physically imposing playing style. In a Welsh team that ground out victories despite some stuttering performances, Jones's dogged attitude came to embody the team and all its successes in recent history. It must have been heartbreaking for him to end his World Cup career with Wales just one penalty decision away from a place in the final.

Kotaro Matsushima, *wing (Japan)*

Of all the Japanese players who helped engross the host nation in this tournament, it was winger Kotaro Matsushima who embodied the high-octane, high-risk rugby played so wonderfully by Japan and celebrated so triumphantly by their supporters. A former team-mate of Cheslin Kolbe's in South Africa, he brings a similar threat when unleashed in space and an incredible flat-out top speed. His anticipation in reading the game and running support lines, his work rate and energy off the ball, and his deft handling skills in offloading out of contact made him a superstar of the tournament.

Cheslin Kolbe, *wing (South Africa)*

Having graduated to fifteen-a-side from the world sevens circuit, Kolbe was one of the most dangerous players in Japan with ball in hand. Unsurprisingly, he has been compared to Jason Robinson: he possesses the same twin virtues as both an elusive and explosive runner. He can bounce through tackles or rely on the turbocharger to get out of danger, squeezing through impossibly tight spaces. He is a Champion for proving once and for all that even in the modern, power-based game, there is room for smaller players – provided they are technically accurate in their skills and dynamic in their movement.

Christian Leali'ifano, *fly-half (Australia)*

There are some Champion athletes who possess a strength of mind that can defy logic and truly inspire. A few years before the Japan World Cup tournament, Australia fly-half Christian Leali'ifano was suffering from leukaemia. He had to endure two bouts of chemotherapy and a bone marrow transplant to beat the condition. At his lowest point he was too weak to lift his own son. Yet he found the determination and resolve to push his body through a gruelling strength-rehabilitation programme not only to make a full recovery, but to get in the condition of an elite professional rugby player. That is an extraordinary achievement and it makes him a Champion by any measure.

CHAPTER VI

RIGHT WINGER
Speaking one language

'The art of communication is the language of leadership.'

James Humes

Winning behaviours: Consider the dimensions of a rugby pitch and imagine where each player spends the majority of time during any eighty-minute match. Now consider the architectural framework of Twickenham Stadium and what this might mean for a winger, positioned on the flank, lurking on the periphery, biding their time to pounce on an opening or burst on to an inside channel and hunt for the ball. The winger is ultimately exposed and closest to the noise of the crowd. While this position requires pace, speed of thought, reaction and fast footwork, most of all the right winger needs to be a star communicator – it is the only way he or she can stay connected to the team. Perhaps counterintuitively, although physically isolated, the right winger serves the ultimate support function in communication. There is nothing more important in team sport – or in the successful operation of any organisation – than communication. Vocabulary and language play a fundamental role in ensuring cohesion and fluency in any working environment. This position is high-profile and high-performance, as so often at the decisive moment it falls to the winger to execute in the 'red zone' and finish off a team move. The difference between success and failure lies on such tight margins.

Our drop-goal routine came down to a single word. After years of training, strategy, process, repetition, just one word, spoken under the greatest pressure conceivable in professional sport: 'Zigzag'.

It was the only prompt necessary for everyone to know what to do, a routine we had drilled on the training pitch and a scenario we had explored time and again in team meetings. The entire team operating as a fluid and holistic entity, all catalysed by speed of communication.

Our half-time operation was similarly clinical, with the single aim of efficiently communicating simple messages – no overloading of information. I am suspicious of coaches who talk for ten minutes at half-time, going through the intricacies of how the match has unfolded in impossible detail. What is the point in showing off how much you know at that particular moment in time? What is the need for that information? Who are you trying to impress? A winning culture is not about big words. If anything, it is about clarity of meaning conveyed with authority and simplicity. If I cannot communicate to my team what I want out of a training session in one minute of speaking, then something is wrong.

To this end, one of the first key points to make is that when you are starting from scratch, you must have one-on-one meetings in private with every member of your team. Talk to them. You must invest in that time. You must be clear on what you want to get across. The first time my England team walked into the changing rooms at Twickenham, there was a new sign in the home end: WINNING, THAT IS WHY WE ARE HERE. It was a simple reminder, written in simple language, but its impact in communicating a common goal was tangible.

Any teacher will tell you that the first and simplest rule of behaviour management is that you do not tell students what not to do, but you model and reinforce good behaviour. The language you use in the classroom is essential to that, and so is the language you use in your business.

And it cuts both ways. One of the biggest problems in broken businesses is also found in broken teams: working in silence. High-performing teams and high-performing businesses have a common language, a shared understanding. Furthermore, great leaders can detect what's being left unsaid and identify issues that are not being communicated. It's important to find the balance in your organisation between words for the sake of noise and a corrosive, restricting silence.

Communication versus connection

Communication is not the same as connectedness. Successful cultures require meaningful communication, rather than frequent chatter. 'Phatic talk' is a term used by linguists to describe the small talk that takes up so much of everyday life: at the checkout till at the supermarket or in the lift at a hotel. It is the type of communication that fogs up so much of a company's day-to-day operations. We offer social pleasantries, but beyond observing convention and being polite, the conversation is not meaningful.

Without exception, the Champion athletes I have spent time with do not bother with this interaction. They talk when they have something of value to say. When you are working in the velodrome with Chris Hoy, you are not talking about the weather.

Power in the personal

Think about the best and the worst bosses you have worked for. Which of them knew you and your life better? Who could predict your response to professional challenges with greater accuracy? Who had no interest in or knowledge of what happened in your world when you logged off for the night? The author William Hollingsworth Whyte wrote: 'The great enemy of communication is the illusion of it.' The best cultures will find a way in their day-to-day communications to supplant meaningless chatter with meaningful connection.

During the celebrations of the fiftieth anniversary of the moon landings, there was a powerful illustration of this sense of connectedness in a team, a connection that defies even language itself. The flight director of the lunar landing, Gene Kranz, was the man in charge of the final descent and successful safe landing of two men on the moon. His job required him to listen to three separate audio feeds at once, all fed through a single earpiece. Imagine sitting at a desk in an open-plan office, trying to listen to the details of three simultaneous, complex conversations at once. Now add in the pressure of 530 million people watching you do it worldwide. It seems impossible. But Kranz had such intimate knowledge of his team that, rather than listening to the words and substance of each strand of audio, in the most chaotic moments of the landing – and especially in the final thirteen minutes of the *Eagle*'s lunar descent – he was simply listening to the inflections of his team for signs of additional stress or concern.

He knew his team so well that a minor change in their voice would alert him to a possible life-or-death situation.

Making a statement

Actions speak louder than words, of course, but words can define and direct the actions of an organisation. You need a blueprint, a statement of intent, off which to hang your behaviours.

Here is a model from BloombergNEF, a research organisation that specialises in the energy transition away from fossil fuels. Their challenge is significant – half the emissions in the atmosphere today were created in the last thirty years – but they are leading the charge to help industries and countries move to cleaner technologies. The landscape is forever shifting, the market forever evolving. Businesses are recognising that they can no longer divorce themselves from the global concern, especially in the age of climate emergency. Transitioning to a low-carbon future is a dynamic challenge and BloombergNEF needs to align this imperative with objective analysis and an innovative approach to new technologies.

To succeed at BNEF we need people who can work in an independent manner and show initiative to develop their own viewpoints, yet be collaborative with colleagues. We don't rely on the status quo, we look for innovative yet pragmatic thinking that turns big ideas into real insights and impact. Working at BNEF sometimes feels chaotic; we need teams that are both dynamic and structured to generate the unique perspective our clients really value. Our teams are diverse, creative, focused, and fun!

This is an example of the right language capturing the modus operandi of a high-performing environment.

Getting it wrong

The wrong language, on the other hand, can derail your operation and motivate your opponents. Towards the end of England's Black Book, there was a page in which I included quotations from rival players who had unwisely spoken out to the press in an inflammatory way. They included the following examples:

- Andrew Mehrtens, the New Zealand fly-half, writing a year almost to the day ahead of the 2003 World Cup final, said: 'England get a decent win about once every four years at Twickenham. They are pricks to lose to.'
- Imanol Harinordoquy, the imperious France No 8, said of England during the 2003 Six Nations: 'I despise them as much as they despise everybody else. As long as we beat England, I wouldn't mind if we lost every other game in the Six Nations.'
- In June 2003, after England's phenomenal victory in New Zealand despite being reduced to thirteen men, Michael Laws wrote the following in the *Sunday Star Times*: 'The rest of the

pack were simply giant gargoyles, raw-boned, cauliflower-eared monoliths that intimidated and unsettled. When they ran on to the field, it was like watching a tribe of white orcs on steroids. Forget their hardness – has there ever been an uglier forward pack?' The headline was worse: 'White Heat, Black Daze: Gargoyles spit on our pin-up boys.'

- That same month, Australia's scrum-half, George Gregan, said: 'We don't care who wins the Rugby World Cup, as long as it's not England.'

Each of these soundbites served as a reminder of the value of our Teamship principles. In any elite, high-pressure environment, you see people at their strongest and at their weakest. Players, therefore, need to know that they can operate in a safe space without fear that those weak moments are going to appear in a book or on the front pages. I have never seen any organisation fulfil its goals if it does not have the background – and the boundaries of communication – right. Vocabulary is essential here too: the wrong word choice can derail a team.

'Dad's Army' was a label that stuck with the England team in 2003, but we did not mind that in the end.

Language and loyalty

Through language also comes intimacy, and intimacy brings loyalty. Successful communication is about not only words but personal investment. During my time as England coach, most players would come to the house to visit us. First of all, it was useful to have meetings in the privacy of my home. I liked the players to meet Jayne, meet the kids. My idea was that they would be able to make more sense of me. I would always end those visits the same way: 'You now know where I live and where I am. If there is anything you ever need, any time you have something you are worrying about, anything goes wrong, you know where I am. Twenty-four hours a day. I'm not going to hide from you and I'm always going to be honest.'

In my whole time as England coach, seven years in all, I only had four players who needed to come and see me – and never once was it a rugby problem.

Here is something Jason Leonard said in *The Daily Telegraph* ten years after the 2003 World Cup final: 'I always felt I wasn't so much happy for myself but happy for my team-mates. There were certain people around the room that had problems in the couple of years in the lead-up to the final and they had overcome those hurdles. It was a very tight team and still is.'

That, for me, sums up the bonds of a winning culture.

Difficult conversations

Communication regarding selection is always the hardest conversation to have within an elite team environment. Leaders in business will have equally challenging contexts in which to deliver news that can affect lives and livelihoods. There are some essential rules.

1. Wherever possible, always tackle these conversations face-to-face. You should never deliver the worst news via text or email.

The harder the conversation, the more important it is that you face it head-on, in person.

2. Do not make small talk. The person on the opposite side of the table wants to know one thing: whether they are starting against South Africa at the weekend or not. They do not care what you think of the FTSE 100. Get straight to the point.

3. Be honest. People respect honesty more than anything else. They do not want euphemisms to soften the blow. Half the time they are in a daze of disappointment and not even listening to your justifications.

The hardest questions to face are always the same. 'What more do I need to do?' 'How can I get back in the team?' Sometimes they are tough to answer because there is no answer. There is nothing that can be done. Sometimes, however, there is a specific weakness, or the decision is based on tactical requirements (you are picking speed in the front row over muscle mass for a particular strategy, say). In those cases, where possible, you must depersonalise the conflict and explain the evidence for your decisions. Selection is not always an empirical measurement, of course. In the 100 metres, you pick the fastest athlete to represent the team – the clock makes the selection – but team sports are infinitely more nuanced and complex. Selection requires putting together a dynamic blend of attributes to ensure the team is exponentially more powerful than the sum of its parts.

From 1999 to 2003, England went four years – an entire World Cup cycle – without losing at home. The single biggest change in our culture was without question the quality of communication.

Communicating with the media

From my first day in the England job, I was determined to be brutally honest with the media. But, frustratingly, as soon as I was, I was labelled as naive and dismissed as ingenuous. In truth, I was neither of those things. My ambition was simply to be as transparent as possible, never to fudge the issue. In business and in sport, your rivals will respect that more than anything.

At the 2019 Women's Football World Cup, after an incredibly challenging and anarchic quarter-final against Cameroon, during which Cameroon players behaved deplorably in the face of legitimate VAR interventions and a 3-0 defeat (including almost staging a walkout), England manager Phil Neville was statesmanlike.

Within minutes of the final whistle he said the following: 'I came to this World Cup to be successful but also to play a part in making women's football globally more visible, to put on a show that highlights how women's football is improving. But I sat through ninety minutes today and felt ashamed. I'm completely and utterly ashamed of the opposition and their behaviour. I've never seen circumstances like that on a football pitch and I think that kind of behaviour is pretty sad. Think of all those young girls and boys watching. I've got to tell the truth and say that I've never seen behaviour as bad as Cameroon's on a football pitch before. It was like being a kid when you lost and you went home, crying, with the ball. I didn't enjoy the ninety minutes, I just felt sad. I can't gloss over it and fudge it, I have to tell the truth. England players would never behave like that, but if they did, they would never, ever play for England again. I would say to Cameroon, get your ship in order first before you start throwing stones.'

His players would have loved his forthright honesty and un-wavering demand for certain standards of behaviour. He did not mince his words or talk about the quality of training. Managers quickly lose their connection with both players and supporters if they constantly try to say the right things and offer the right soundbite, hiding behind a mask of bland cliché.

The art of deflection

Sometimes it is right not to answer the question. At other times it is important to manage the conversation. One thing I used to do was plant the odd question in order to get the right informa-tion out there. It would always be something I wanted the opposition to read and it meant I could manage the narrative leading up to a big fixture.

I remember sending a text to the *Daily Mail* rugby corres-pondent Peter Jackson ahead of a pre-match press conference in Melbourne in June 2003: 'Jacko, make sure you ask me about the roof!' After a quick briefing, the press conference was opened up to the world's press and – as was typically the way – Peter's hand was the first to rocket into the air.

'Clive, there's a bit of rain forecast. I assume you want the roof of the stadium kept open?' he asked, innocently enough.

I tore into him: 'Why on earth would we want to keep the roof open? We are quicker than Australia, we are more skilful than Australia.'

He just sat there making furious notes and chuckling along quietly to himself, knowing precisely what I was doing. That was a week of stories sorted and nobody was going to ask me about the fitness of key players! We had the roof shut and we beat Australia 25-14, outscoring them by three tries to one. Get on the front foot and control the story. Incidentally, fourteen of those fifteen players would form the starting side for the World Cup final five months later.

Windows and mirrors

As a leader, there is another crucial rule with the media: **windows and mirrors**. When things are going well for the team, you look through the window and praise everyone else. When things go badly for the team, you look in the mirror and blame yourself. The quickest way to lose a dressing room is to get that the wrong way around. The great American college football coach Paul 'Bear' Bryant said this: 'If anything goes bad, I did it. If anything goes semi-good, we did it. If anything goes really good, you did it. That's all it takes to get people to win football games for you.'

> **Windows and mirrors:** Leaders look through the window and praise the team when things go well, but look in the mirror and take the blame when things go badly.

In the 2003 World Cup quarter-final against Wales, Jonny Wilkinson probably had one of his worst games in an England shirt. I fired off another text message and made absolutely sure the first question in the press conference after the game was about him.

'Clive, Jonny had a poor game tonight and France were magnificent against Ireland, thrashing them by more than twenty points, and it was all led by fly-half Frédéric Michalak . . .'

Before he could even finish the question, I jumped in, twisting the story around before any copy was filed.

'Jonny was fantastic tonight. I got it wrong. My preparation was way off and I got the tactics wrong . . .' and off I went, making sure my answers were sufficiently colourful to absorb the attention of the written press.

England's Teamship rules on the media

As an organisation, you need to establish the rules that suit you. We had clear Teamship rules in the Black Book concerning our interaction with the media. For starters, nobody was allowed to 'gift' the opposition any cheap ammunition, especially in the build-up to a Test match. As a high-performing operation, we could not have a thoughtless comment turning into a soundbite that gathered momentum and motivated our opponents. Similarly, I did not want anyone involved in our operation speaking 'off the record'. My ethos was that if we could not stand by our quotes at all times, we looked weak – and if we were worried about being quoted, we should think twice about what we were saying in the first place. Players were briefed to recognise that the press could be critical and, potentially, personal in their hostility or criticisms. The final key idea was one of absolute unity: we must support our team-mates – both players and management – if they were getting any stick from the press.

The power of metaphor and analogy

Rugby players are an intelligent bunch of people. In terms of socio-economic status, they tend to have enjoyed the privilege of a good education. Many Olympians, if not all, are in a similarly fortunate position. That said, they are not necessarily poets and playwrights or avid students of literature. But language is still a phenomenal weapon. Communicating your messages as a leader in a commanding and powerful way is an essential part of establishing and maintaining a thriving culture. This is where creative analogy, metaphor and graphics can be a powerful tool.

We all use figurative language in almost every conversation, often unconsciously. Figurative language – loosely speaking, any non-literal expression, most usually metaphor and simile – is used to capture ideas that seem difficult or impossible to articulate through literal denotation. Asked without warning to describe one of the best moments of your life – to capture the emotional fog of that moment – and you will intuitively reach for simile or metaphor as a means of explaining the feeling. It serves as a map for your audience, providing stepping stones to your meaning. Sportsmen and sportswomen, interviewed on the side of the pitch in the heat of a glorious victory or heart-wrenching defeat, often reach for hyperbole and cliché because they cannot find the right words to literally explain that immediate moment. Hardly surprising, as it is neither their expertise, nor their priority. They are out of breath and out of words.

This is a familiar script:

TV PRESENTER: 'How does it feel to be a world champion?'

CHAMPION 'I can't begin to describe it . . . I don't know what to
say . . .'

TV PRESENTER: 'You must be over the moon.'

CHAMPION 'Yes, absolutely. Wow. I mean . . . Wow.'

We can see the emotion – the intensity of relief, joy, elation, bewilderment – in their tears, in the muscles on their cheeks, in their broken words, but we cannot necessarily connect with it through their words.

I have learned two essential lessons in my time as regards effective communication. The first is that analogy and metaphor can be incredibly powerful tools. When we turned our team meeting room into the 'War Room', that change in vocabulary, that shift in register, was more than sentiment or 'boys playing games'; it embodied a shift in mindset about our attitude and the seriousness of our ambitions. The language denoted our purpose and sharpened our minds.

The power of graphics

The second lesson is the power of the visual aid: graphics, charts, colour. The human brain can process visual stimuli up to 60,000 times faster than the same information being conveyed through prose. Capturing a single key performance indicator in a team meeting with a powerful single graphic – bar chart, pie chart, touch map – is demonstrably more impactful than shouting at your front row for losing three scrums against the head. Not only can you transmit the content or message faster, but it sticks in the long-term memory, enhances comprehension and can even trigger a more visceral emotional response. With that emotional response comes a more intense reaction, and a more sustained commitment to change.

This is not to overload your team with data. You want to achieve quite the opposite. Your job as leader is to select the crucial detail and illustrate this in a memorable way that captures everyone's imagination and aligns the team towards the same new target. We developed seven disciplines and created seven graphics that became visual aids that embodied these seven winning disciplines (see 12: Inside Centre).

Finally, a sense of theatre can be a profoundly powerful communication tool. In the early 2000s we built two towers of scaffolding at either end of the training pitch at our training base in Pennyhill Park so that the coaching team could gain different perspectives on our attacking and defensive shapes – but these also provided another purpose. Tony Biscombe and his team filmed everything we did so that we could put together a video for our final team meeting. The video – edited brilliantly with graphic effects and tailored soundtracks – encapsulated the tone of the week and captured the the most important things that had been learnt. It quickly became one of our traditions – and is now widely practised – but at the time I had simply wanted to bring in the best use of technologies I had seen at successful business conferences.

Breaking the tension

In our final team meeting before a Test match, I would turn to a flip chart displaying the head-to-head line-up of the two teams and the key contests. The overriding message had to be that there was nobody in the opposition you would want in your team. I used to call it my 'key match-ups'.

There was one team meeting, ahead of a Test match against New Zealand, that stands out. Having run through almost all the positions, one of the last match-ups was Austin Healey playing on the wing opposite Jonah Lomu. I was about to ask the usual question: 'Which dressing room would you rather be in?'

From the back of the room Will Greenwood shouted out, 'Sorry to interrupt, Clive, but I'd swap Austin for Lomu!'

The room erupted in laughter. They were close friends, so I knew it was a joke meant absolutely in the right way. It certainly helped break the tension the night before one of our biggest games.

Lesson from Japan: Managing communication

Eddie Jones employed very clear rules of engagement at the Rugby World Cup in Japan: manage the story. It was a masterful campaign, carefully strategised to distract the world's attention away from injury concerns or surprise selection calls. Top-class professionals never let external noise get the better of them, and his players would have been grateful for this strategy – and occasionally amused by its content.

The public media sparring between Jones and Australia coach Michael Cheika ahead of their quarter-final, Jones's contrived (and carefully selected) 'swipes' at the opponents' press, the disclosure of a mystery figure spying on England's training in the week before their semi-final victory over New Zealand – it was all choreographed to ensure that his players were left to prepare for the next game in the way they wanted. After two World Cups of intense scrutiny of player behaviour, Jones stole the attention.

Open communication is also an essential requirement for the integrity of the game and I was surprised by World Rugby's regulation at this tournament that prevented coaches from meeting with the referee before a match. Refereeing is fundamentally about communication and transparency. These meetings present an opportunity to ask questions so that a coach has clarity – each referee has particular idiosyncrasies regarding the timing or binding of scrum engagement, for example – but also a chance to explain your own tactical ambitions. If you believe that the opponents have a weak defensive blindside winger and you want your No 8 and scrum-half to target the blindside off the base of a scrum, then you want the referee to know, so that his positioning does not interfere with the plan.

By shutting down that transparent communication between coach and referee, you cast any dialogue under suspicion. What if a coach sees the referee on the way into the stadium or around the team hotel? By shutting off these conversations you are inviting mistrust, when instead rugby should pride itself on that relationship.

A referee's interpretation of the laws has an enormous impact on the quality of a Test match. The more prepared they can be through open dialogue, the better they are going to be.

CHAPTER VII

OUTSIDE CENTRE

How to build a winning culture: the mindset of a high-performance team

'If you don't believe in yourself, why is anyone else going to believe in you?'

Tom Brady

Winning behaviours: In many respects, outside centre is the most challenging position on the pitch, requiring the execution of the very highest attacking and defensive skills under intense pressure. The outside centre must have the vision to see space beyond the immediate chaos, command real tactical knowledge and possess fearlessness at the breakdown. The performance of the outside centre is reliant on the service of those around him or her in the team. It is a position that requires both sledgehammer and chisel: a capacity for flexibility and adaptability. The mindset and preparation must be flawless, and therefore this pivotal position embodies the culture of the entire team. You do not win the biggest Test matches unless your outside centre is dominant. If this player becomes isolated, their involvement fragmented, then the team breaks down and victory is lost.

I walked out of the team room to complete silence. The twenty-five best rugby players in England were left inside, sitting around the dark wooden table. They did not know what to think. For a while, nobody spoke. As for me, I thought the question was simple enough.

'How do you define time?'

Let me explain what I meant by this question and precisely why I asked it.

First of all, I was not interested in Martin Johnson's take on ancient philosophy. As intelligent as he is, I do not believe he has strong feelings about what Plato wrote about the concept of time. But what I did know is that unless we, as a team, agreed on how we would define time – and therefore the rules around punctuality by which we would operate – then we would not work as cohesively, ergonomically or efficiently as we should.

I started with time very intentionally. I believe that time says more about an individual, or a group of people, than anything else. There is no commodity and no resource more intrinsically valuable than time. How can you work with anyone who does not understand the importance of time?

This first question – *how do you define time?* – became the foundation of our Teamship principles: a collection of winning behaviours, generated in collaboration and in complete agreement with every member of the team, management as well as players. Whether you were the head chef or the rookie fly-half, these were the rules you lived by.

This is not about an obsession with rules. I ran away from naval boarding school because I hated the rules. I was not empowered by the system, or listened to, or involved in any sense. My voice did not matter. As a consequence, I felt no loyalty, no sense of belonging.

Avoid imitations

Never create a '**copy culture**'. One thing that drove me crazy during my time as an England player in the 1980s was constantly being shown footage of the All Blacks or the Springboks, always followed by the same blinkered instruction: *Let's try this!* If your operation is simply engineered towards the imitation of others, you will only ever come second.

> **Copy culture:** A culture concerned with imitation over innovation that will consequently always come second.

I am often asked what model of management I followed in building the England team of 2003, but the honest answer is we created our own model. We started with a blank piece of paper. We did not want to be a poor copy of the All Blacks. If we operated in similar ways in various elements of our play or preparation, that is because we reached that conclusion rationally and empirically, through experiment and through trial and error. Incidentally, when I first started coaching in the 1980s, it seemed that every single rugby coaching book was written by a Kiwi. I wanted to write the England book.

Collaborative rule-making

Individuals and teams perform exponentially better if their culture and environment is matched to their development and the goals they seek to achieve. This winning culture is the necessary mindset of a high-performance team. Weak links will bring about failure and destroy trust. It is each individual's responsibility, as part of the team in which they operate, to ensure they perform to the highest possible standards. In war, there are rules of engagement; in sport and business, there is a need for the same.

Some of the best businesses I have seen operate over the past twenty years treat their employees like highly trained athletes in the way they manage their culture. Professional sportsmen and sportswomen thrive in an environment of open minds, frank discussion and complete confidentiality – and these are the most essential foundations that you need to lay if you hope to build a winning organisation.

The first step is to ask your team to discuss whatever subject you are going to be dealing with. Not only should they do this without your input but, better still, without you in the room. In my example above, I asked the team to get 100 per cent agreement on their definition of time before I returned to the room.

The crucial caveat is that the leader does not give up any

autonomy. This kind of leadership is not about delegating authority but about empowering the team to be a part of its strategy and direction. Teamship rules require 100 per cent agreement, but if I, as leader, do not agree with them, we go back to the drawing board and start again. Similarly, anyone in the room has the right to challenge a rule. They just have to make sure they follow the proper procedure.

There was another way to think about time. With England, I quickly realised it was going to take far longer to make progress as a professional sports team than it would as a business because I only had access to the players for fifty-one days a year – and that included Test matches. Time was a scarce resource that had to be utilised with absolute efficiency. We needed to fast-track our cultural development.

England's Teamship rules on time

We began to generate the Black Book long before 2003. It was the blueprint for our winning culture and contained every one of our Teamship rules. The first standard regarding time was very simple: punctuality was essential. In fact, the players came up with an idea called 'Lombardi time', which meant being ten minutes early and ready to start whenever on England duty.

This is what the team had come up with when I was out of the room – and I loved it. As an American football coach, Vince Lombardi was celebrated for his relentless pursuit of off-field standards. In his own words: 'Winning is not a sometime thing; it's an all the time thing. You don't win once in a while; you don't do things right once in a while; you do them right all of the time. Winning is a habit. Unfortunately, so is losing.'

Habits set standards of behaviour and slipping standards have an insidious impact on performance. Discipline with timekeeping is a non-negotiable. This was a tiny but essential moment in our evolution as a winning culture. Do not lose sight of the fundamental difference here between respect and deference; once the Teamship rule is signed off, it becomes sacrosanct.

The Teamship model

Leadership in a winning culture should be far away from a dictatorial 'I know best' approach. Such an antiquated attitude is self-limiting, self-defeating and, essentially, beatable. It's also alarming how many business leaders seem to think their team or employees should be able to intuit the rules under which they are expected to work and behave without ever being told. Any opponent who has even done the most superficial collaboration in their preparation will easily defeat a lone leader. Instead, the leader of a winning culture works tirelessly to ensure they have 'the right people on the bus' and then, most importantly, that they are 'sitting in the right seats', and trusts them to get on with the job. It empowers people, stretches people and – without exception – brings out the best in them. It is no good having fantastic talent at your disposal and picking them in the wrong position.

You allow people to make mistakes, but ensure they are not repeated. This empowers individuals to take ownership of performance, which encourages the creation and development of leaders

England captain Will Carling cuts a dejected figure after losing the 1991 final to Australia.

South African president Nelson Mandela hands Francois Pienaar the Webb Ellis trophy in 1995.

New Zealand's Michael Jones sprints round the French defence at the 1987 inaugural tournament in which the All Blacks would go on to become the first champions.

England's Jason Robinson is scrag-tackled by Scotland in an old-fashioned baggy shirt during the 2001 Six Nations before the kit was redesigned.

South Africa fly-half Jannie de Beer kicked five drop goals to end England's campaign in 1999.

In the 2003 World Cup quarter-final Robinson slices through the Wales defence in a skin-tight shirt that prevents tacklers getting any grip on loose fabric.

Captain Martin Johnson, leading by example, charges through a gap during the World Cup final.

Jonny Wilkinson kicks his iconic winning drop goal with the score at 17–17, deep in extra time.

The team savour the feeling of being crowned World Cup champions straight after the ceremony.

This disastrous Olympic dive from the previously unbeaten Chinese synchronised pair captures the importance of T-CUP.

England wing Mark Cueto was ruled to have put a toe in touch by the TMO in the 2007 final against South Africa.

Wales captain Sam Warburton was sent off for this tip-tackle during their one-point semi-final defeat in 2011.

Brian O'Driscoll leads Ireland's effective choke tackle technique at the New Zealand World Cup.

Japan's Karne Hesketh dives to beat South Africa after the buzzer in a 2015 match dubbed 'The Miracle of Brighton'.

Wales scrum-half Gareth Davies snipes an intercept try against Australia in their 25–29 pool-stage victory in Japan.

Japan winger Kotaro Matsushima would quickly become one of the stars of the 2019 tournament.

Owen Farrell was on the receiving end of a poor challenge in England's win over Argentina.

Springbok winger Cheslin Kolbe was one of the smallest but most explosive ball-carriers in Japan.

Fly-half Johnny Sexton stretches over the line in Ireland's 47–5 victory over Samoa.

within the team. You end up with a group of leaders, whose combined expertise makes the team immeasurably more powerful than a single, inward-looking commander at the top.

I have seen too many excellent sporting teams – and business operations – failing because of a lack of understanding of how to work effectively. The leader's job is to identify the areas of the organisation that are critical to success, but then it is vital that the people responsible for acting in these areas should establish their own standards. This Teamship model allows a leader to lead in a totally different way, by letting a team set their own standards: our rules, our standards, put in place by the team, signed off by the leader.

How to begin

To get the process right, you start with the easy things. *What is our institutional attitude to punctuality? What are the consequences of getting to a meeting late – for the individual and for the team? What is our attitude to dress and appearance?* When I was first in charge of England, this collaborative and mutual generation of principles was especially necessary if you consider the unique context of a national sports team: I was running a business with no employees, because the players were contracted to their clubs. Therefore, it was critical to create our own identity.

Once you have agreed collaboratively to those essentials, you can move on to much more interesting and complex ideas, such as diversity and inclusion, harassment – difficult topics about which a successful culture must have a clear and documented policy. There is a celebrated saying: 'If you want to go fast, go alone. If you want to go further, go together.'

The following mantra has proved successful in every business or sporting context in which I have worked: *Tell me and I'll forget, show me and I may remember, involve me and I will deliver.* The Teamship process is about involvement from start to finish. The rules only work if you have absolute investment from all parties. I reiterated our Teamship very clearly in the 2003 Black Book. I defined it then as the values and mindset which allow high-performance teams to flourish. It listed the necessary behaviours within an operational culture that empower individuals to take ownership of their own performance, working within a group that values honesty, transparency, efficiency and enjoyment. Peer pressure is often used as a pejorative term with negative connotations. I explained that we were going to subvert that norm and harness peer pressure in developing a sense of team spirit and identity.

I wanted us all to work together as 'One Team'. There could be no great England team unless every individual component played their part, so we functioned as a holistic, cogent entity. I wrote at the time that although the ideas of Leadership were well established and well understood, Teamship was a foreign concept outside of this England team. And it was this that would make us a winning culture.

Where other teams – full of talented individuals and with all the requisite resources to excel – had failed, we would operate as 'One Team'. From here, it would be the basis of how we operated.

I remain convinced that our outstanding commitment to

Teamship principles provided the foundation of our 2003 success. It was our greatest strength and sustained our performances over a period of time. The rules were never formalised until they had been discussed and agreed to by all parties concerned: players, management, coaching, fitness/nutrition, medical, IT and admin. Nothing went into the Teamship Rules unless it had complete agreement. Similarly, the rules were open to constant review and revision.

The document was then signed by Martin Johnson on behalf of the players, and by me on behalf of the management. It can be described as the blueprint for how we worked together as a team, or as the collective standard of behaviour understood by everyone in the team environment. It was our operational manual.

Actions not behaviours

Here is the most crucial rule of all: Teamship is not about values, but a list of actions or behaviours. You need a team ethos, of course. That is your starting point: *What is our collective attitude about* x? But this philosophy then has to be drilled down into individual agency. It must be accountable; it must be practical; it must be measurable. Anybody is welcome to say no. In fact, I was always more interested in those who said no rather than yes because they might be right and we, as a team, might be on the brink of a different and innovative approach.

This process of collaborative creation also ensures that the leader's vision and the organisation's strategy are completely aligned and, furthermore, that operation is centred around action and behaviour, rather than abstract nouns and values. That reciprocity between leader and team becomes the most extraordinarily powerful asset in your organisation: complicity over coercion.

It is also a precious culture to be a part of. When unseen people – the backroom staff supporting the few who earn the accolades, the tireless juniors crunching the numbers to ensure the sums are correct for the next big pitch – are sacrificing everything and working selflessly with the courage to risk everything and daring to dream, that is when you know you have established a winning culture.

Fast-tracking

It is essential to record these rules for a number of reasons. Documenting this process ensures that any new member of a team can be instantly educated in the fundamental expectations of the culture.

When a new England player arrived at Pennyhill Park for duty for the first time, I welcomed him at the door and then sent him to the team room with the Black Book to read from cover to cover. Because everything was documented, new team members could be fast-tracked. They knew before their first training session precisely what was expected of them.

An evolving process

Values are your starting point, but it is actions that bring these to life and make the difference to your culture. In 2007, the RFU established a task force to identify and articulate rugby's core values. They identified five principles which lie at the heart of the game in England: Teamwork, Discipline, Enjoyment, Sportsmanship and Respect. The problem was that these values were never consolidated with measurable actions and behaviours at every level of the game. There was no sense of Teamship.

You cannot start the Teamship process in a room with 2,500 employees, or 250,000 employees. If, for example, you are dealing with a multinational corporate, you start with, say, your sixteen-person team in the Japan office. They then share the best ideas and suddenly the creation of a winning culture becomes a collaborative process. Better still, you share these ideas with your clients around the world. As the process expands, any employee can put forward a Teamship rule within the community of colleagues (in a later chapter I will illustrate the power of modern technology to this end).

The cementing of a Teamship rule goes as follows: 'I need your support on this. If you don't agree, tell me why. But if you can't tell me a better way of doing it, it sticks.' If anyone disagrees, they have to come up with a credible alternative. Some players I will forever remember for their sheer fearlessness. Others for their inventiveness. Martin Johnson for his willingness to experiment. His response was always the same: 'Let's get on with it.'

Testing your culture

The value and power of Teamship proves even more essential when things do not go your way. I will never forget announcing the 2003 World Cup final squad. That single moment in my most important team meeting illustrates the brutally binary world of elite sport. Think about this: fifteen of the players in the room are about to get the best news of their professional lives. Seven are going to be told they are on the bench, but they are at least involved in a World Cup final – they might feel disappointed at not starting, but they are still putting on a World Cup final England shirt and have their place in history. Eight men in that room are being given the worst news of their professional lives. They have no place in the match-day squad. Better yet, the world's press are waiting outside, desperate for a soundbite insulting the England rugby coach.

Walking into that team meeting in the War Room of the Manly Pacific Beach Hotel on 19 November 2003, I knew one thing: how those eight players reacted to that news could define whether we were capable of winning the World Cup.

But I also knew one other thing. The strength of our Teamship rules came from being built on a foundation of loyalty and collective investment. The players had always known that I regarded selection as one of the most important responsibilities of the head coach, and that decisions would never be taken lightly, or without full and fair reflection and discussion. Players also knew that my established selection criteria had a clear emphasis on three ideas: form, fairness and the irrelevance of age (old or young).

There were three rules on selection in the Black Book. Firstly, any player not selected had to immediately congratulate the team-mate selected ahead of him with a hand-shake in the team room, no matter how challenging or painful that might seem.

This would engender fundamental respect for the team ahead of individual upset. Secondly, selected players were expected to publicly recognise the role of the whole squad at all times. The final rule was that any discussions about selection issues must be done privately with me at the appropriate time.

I also held myself to certain standards of behaviour regarding selection. Whenever possible, I always communicated the bad news to the disappointed players twenty-four hours before I made any official announcement, only failing to do so when timings made it impossible.

On the day, the reaction of those eight players did not surprise me, but I still feel enormously proud of them and grateful to them. Their dignity in the face of devastating news, and their loyalty in ensuring the twenty-two players involved were as well prepared as they could possibly be, catalysed our performance in the final.

Wind the clock back four years and that had not always been the case. Before we had properly built our Teamship winning culture, England were exposed to breaches of discipline that completely undermined the shared ambition of the entire set-up. After the 1999 World Cup, one player wrote a highly critical book. I was already down after the tournament – and then that happened. You see a headline like that and it stings. That same player has since become a very good coach. He called me a few years later to say he totally understands it now. As a head coach, with players talking to the press every week, he now recognises the need for these rules.

Incidents like this proved to me that I needed 100 per cent

investment. It could never work if even one individual felt they could go away and write whatever they wanted about that environment – there could never be trust.

Using your judgement

The creation of Teamship rules is a painstaking process. I am not necessarily the best coach in the world at generating new ideas, but I pride myself on being able to recognise good ideas and, furthermore, putting the necessary mechanism in place to make them happen, quickly and efficiently. Leadership is about listening to ideas, recognising the good ideas and making the right decisions to make them happen. That is my skill set.

The seven steps to winning

I have found success in sport by applying business principles to the management of professional sports teams. Here is a summary of the seven processes that generate a winning culture:

1. Set the vision, inspire the team
What is your most ambitious end goal? Break down that vision into the constituent parts necessary for its achievement. I needed a team with the same level of ambition and the same level of excitement about our potential.

2. Design the experience that supports your goal
Create a culture that nourishes this vision. Don't accept the

existing modus operandi of the organisation or team, but design one specifically to match what it is you seek to achieve.

3. Build an infrastructure of effective systems in the core parts of your business

Establish your world-class performance standards in each area to ensure you can measure and manage your progress. For the England rugby team the areas were Leadership, Coaching, Fitness/Nutrition, Psychology, Medical/Recovery, Analysis/IT and Management. After 1999, I ensured I hired the right coaching team, absolute experts in the game such as Andy Robinson, Phil Larder and Dave Alred.

4. Lay the foundation for a strong elite team culture

This is where you collaboratively build your Teamship principles, so that everyone is fully invested in a 'this is how we do it here' philosophy. It is a living, breathing, dynamic part of your organisation. But it is also a framework that is open to continued improvement, development and evolution.

5. Think: Mindset

Ensure the attitude and mindset is spot on at every level of the organisation. Identify and remove energy sappers and rocks. They have no place in a winning culture.

6. Plan: Organisation

Leave nothing to chance, but try everything. Prepare carefully for any new initiative and implement it in good faith – but do not pursue a lost cause. In the early days of England rugby, for every one impactful idea, nine were ultimately inefficient or 'loss-making' to our culture.

7. Do: Coaching/Playing

Within the cycle of your business or operation, identify when you can implement and experiment with revolutionary and progressive ideas, and when you cannot afford to destabilise your operation. Draw this up on a calendar and plan your research and development operational phases.

Starting with the basics

The first building blocks are your **basics**. These are so often overlooked. A business has to understand what its basics are. I would define them very simply as follows: 'What are the things we have to get absolutely right in order to be successful?' When I started with England, I did not fully understand that. Once you know your basics, you hire the very best people you can to look after them. That's why I had a coach whose fundamental job was to ensure that England had the best scrum in the world.

> **Basics:** The things you have to get absolutely right in order to be successful.

When golfers walk the course, they fret over their swing for eighteen consecutive holes, worry about the wind direction, waste an age stressing about club selection; but the fundamental basic in golf is your set-up. It should be the only consistency for every shot you make. Yet the vast majority of amateur – and professional – golfers regularly forget to prioritise this absolute basic of the game.

If I walked into your place of work tomorrow and asked everyone what their basics were, could everyone answer? More tellingly still, would everyone's answer be the same?

Sometimes you need to step away to get some perspective. Teamship comes from working 95 per cent *in* the business and 5 per cent *on* the business. Successful business people are obsessives. You may be driven, you may be working at full capacity and at all hours of the day. But you need to step away for 5 per cent of the week and find a couple of hours to think strategically. Come up for air and get some space. Get out of the office and ask yourself: *What else could I be doing to make the team do this even better?* You may think you do not have the time, but I promise you this: one day soon, your competitors will do this and they will beat you.

I would make this the first provision in a contract, especially at the start of any new coaching relationship. It will only work if you have 5 per cent of every week protected for the space to conceptualise your strategy. Without it you – and therefore your business – will become dull and predictable.

Building with critical non-essentials

Once you have established your basics and collaboratively agreed your Teamship principles, it is time to explore one final question: what are your **critical non-essentials**?

> **Critical non-essentials:** The components that are not strictly necessary but differentiate you from your competitors and give you the winning edge.

When I was working for Xerox in Sydney in the 1980s, I heard about a dentist who was changing dentistry. While I had no interest in retraining, or swapping gum shields for gum plaque, I was very interested in finding out what it was that he was doing.

Dr Paddi Lund's story was a simple one. A few years previously, he had been unbelievably unhappy and found himself in a dark place. He hated being a dentist but he could not afford to retrain. One morning, he decided to go for a walk and think through his business and his life. He made a list of priorities and his number one was that he and his staff should enjoy the job.

So he came up with a list of the critical non-essentials he needed to put in place to make sure that happened. The first thing he did was write to his patients. Eighty per cent of his clients received Letter No 1. It was a very frank and forthright summary of his feelings: *Because of you I was close to the brink. Please do not come back to my practice. Find another dentist.* The recipients were not selected at random. He painstakingly went through his database and made a note of anyone who was consistently rude or late or who had upset him. That process enlightened him to a brutal truth – those customers were making his life miserable.

But that was not true of all of them. Letter No 2 was sent to the remaining 20 per cent and it contained a very different message: *You are a valued and delightful client, I would love to continue to be your dentist.*

What a statement! What courage. It was not easy to become a patient because you had to be referred by an existing client.

When you arrived for an appointment, the door was locked and you had to ring a bell. If you think that sounds unwel-coming, you have missed the point – the entire idea was to make sure you were personally welcomed on arrival. When you are invited to a friend's house for dinner, you do not just let yourself through the front door. You ring the doorbell and are greeted with a smile.

His second rule was that if you arrived a moment late for your appointment, you did not get treated. You could come in and enjoy the books – and he would still bill you, of course – but if you lacked the courtesy to be punctual, implying that your time was more important than his, then you forfeited the right to be seen by him. It is one way to ensure nobody is ever late!

Those who were on time, however, got to enjoy a happiness half-hour. You could eat and drink in the waiting room and make yourself at home. While everyone else who is off to the dentist flosses in the bathroom mirror until their gums bleed – here you were handed a bacon sandwich and a coffee. Now, if he had been a useless dentist, none of this would have mattered. But he was excellent and people wanted him to look after their teeth. With those essential basics in place, he could focus on the critical non-essentials.

This applies to rugby and business, too. The number one thing is to get your basics right and get your team together – that is a critical essential. You cannot mask a crap lineout with a bacon sandwich. You do not *lead* with critical non-essentials, or you will throw off the balance of your whole organisation. But once your scrum is as good as South Africa's, and your counter-attack is as clinical as New Zealand's, then you can build on that foundation by beginning to strategise your critical non-essentials.

England's critical non-essentials

With the England team, my focus was on trying to do a 100 things 1 per cent better: I called these the **'one per-centers'**. Little improvements brought big change. Sir Dave Brailsford adopted a similar philosophy with his 'marginal gains' mantra with the British cycling team. When you are

---

One per-centers: Identifying small shifts in behaviour that collectively have a profound impact on performance.

---

coaching a national team, countless people call you up and try to sell you stuff. Most of it could be dismissed pretty quickly, but anything I thought we should consider saying yes to was discussed with the team in the War Room. That is where Martin Johnson was so influential. He'd raise an eyebrow and, with a glint of humour in his eye, just say: 'Get on with it, then. We'll tell you if it's any good.'

At the time, some of our critical non-essentials were blown completely out of proportion by sections of the media, but they differentiated us from our opponents in the following ways:

Taking a barrister

When we went to the World Cup in 2003 we took one of the leading barristers in the UK, Richard Smith. We ended up in court after accidentally – and very briefly I might add! – putting sixteen men on the pitch. If the IRB, now World Rugby, had really wanted to, they could have docked points from us. It's at times like that you realise you do not want to be 10,500 miles away from home without your best legal advice. Previously, the home team provided the legal help! Most international sports teams now always travel with their own legal representation.

Taking a chef

We took our own chef with us from Pennyhill Park. No other team had a travelling chef. But he was more than just in charge of food; he was in the kitchen, sleeves rolled up and looking after the nutrition of the team. Players could ring him any time of day to get the fuel they needed to recover and prepare for the next game. Even more importantly, he was in charge of hygiene. I certainly was not going to allow our World Cup dreams to be ruined by an untimely bout of food poisoning in a Sydney hotel. The world had already seen that happen at the 1995 World Cup when the New Zealand team were struck ill before the final.

In-house testing

I was absolutely paranoid about drug-doping. I was not suspicious of anyone – I knew for a fact that nobody in my team was doping – but I was militant about making sure they all understood the facts. Every player knew we would test them at any time. I am not talking about IRB testing, but in-house testing. That was the level of scrutiny I wanted. Young men sometimes believe they are indestructible, and they can be easily swayed. What I wanted everybody to understand was that when they were working out and a mate who was into body-building or a club team-mate said 'Have you tried this pill?' they should know instinctively and unhesitatingly to say 'No, thank you.' Even if the packaging insists it is legal and approved – under no circumstances do you ever take that risk.

Security team

We took a security team with us. The profile of players changed with the advent of professionalism, and as the team became more and more successful, so the attention grew and grew. I just wanted players to be able to go for a walk on Manly Beach with their family and friends and not have to worry about any hassle. In the build-up to a knockout Test match, there is nothing worse than feeling imprisoned in the team hotel. It is claustrophobic and utterly detrimental to getting in the right mindset for the match. The security team we worked with were admired by the players for their professionalism and discretion – for the most part, nobody even knew they were there. This is also now common practice.

Training with referees

Too many players do not know the rules. Sit players down today and make them take a quiz, and you would be staggered at the number of players who do not know the laws. Refereeing them properly in training was a huge operation. During our training week we used to have international referee Steve Lander emulate the quirks and idiosyncrasies of the next referee: whether he was especially strict on ball presentation, say, or on supporting your body weight as the jackal at a ruck. Nobody else had a referee with them. Even in training, if somebody got penalised for being offside, I would go nuts. Sometimes I even asked Steve to referee intentionally badly. I wanted my players to understand that you are offside because the referee says you are offside! In the 2011 Rugby World Cup in New Zealand, referees were focused on spear- or tip-tackles in which players were tipped over the horizontal. In the 2015 Rugby World Cup in England, there was a clear and explicit focus by the referees on the dangers of neck rolls and low-diving 'cannonball' tackles. Players very quickly had to adjust their tackle technique and their approach to the contact area to avoid being sent to the sin-bin. It was fascinating to see which teams were quickest to respond to this directive. The 2019 World Cup will be remembered for the World Rugby directive on high tackles which defined so many games. All teams trained with referees ahead of the tournament, but not all teams put this learning into practice.

Training facilities

Pennyhill Park was transformed from a five-star luxury hotel into a high-performance centre. I was so lucky in the people who worked there. In my early winters at Pennyhill, when the practice pitch was frozen and unplayable, we had been reduced to training in the garden at the team hotel. But the owners, the Pecorelli family, were so open-minded, innovative and flexible, and we turned it into an outstanding centre of excellence that the England rugby team still use today.

Our Twickenham fortress

Our final critical non-essential was Twickenham Stadium, a ground that was to become our fortress. I wanted it to become the number one rugby venue in the world. When I first walked into the home changing room, it seemed to be built of a couple of breeze blocks and some pegs. I knew I wanted to transform it. A fresh lick of paint, some inspirational quotes, a reminder of the team's history and of what was at stake and it suddenly felt like a room in which an elite-performing team could prepare for a Test match. We didn't lose a game there in four years between World Cups. It was a while until the opposition changing room had the same treatment!

Creative financing

People always think it is about money, but Francis Baron, who was chief executive of the RFU, said no to me far more often than he ever said yes. However, just because the person who holds the kitty says no, that does not mean the answer has to be no. Whether you are dealing with your chief executive, your investors or your bursar, consider finding a way to fund the idea creatively. Use your contacts, sell the idea to sponsors, crowd-source funding. The RFU did not pay for our chef or our barrister's travel to the Rugby World Cup in 2003, but I found ways to finance the trips.

There is always a distinction between low cost and good value. Price is no mitigant for failure. I once put up the entire England squad – players and management – across several of my own credit cards on tour in South Africa because I simply was not prepared for an elite sporting operation to stay in the quality of hotel provided. The opposition had also moved their own Under-21 side into the hotel. That was the final straw.

Meaningful relationships

I wanted to create the bonds of a club culture within the confines of the England set-up. I wanted to get to know the players as well as possible in as short a time as possible. I knew from the world of business that if you want a happy employee, you have to know more about them. If you want an employee to feel a sense of belonging and to thrive professionally, then you have to make an effort with meaningful communication.

Early on with England, I realised that the players' partners were being thought of as an afterthought, almost surplus to requirements. On match days nobody knew where they were sitting in the stadium and the players did not see their partners until after midnight. No one had considered making them a part of the England team. We flipped that on its head and made girlfriends, partners and wives the VIPs of the day.

We analysed the experience of partners in the week of a Test match and worked out how to make that week enjoyable. Jayne helped us run alternative tours for partners to ensure travelling was a smooth and stress-free operation – even for away tours to South Africa, New Zealand and Australia. It took a huge amount of planning and logistics, but the whole purpose was to create a new environment for the England team. Changes of attitude, treating people as if they mattered and recognising and marking their importance – these behaviours had a demonstrable impact because the players knew that their partners and children and parents were being looked after.

We made post-match dinners mixed occasions, so that partners were part of the experience. Jayne and I met privately with each president of the RFU at the beginning of their year in office. One of the key points of the discussion was to secure a box at Twickenham so that partners with children could enjoy the match-day experience. In seven years, no president ever refused that request.

We worked hard to ensure that players understood the value of this, so it was not a distraction. In terms of bonding, this was a huge part of that process. I arranged for Nike and Eden Park to send thank-you gifts to partners and to say how much we were looking forward to their support ahead of the next major tournament.

Families understand the sacrifice players go through in terms of the commitment necessary to maintain their levels of fitness with nutrition and lifestyle. In terms of rehabilitation – and bearing in mind that significant injury is one of the most profoundly destabilising and emotionally distressful things a professional sportsman or sportswoman can face – there was a support structure and network of care in place.

Basics first

One final point to reiterate: we did not win the World Cup because we had a lawyer and a chef. We started with the basics. We won the World Cup because we were the best team in the world. These critical non-essentials were put in place to ensure we were in the best position to prove that on the night of 22 November 2003.

This is all standard stuff now, but at the time it set us apart from the opposition. It was innovative and pioneering. If you are going to be the best on the pitch, it can only help if you pursue best practice off the pitch.

Lesson from Japan: Training culture

Japan's winning culture was built on their training culture. Everyone within the operation understood exactly their principles of performance. Jamie Joseph and his coaching team came up with a blueprint for victory – a furiously high-tempo game – and then designed a training year around it, doing more 'fast training' than any other team (replicating skills at a higher speed than during a match). They did not just focus on the speed of passing, but on being able to replicate that speed quicker than anybody else. Their tactics were drawn up to offset their lack of power with speed: speed of thought, speed of attack, speed of feet, speed of hands.

They refer to their training as 'conditioning overdrive'. In their ten-day summer camp, they were operating a six-session routine, with set-piece drills after dinner. These included physically punishing sessions – wrestling and ju-jitsu – to develop tolerance against injuries. They would build up lactic acid in the legs on the Wattbike (an exercise bike with varying resistance levels), then, after players had reached a state of exhaustion, they had to complete rugby sessions on the training pitch.

Their ambition for ball-in-play time was remarkable. Most Test matches sit around the thirty-minute mark for ball in play, but Japan's ambition was to keep the ball in play for forty-plus minutes – a punishing 12.5 per cent increase on what their opponents were used to tolerating. That is why their accuracy had to be so precise and why they seldom kicked – relinquishing possession gives the opponent a chance to slow the game down.

Their ruck speed was equally impressive, dynamic and precise, providing a slick platform for the scrum-half to shift the ball away from contact and prevent the chance of a counter-ruck from more heavyweight opposition.

Japan's defensive technique was considered old-fashioned before the tournament but was profoundly effective. By tackling low and around the knees, rather than attempting chest-height power shots, they felled opponents quickly, competed for the ball and dictated the tempo of matches. Five of the top six tacklers from the sides who reached the quarter-finals played for Japan.

Beyond their training, the management of their players was also exemplary. For starters, many of their most influential players at the tournament played very few Super Rugby matches this season. Michael Leitch, their leader and talisman, did not play a single game for his Sunwolves team. That preparation was key. By the third week of the tournament, before the typhoon disruption and while all teams were still in the competition, Japan led the statistics for collective tackles and most carries, were second in tackle completion and third in passes made. They played an 'all-court' game with no numbers on their back. By that I mean that no player was limited by a prescribed role in open play because of their set position. Instead, every player had the freedom to flourish.

In 2003, England were the fittest team in world rugby and, for the 2019 tournament, Japan were working with the same strength-and-conditioning expert in Calvin Morriss. They put an emphasis on skill and fitness and will be remembered as one of the standout teams of the tournament.

CHAPTER VIII

INSIDE CENTRE
Performance behaviours: 3D Learning

'The greatest leader is not necessarily the one who does the greatest things. He is the one that gets the people to do the greatest things.'

Ronald Reagan

Winning behaviours: The central position of inside centre is incisive and impactful, relied on time and again for gain-line advantage and momentum that puts the entire team on the front foot. In the context of big business, the CEO does not have time to run the day-to-day operation or oversee every mechanism within a functioning team, but the inside centre is the eyes, the ears and the engine. Measuring the key performance indicators of this position will offer a fair representation of the team's performance. This player also defends the No 1 channel of attack from the most heavyweight of competitors; aggressive defence here can change the momentum of the match and turn a bad situation on its head (on the rugby pitch, quite literally).

Could you break down your business into a range of essential disciplines?

By the time the England rugby team became the number one team in the world, the coaches and I had divided the game up into seven disciplines, neatly encapsulated by seven illustrative graphics. One of the key skills we developed as a team was capturing information and knowledge to inform and enhance future practice. The collection of rugby brains I had at my disposal was unrivalled and every coach offered insight into every discipline.

Andy Robinson came in as England coach and my number two. He had won a Heineken Cup with Bath and we had experienced coaching together with both the England Under-21 team and at Bath, sharing a belief in an expansive, dynamic brand of rugby based on fitness and imagination. Phil Larder – who was assistant coach and a specialist in defence – had a wealth of experience coaching rugby league, including the Great Britain team. Dave Reddin was in charge of fitness and conditioning. He had worked at Leicester Tigers and with England's Under-21 development team. Dave Alred had a breadth of experience across a range of sports, including American football. He was a kicking coach with an expertise and insight in psychology. Tony Biscombe had been in charge of video analysis and technical support at the RFU for years. We drew on that pool of knowledge to harness our collective understanding of the game. In addition, we utilised the vast experience of Phil Keith-Roach as our scrummaging coach and Simon Hardy as our lineout specialist.

In the seven graphics, every word was encoded with all manner of intricate detail and nuanced understandings of our processes and behaviours, but the key words themselves were all that was needed to signify and embody this knowledge. These graphics were then brought to every team meeting and used as a reference tool.

Every aspect of the game was divided into a specialist discipline and that specialism was covered by an expert. Better still, I appointed a role to each player in the team, so they became specialists in this area. For example, Neil Back and Mike Tindall were in charge of our defence. Before and after every game they would lead the team meeting on this discipline and we would not move on until they were happy. It is a basic teaching skill and a basic proof of learning – if you are able to explain something to somebody else, or better still teach the concept, then you know it. At this stage in our evolution, we had fifteen teachers in our starting team, all experts in their field and specialists at passing on their accrued knowledge.

There were seven disciplines, divided by the sections of the game as follows: 1. Team Defence; 2. Team Basics; 3. Team Pressure; 4. Team Attack; 5. Team Tactics; 6. Self-control; 7. Leadership.

Each graphic would then drill down into more refined detail. For example, the graphic on 'Team Pressure' would outline everything from our offloading principles in contact to our focus on the sheer pace of our game; 'Team Attack' would cover everything from our driving maul principles to our multi-phase attack; 'Team Defence' would assert the need to dominate the opposition with our shape as well as our emphasis on winning the collisions. The embryonic structure of our entire game – from decision-making in critical situations to our rucking principles – was neatly captured and illustrated. Finally, each category was defined by its own mantra, from 'They have no hiding place', to 'Give them nothing'.

Players had key responsibilities for different disciplines. For the 2003 team, that split was as follows:

1. **Team Defence:** Neil Back, Mike Tindall.
2. **Team Basics:** Trevor Woodman, Steve Thompson, Ben Kay, Ben Cohen, Jason Robinson.
3. **Team Pressure:** Phil Vickery.
4. **Team Attack:** Lawrence Dallaglio, Mike Tindall.
5. **Team Tactics:** Jonny Wilkinson.
6. **Self-control:** Richard Hill, Matt Dawson.
7. **Leadership:** Martin Johnson, Josh Lewsey.

These disciplines were the consequence of years of institutional learning from the best coaches and players in world rugby – an embodiment of collective wisdom accrued through a process of **3D Learning**.

What is 3D Learning?

The 3D Learning model is a tiered process for learning that is split into three distinct but related components: **Discover**, **Distil**, **Do**.

Discover – Capture and share knowledge and information.
Distil – Identify the key points and create checklists.
Do – Leverage those key points through deliberate practice.

Step one: Discover

In discovery mode, you capture and share as much information and knowledge as you can, by whatever means necessary. This might mean capturing data using the latest analytical software or technologies; this might mean the most comprehensive market-research process your organisation has ever undertaken; this might mean re-examining every failing loss-making scheme from your most entrepreneurial employees. '**Capturing**' is doing any research or investigation you can within your own company and within your sector. '**Sharing**' is looking beyond that immediate horizon – by inviting different people from diverse backgrounds into your environment.

Think about it like this: if you are going to write a book, you need to know its contents, so the best place to start is with the contents page. By that I mean that conceptually you need to have complete clarity on what you are trying to capture or document in that book.

What is essential, at this phase especially, is that you should never shut down an idea without solid reason and you should always

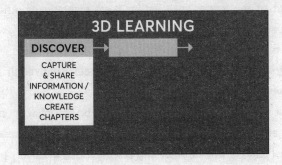

be open to a mass of information. Anyone who has worked in consultancy understands the power of alternate perspectives. One way to obtain these is to simply sit in a room and brainstorm ideas. In the context of rugby, they could be about anything from tackle technique to patterns of attack. In the context of business, they might be about enhancing customer experience or stream-lining your production line.

As England coach, the first thing I knew I wanted to do was to tap into the different approaches taken by the twelve Premiership clubs. I knew we could create bucketloads of infor-mation about different methods and then cherry-pick the very best. In the amateur era, players had regarded such an idea as disloyal. But I quickly explained what nonsense this was: any sense of secrecy or protectionism had no place if we were serious about being the best team in the world. Without pooling your best ideas, you are already taking to the field with a handicap.

Similarly, do not underestimate the value of new people joining you. In the first team meeting for any new England player, I would ask them to stand up and give a presentation about an element of the game, even if they were eighteen or nineteen. (The fearlessness of kids can be a real asset, too. The average age at mission control during the Apollo 11 moon landings was twenty-seven. In the words of one engineer: 'We didn't know what we didn't know, so we just did it.')

Some CEOs I have encountered seem to be sheepish or embar-rassed about the idea of not having all the answers themselves. The best leaders will embrace and celebrate this discovery phase.

Do not mask it. In my first meeting, I made it clear to the whole room: 'You're all out there working with great coaches at your clubs. Bring that knowledge to the England camp.' This philosophy is completely transferable to a professional context in which the pool of talent will have arrived from a broad range of companies and different operational cultures. Harvest the best institutional ideas from everyone's historic professional experience. How much free wasted knowledge is already lurking in your organisation if you have not yet tapped into this resource?

In my first England camp, when the players came down to lunch, they were not wearing their club colours, but you could tell precisely who played with whom. There was a Leicester table, a Northampton table, a Bath table, a Harlequins table. It was as if there was some kind of unspoken seating plan and, in the circumstances, it was absurd and unacceptable. From that moment on, I demanded a complete cultural and professional immersion. This was where our concept of **One Team** began. Jason Robinson is a devout man of faith. Does that mean the entire England squad had to attend prayer three times a day? Of course not. Does it mean everyone in that squad is entirely respectful of his Christian beliefs? Of course it does.

One Team: A unified commitment to the shared goals of a team or organisation ahead of individual ambition or preferences.

During my seven years with England I must have invited more than fifty people to come and stay with the team at Pennyhill Park. I was hell-bent on discovering the best possible way to achieve the optimum outcome in every facet of our game: 100 things 1 per cent better. The deal I offered visitors was a very simple one: come and spend twenty-four hours with me and my team – no holds barred, nothing is off limits – but, in return, when you leave, I want one idea or one thought about something we can do better or differently.

To be honest, it used to infuriate me when a CEO or a head teacher, who had not played rugby since retiring from the Under-10 team at school, came up with a better idea than we had about how to run an elite rugby team. But only for a passing moment. Then I realised we had just got even better. Humility is an often-forgotten quality in a great leader of any winning culture: the grace and virtue to admit to a failing or to recognise that somebody else has a better idea. That is not a weakness but a fundamental strength. Successful leaders must possess the humility to recognise that they need help.

In the England rugby team, the statistical side of the 'capturing' element of the discovery phase involved crunching the numbers to work out some very clear key performance indicators. Simple top-line targets ensured complete cohesion across our operation: we had to win 100 per cent of our scrums; we had to win 85 per cent of our lineouts; we had to win 100 per cent possession on receipt of kick-off; and we could not give away more than ten penalties across eighty minutes of a Test match. We discovered that hitting these targets would win us Test matches. These, then, are the elements that you spend more time on in training, that you invest more money in, that you dedicate your professional life to improving.

Step two: Distil

After discovery comes distillation. During this process you filter down all the information into key points. It is crucial to slim down the content, identify and prioritise the salient detail, and use simple language. The seven England disciplines were the product of this distillation process. Simple language does not simplify your knowledge, but it does purify the process. So many leaders are scared of simplicity. Don't be.

Distilling ideas into communicative one-liners that act as a referent to a complex idea is a profoundly important job. If done well, there is a slick and impressive elegance to this process. With an estimated total value of more than $260 billion worldwide, the global consulting sector remains one of the largest markets within the professional services industry. A consultant will not be able to contribute too much during the discovery phase of the process, but can play a part in the distillation phase: drilling down to key functions and key points. It is little wonder there is so much commercial investment in such an integral part of any business model.

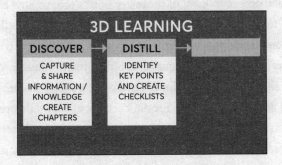

The distillation process with England led to all manner of different strategies. We recognised that the time it took for a tackler to get back into the defensive line had a demonstrable impact on our gain-line statistics; that defences had no systems for dealing with non-standard attacks; that if attackers did not take up their final position until the last few seconds, defenders could not work out or communicate possible options; that a move could be broken down to its raw geometry (starting position, pace, angle, depth, distance).

Step three: Do

After distillation comes doing. The doing stage consists of your actions and your standards of operation: your winning behaviours. You identify your key points and you work out how to train for them, isolate them, practise them, to enhance your performance. At the top end of competition, whether you have a Six Nations match against Wales in Cardiff on Saturday or a make-or-break pitch to an investor that will define the financial future of your company, your competitors and rivals will probably have had access to most of these key points too, so how are you going to do them better? How can the doing phase influence your key performance indicators? Does it improve the bottom-line profit? Or, in the language of Sir Matthew Pinsent, one of our greatest Olympians, does it make the boat go faster?

You are not tapping into the dark secrets of your industry here, but designing a process that ensures clinical efficiency in harnessing maximum potential from your team. For example, I once visited Colorado to observe an NFL operation and recognised the value in redividing the coaching. Rugby had traditionally always followed a 'forwards/backs' coach model, but I recognised that the professional game needed something different, and I was excited by the American football 'defence/offence' model.

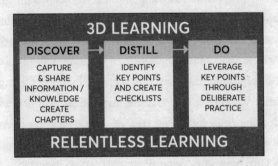

The coaches I worked with were not yes-men. They were committed to being the leading expert in their particular specialty or discipline, and they questioned everything. Phil Larder had been in charge of England and Great Britain's rugby league teams, and then spent time with Leicester to hone his knowledge of the union game. While no other side had a defence coach, we had the best expert in the northern hemisphere designing our defensive strategies.

Dave Alred, meanwhile, was not just our technical kicking coach. There is no point kicking if you cannot catch, so he became our leader on catching high balls. He had learned a lot from Aussie Rules and so the 'forward pass', as we called it, became one of our key attacking options: a lateral kick-pass from first or second receiver to a player on the wing. That option transformed our ability to penetrate defences because it forced our opponents to stand wider and spread more thinly across the width of the pitch. If you can weaponise every channel on the pitch, then there is space everywhere.

To improve our catching, we shipped over 'turtle' padded shields from Australia that help you learn to climb up the back of an opponent to win a high ball in safe training sessions and we repeated this drill until our execution was technically perfect. The catching skills of Josh Lewsey and Ben Cohen became world-class. By combining this new skill with the increased 'hang time' that Jonny Wilkinson was training himself to produce with his high, floating drop-kicks, we created a new weapon in modern rugby – a way of retaining possession and breaking the gain line both at kick-off and in open play.

This is a microcosmic example of the wider impact of the 3D Learning model and working with expert coaches. Coaches like Robinson, Larder and Alred were fundamental in educating players to become conscious of how their own behaviours would enhance or undermine performance.

This 3D process facilitates both the understanding of your content, but also the organising of your essential structures: it is a way to organise your expertise. Businesses go wrong when this balance is off.

Strength and conditioning

When I first set out as England coach in 1997, the game was evolving into professionalism, but it was not an instant switch.

I knew very early on that the single greatest distinction between the amateur and professional eras was going to be the physicality, fitness and physiology of an international rugby player.

England were behind on strength and conditioning and the wake-up call was not long in coming. I took over the role in September, and in November and December our schedule saw us face South Africa, Australia and New Zealand, twice. In the last game of that autumn campaign, we drew with the All Blacks 26-26, and by the time I got down to the England changing room, everyone was celebrating. I could not believe the reaction. At half-time, we had been winning 23-9 – a 14-point cushion against the All Blacks! We had been dominating them, smashing them physically up front and playing with guile out wide. But the second half proved we were nowhere near ready to win a World Cup. We were not fit enough either physically, as proved by our stalling on the way to making history, or psychologically, as demonstrated by our disconcertingly elated response in the changing room.

There are three non-negotiables as England coach: conditioning, skills and selection. It wasn't long before Dave Reddin joined us and his brief was the simplest I have ever written. It was essentially a one-line job specification: *England are going to be the fittest team in world rugby.*

Making a point

I was not averse to a bit of theatre, either. The following year we were still way off being fit enough. We had just been heavily thumped by the All Blacks in Dunedin, 64-22. Although we had a depleted touring side through fatigue and injury, and although we had been reduced to fourteen men, fundamentally our biggest problem was clear: we were demonstrably less fit than the rivals we wanted to overtake.

Josh Lewsey had made his debut in that game and I was walking around the changing room afterwards, catching a few players for a quiet debrief. This was a young side that needed a bit of support and attention at such a dark moment. Then I saw Josh with his top off! He was absolutely chiselled: a perfect specimen for rugby. He looked like a Renaissance sculpture. In fact, he looked like Michelangelo's *David* had spent a summer in the gym!

I walked over to him and spoke to him quietly: 'Josh, congratulations on your debut. I'm sorry you were on the receiving end of that in your first game in an England jersey. You didn't deserve that. Listen, this might sound like an odd request, but do you mind if I make a point about your body?'

Not only was he versatile as a player, but he was a fiercely competitive bloke and he had no problem with being an example for the rest.

I asked for silence in the changing room.

'Right, can I have your attention for a second? Nobody wants to repeat what has just happened out there ever again, so listen up.'

I pointed at Josh, who was wearing nothing but his towel.

'This is as fit as you all need to be.'

It was good fun at the time and a bit of banter to lighten the mood after such a horrible game to endure, but despite the humour there was a very serious message. Unsurprisingly, Josh was one of the few survivors from that 1998 'Tour of Hell' and became an integral member of our 2003 team.

Everyone's skin should fit

From that moment on, we had a saying in the England camp: *Everyone's skin should fit*. That meant no excess fat, that your physical conditioning should be painstakingly tailored to your positional assets and needs: explosive sprint power for the centres, neck strength for the front row, a long-distance engine for the back row. Everyone knew the targets they had to hit in the gym, and assessment was based not on subjective judgement but on empirical assessment.

I still believe that the 2003 team were far fitter than any team playing today. If you look at footage you will be shocked by the speed of the game and, therefore, the athleticism and dynamism demanded of the players. Over the past decade, modern rugby has morphed even further away from a game for aerobic athletes to a game for power athletes, and this can be to the detriment of the quality of rugby being played. People remember the England team during that era as a big powerful team, but we actually built our game plan around an aerobic, mobile pack of forwards who could keep up with our ambitions to play the quickest brand of rugby and outrun (and outlast) any opponent.

The strength-and-conditioning culture became contagious, and we leapt from the 'discovery' phase to 'doing' in a matter of months. You could not imagine the number of hours Jason Leonard spent in the gym hanging weights from his neck to improve his power at the scrum and minimise the chances of injury. It is not down to good fortune alone that his body was able to endure 114 front-row caps over a decade and a half of Test rugby.

Testing days

On testing days in the England camp, the edge in training was palpable. It was intense. The players used to drive each other to the brink, pushing each other to their absolute physical limits. I remember Neil Back doing a bleep test on the Twickenham pitch. I thought his heart was going to stop before he would let his legs stop moving. There was one time when a testing session nearly came to blows – and that was only because senior players suspected someone of taking it easy. I have not seen athletes consistently push themselves that hard, aside from when I was working with Olympic rowers and cyclists, who can extend themselves in training to a physical limit in which they suffer from tunnel vision and their lips turn a cartoonish blue.

Working hard was half the battle, but the other side of it was nutrition. So much of rugby culture in this regard was stuck in the amateur era. We started working with a Harley Street doctor named Dr Adam Carey – one of the leading sports nutritionists in the world – and he followed a sample of players and did a comprehensive review of their eating habits. More discovery, but this was 'sharing' because it was an expertise we lacked in the current England set-up. He told me very simply that their diet was all wrong. 'It's a complete mess, Clive. You're putting two-stroke diesel into Ferraris here.'

If you look at pictures from 1999 onwards, the players can be seen to change shape from month to month. They became leaner, put on muscle and lost weight. It had a profound impact on our match-day tactics too. It meant I never had to worry about substituting any players simply because I was concerned about their fitness or energy. In that respect, has the game has gone backwards? Nowadays, laptop coaches are making predetermined substitutions at predetermined times because players can no longer last the distance. They are not responding to the narrative of a game, but simply pandering to the statistics. Inexperienced coaches often take players off without a reason, but substitutions are absolutely key and should be part of a clear strategy based on what is going on during the game – never preplanned. It is extraordinary how many coaches make sweeping changes in the sixtieth minute of Test matches – it is a fundamentally flawed strategy. If power teams continue to dominate the global game, then the sport will regress. The only thing in rugby you cannot defend against is out-and-out pace: you cannot tackle what you cannot catch.

Before you get the idea that the England players were monks, there was always one 'secret' treat day in a training week. On Friday afternoon, the players would sneak off to Dave Reddin's room at the team hotel. At 4 p.m., like clockwork, the team room would quietly empty out and everyone would disappear to enjoy cake and chocolate.

Lesson from Japan: 3D training

The best rugby environments are learning environments and the best rugby coaches are obsessed by the pursuit of knowledge. The likes of Eddie Jones, Warren Gatland and Steve Hansen are always striving to innovate their training and playing style to harness the collective talent available. Training is designed as a means to achieve a particular outcome.

Alongside Japan, it was England, Wales, South Africa and New Zealand who led the charge over the past four years with innovative training methods – no surprise, therefore, that it was these four sides who lasted the distance in the tournament. Japan had to generate size and strength, as they weighed on average around 10 kg less than their tier-one opponents in each respective position. South Africa, by contrast, had to work on the athleticism and endurance of their naturally bigger forward pack. Rassie Erasmus demanded his players did not lose any gym strength, but increased their aerobic fitness and mobility around the pitch.

England's challenges were different and Jones came up with some creative ideas to combat them, such as using speakers during training to generate crowd noise (and even blast out rival anthems), or refereeing games himself in training and targeting particular players with punitive calls. To develop the endurance required in a World Cup campaign, England's players were put through double training sessions ahead of the Italy warm-up match so they played under fatigue. Practising skills under pressure and exhaustion is vital for both the mental and physical preparation for the latter minutes of a knockout World Cup match, so skill drills were scheduled immediately after heavy workload in training.

Even during the tournament itself, New Zealand systematically fatigued their players before their last two pool matches, against Namibia and Canada, before a fortnight of tapering in the build-up to their outstanding quarter-final demolition of Ireland. Tapering training and managing workload is essential.

In 2003, after the Wales quarter-final, we knew the players felt lethargic, so we adapted our plans and moderated training to prepare for France. The coaches who are committed to this flexibility – who are willing to keep returning to the Discovery phase of 3D learning – are the ones who win.

CHAPTER IX

LEFT WINGER

Transparency, innovation and room for the rookie

'You can't depend on your eyes when your imagination is out of focus.'

Mark Twain

Winning behaviours: This role exists for your firecracker: a different personality who brings fresh air, new ideas and a sense of balance to an organisation or team and counters mainstream thinking with a complementary skill set. In fact, the greater the difference, the better. Moreover, as a progressive operator, this player offers assets that your opponents do not yet know how to manage or predict, bringing you an immediate competitive advantage. Harnessing expertise and perspective from outside your immediate environment is an essential contribution to any winning team – sporting or business – as is always being open to trying something new.

No team can have innovation without the risk of failure, or creativity without a sense of vulnerability. But real courage comes from embracing the possibilities of such weakness. Some of the best ideas that we brought into the England culture came from the Royal Marines, from entrepreneurs and from an Israeli graphologist.

After the inquisition into the 1999 World Cup was finally over and the cycle was about to begin again, I made a very simple decision: this time it was going to be different. This time I was going to do things my way. My two years in charge had taught me a big lesson. If you are put in a position of authority but not given complete control, you are always going to get the wrong result. This meant at the RFU and with the team. From hereon in, there were not going to be any shortcuts.

Setting my stall out

Forthright honesty was going to define the next four years, so I started the next team meeting as I meant to go on.

'You will get one chance to make history. We have the talent to win a World Cup, but to do it I need your help.

'First of all, as a former player I need to warn you of one thing. Your time will go in the snap of a finger and you'll miss it.'

It was a tasty meeting and it was the time when we realised we were all in this together.

There is no such thing as a dumb idea

The single biggest factor preventing a team from flourishing is fear. I knew England could not be the best team in the world if we had a culture in which an idea could not be voiced. It is not a weakness if a player – or a junior employee – knows better than the boss. There is a saying in the Royal Marines that it's the guys on the front line who know how to win the war. The generals back at base camp do not have the full picture.

We established a rule inside the England camp: *There is no such thing as a dumb idea.* If you have a fresh suggestion, do not be scared to say it. Anybody who has seen me operate, working at Xerox, my own company, England rugby or the BOA, knows that for me there is only ever one immediately sackable offence: not sharing an idea for fear of ridicule. You might risk being on the receiving end of a bit of banter, but your potentially silly idea might also be the game-changer that can revolutionise performance.

As a leader, you must focus on curating an environment in which people feel empowered to speak, in which the hierarchy is based on respect but not deference. In fact, some individual teams at Amazon work with the mantra *People with opposing objectives get things done.* Conflict and competition, harnessed in the correct manner and played against a backdrop of a Teamship culture, drive performance.

Pride is inimical to a winning culture and will be the downfall of any aspiring leader who is more concerned about self-promotion than team performance. The killer idea that can propel a company to the FTSE 100 might come from the summer intern who has been in your building for twenty-four hours. If Shane Williams and Jonah Lomu can play in the same position on the rugby pitch, there is still room for invention in the modern game. I brought in Jason Robinson from rugby league when everyone told me he would never understand the game, and we suddenly found a stick of dynamite in our attacking line.

Innovation with unintended consequences

Not all innovative thinking will improve performance. Will Greenwood was a refreshingly inventive, outside-the-box thinker as a player. He certainly took an inventive attitude to our very first game using ProZone statistics, an emerging technology that could track a range of speed, movement and distance data on each player during a game.

After months of investment and development, at the first stoppage of the very first Test match in which we used ProZone, I saw Will Greenwood sprinting back and forth across the width of the pitch. Everyone else was catching their breath but Will was doing shuttle runs. I called down to the team doctor urgently and – convinced Will was demonstrating the early symptoms of some dreadful concussion – got him straight on to the pitch.

Moments later, the doc called back. 'He's fine, Clive. He says he's running off a dead leg.'

The game resumed but at the next stoppage, off Will went again. I was perplexed, but the doctor reported he had told him exactly the same thing: 'No problem, I'm fine.'

After the game, I collared Will in the changing room and asked him what on earth he had been doing in the middle of a Test match. He responded with typically forthright humour and honesty: 'I was just trying to get my ProZone stats up!'

I think he still holds the record for mileage covered at sprint speed in a game.

An important point of a silly story is that innovation can take you in all manner of surprising directions, but only if you think differently. A mistake so many businesses make when they attempt to be relevant or contemporary is to simply 'download' their paper content into a digital format. I am frequently astonished by the number of businesses who assume they have successfully digitised their operation because they have built a website. This is lazy and thoughtless. That process is not modernising your modus operandi or adapting to a new environment; you are just shifting the medium without actually assessing for a second the value of this new technology, or considering how it might undermine your existing business model.

Technology offers entirely different functionality and therefore the nature of your business – the way you interact with customers and clients, the elements you choose to invest in and promote, the resources of most value – may all shift. Building an app is not innovating your business. Designing an app for your customers of the future is innovation. In our modern world, we have a tendency to seek to homogenise our identity and experiences, but a thriving winning culture will actively embrace and therefore utilise our differences.

One final warning. I have learned in both business and sport – after successes and setbacks – that innovation and ingenuity are relative terms. In a new start-up with a small team there is scope for transgressive, experimental, risky manoeuvres, and your team are much more likely to be fully on board with such a plan. But the bigger the institution, the more entrenched it will be in its operations and the more realistic you will need to be in launching innovative initiatives. New strategies will attract attention, often adverse attention at that, so you need to be willing to face criticism and you need to believe fully and unhesitatingly in your vision.

Touch of genius

Jason Robinson was an explosive athlete but a gentle personality. He had a challenging childhood and that upbringing gave him a sense of humility and perspective that I instantly warmed to when we first met. While I was persuading him to switch codes from rugby league to rugby union it was all very secretive. I called him up out of the blue and told him we were three years from a World Cup and I thought he could be an important part of what we had set out to achieve. I met Jason at a service station for a face-to-face meeting and I was immensely impressed. Neither of us spoke money; he was interested in the game.

I had tried to sign four rugby league players before the 1999 World Cup, but the idea never materialised. Once union went professional, as with any business, there was always going to be a competition for the best assets available. And Jason was the best asset available. When the top league players were out of contract, I wanted to make sure that those players were aware of exactly what was happening in rugby union, and especially what an exciting place the England camp was. Prior to that, rugby league players would not have wanted to switch unions because they assumed they would never get the ball – but the game, and the way England were playing, was changing.

At the end of our meeting I made one last important point clear to him: I could guarantee him no place in the England team. Throughout his eight years in league, he had won a Super League crown, three Challenge Cups and a World Club Championship, but he was about to learn a new sport altogether. I always knew he could be a star but, in a perverse way, I also knew it would be good for union if he failed to secure a place in the side, because it would prove that we were producing players good enough to keep him out. He understood the deal and he relished the challenge.

Jason changed the way the full-back position was played. He had not yet mastered the tactical intricacies of the breakdown, but he knew how to beat the man in front of him, always breaking the first tackle. Instead of following conventional expectation, his attitude was 'I can run the ball further than I can kick and secure ball retention, so why on earth would I kick it?' I remember him trying to teach a bit of footwork to the forwards at the end of one of his first sessions. He was stepping around them as if they had been glued to the grass and he was growing increasingly infuriated that they could not follow his instructions. I enjoyed it from the sidelines because nobody could begin to imitate or emulate the magic in his boots.

The revolutionary kit design

Jason's debut was magnificent. He came off the bench against Italy and again against Scotland in the 2001 Six Nations. On a counter-attack, against a broken defence, he was untouchable. But on the Monday morning after the Scotland match, I received an email from him: 'Hi Clive, I really enjoyed the game but I'm just watching the footage. Take a look at the tape.' It was typical Jason: he had spent Sunday night going over clips and evaluating his performance. As he did so he wrote down the timings of some of the key moments. There were four occasions in that game when he had made a clean break only to be scrag-tackled by a Scottish player who managed to grab his shirt and wait for reinforcements while holding on for dear life.

It was another moment in my career when I was stopped in my tracks, paralysed by sheer disbelief. *Why are we being so stupid? Why are we wearing baggy shirts with collars? Why are we arbitrarily following conventional kit designs without challenging and asking why? And why am I handicapping my best attacking weapon and providing opponents with handles to catch him?*

As I began to think about this problem, I searched online for images of Cathy Freeman's Nike outfit. It was the iconic skin-tight all-in-one suit that even has a hood: one of the defining images of the Olympic Games in Sydney a year earlier. I thought to myself:

Just imagine how difficult it would be to stop Jason Robinson in that! Sometimes the best feats of ingenuity hit you in the face and make you feel embarrassed by just how obvious they are.

As soon as I got to the office on Monday morning I headed down to Paul Vaughan, who was our business operations director. I told him I wanted to speak to Nike because I had an idea to make our kit skin-tight. I could not believe his response.

'Oh, yeah. Nike wrote to me a year ago with the idea of skin-tight shirts.'

I was incredulous. 'Why didn't you tell me?'

'Don't be ridiculous, Clive. It cannot happen. Sales of replica shirts would fall through the floor! Most fans cannot wear that – they drink too much!'

Putting commercial prospects ahead of team performance was anathema to everything I had worked so hard for, everything our Teamship rules protected. Suffice to say, I went nuts. Besides, I knew damn well that lifting the Webb Ellis trophy in three years' time would do a hell of a lot more for shirt sales than a slightly looser cut around the collar. That flawed logic was the greatest catalyst for institutional innovation that the England team could have had, because it was then that I realised the battle we would face to ensure we operated with the ingenuity necessary to lift the World Cup trophy.

In the end, it turned out we were not allowed to design an all-in-one strip, as IRB laws stipulate that players must be wearing shorts and shirts as separate garments. But I did have a little bit of fun with the idea. For a team meeting soon afterwards, I superimposed Martin Johnson's face on the body of

Cathy Freeman running in her lime-green all-in-one. Martin definitely raised his eyes at that one . . .

Ensuring the shirts were perfect involved a slow and laborious process of research and development – and Nike were brilliant at working with us in complete confidence. Secrecy was essential. I did not want any opponents finding out in time for them to follow suit ahead of 2003. We deserved to reap the rewards of our own innovation. The first prototypes were so tight you literally had to peel them off and players had to line up in the changing room so that we could help.

The shirts made their official debut in August 2003 during our World Cup warm-up match in Marseilles. I was essentially putting out a second team that night as the bulk of the squad were bolted on, but for a small handful of players this was a huge game as it was their last chance to fight for a place. However, the intensity of the occasion soon descended into hysteria as it quickly became apparent just how difficult it was to put on these shirts. It was like a queue of F1 cars at a pit stop ahead of the warm-up! Worse was to follow. Minutes into the game, the numbers started to detach themselves and roll up the shirts and both the referee and the commentators were growing increasingly infuriated because they could not tell the players apart. The numbers had been ironed on for that game, but by the time of our first World Cup match they were properly stitched. It was an important test run.

The final part of this story involves a crucial moment in the 2003 quarter-final against Wales. Jason Robinson changed the game with one of the most explosive runs in World Cup history, finding an invisible path through red shirts with a breathtaking change of pace. Watch that run again and you will see how many Welsh players try to put a hand on him – but they cannot catch the fabric of the shirt and scrag-tackle him. If we had been wearing the baggy shirts of the previous season, we would never have scored from that attack, and we might well have crashed out of the tournament.

But it was not just a piece of exhilarating pace. Because Jason's zigzagging run was so spectacular, people often overlook how it ended. The final, deft pass to Will Greenwood in the corner is a sublime piece of skill, executed perfectly, and a textbook example of T-CUP. Despite the context and all the pressure, Jason checks his run and moderates his foot speed to stabilise his pass, shifts his grip on the ball to shape the flight, and anticipates the direction and velocity of Will's run before floating a long pass with pinpoint precision into his path, off his left hand. He does not pass where the player is; he anticipates where the player is going to be.

T-CUP: Thinking correctly under pressure, ensuring that the stakes in any given situation do not affect the quality of performance.

Change Thinking!

This development of the kit came to embody our mantra of '**Change Thinking!**'. I was determined to think differently, and laterally, about old problems or situations usually taken for granted,

Change Thinking: Taking a different, innovative approach to old problems often assumed to be the way things are.

inherited without challenge or assumed to be simply the way things were.

If you look at pictures of Jason in the 2001 Scotland game and in the 2003 quarter-final (see picture section), apart from the shirts, there is one other distinction that nobody seems to notice: the colour of his boots. I wanted all my players to wear black boots for a simple reason. If you are the referee and you are looking up at a line of defenders who are creeping forward on the offside line by a matter of inches, then a luminous boot is far more likely to catch your eye. Despite modern fads and sponsorship deals, if I were England coach I would not allow my players to wear fluorescent boots. I understand players have lucrative financial deals in place and the latest trend is high-visibility, multi-coloured boots, but this is a decision based on performance. Most penalties in rugby are given for offside – why give the referee an excuse to penalise you? It comes down to those marginal gains, those 1-per-centers, that make the difference.

Compared with England's dazzling white strip, New Zealand's all-black kit can already offer a small advantage when a referee is peering into the darkness at the bottom of the ruck. So why give yourself a further disadvantage out in the line, too? The only exception to the black-boot rule was the back three – I wanted them in white boots. I thought players like Jason might get an edge by wearing white boots as they frequently brush the touch-line and that colour might affect a borderline decision.

I initially had problems when challenging accepted practice in another area: when I asked if England could train on the Twickenham pitch to ensure we had the competitive edge in terms of dealing with its idiosyncrasies. Each stadium 'plays differently' when it comes to judging distances based on the shape of the seating, proximity to pitch, the gusts and movement of the wind, grip and traction on studs and so on. Sir Alex Ferguson's Manchester United side were regularly training on the Old Trafford pitch, so why were we having such a battle?

Transferring leadership

Somewhat counterintuitively, I have no qualifications to coach rugby but I am a fully qualified UEFA football coach. In fact, when England won the World Cup, my only existing formal training was in teaching. Because of that, I did not believe there was any logical reason why I could not coach football – and I still don't.

After the 2005 British and Irish Lions tour, I joined Southampton Football Club as performance director. When I had signed the contract they were a Premier League team, but by the time I joined them they had been relegated to the Championship and the entire set-up was under an inordinate amount of pressure to earn promotion back to the top flight as soon as possible.

I am very critical of the style of coaching when I earned my FA badges in 2004 and 2005. The qualifications I was put through were absolutely 'by the book'. You had to tick boxes. I remember during one assessment I tried to experiment with a different style, beyond the prescriptions of the textbook, and the assessor said to me: 'I'm sorry, Clive. I really don't want to fail you. Please do it how you're supposed to.' You had to do it the FA way and there was simply no room for entrepreneurial spirit or a challenging attitude. I kept my head down, got my FA badges and moved on. In more recent years, I have been asked to lecture at the FA base, St George's, on a number of occasions, educating football coaches such as Gareth Southgate and Ryan Giggs about very different styles and approaches to management. I never realised how different my coaching style was until I entered the world of football.

There is a clichéd stereotype that surrounds young footballers. And while it is true that many of them turned their back on formal education at a relatively young age and are suddenly earning an extraordinary amount of money, there was another difference I saw between young footballers and rugby players that really surprised me.

My time at the Southampton academy coincided with a halcyon era when it was a dynamic factory of emerging footballing talent, led by a couple of teenage lads: Gareth Bale and Theo Walcott. But rather than fitting the stereotype of petulant, demanding, egocentric young footballers, they were everything I would want from an aspiring young sportsperson: passionate about the game, competitive to a fault and united by an ambition to be great footballers. People forget that football is a tough, physical game and this was certainly true in the style of training I saw in the youth set-up at Southampton. They were respectful to the adults and coaches around them and they were always punctual.

I remember my first team meeting at Southampton. I was expecting players to rock up late in flip-flops with headphones on, but everyone was bang on time and looking smart in their team training kit. There was, however, one major problem.

Nobody said a word! They were completely and utterly submissive. They never said a critical word, nor did they challenge anything. The only memorable sound at any team training session was the coach effing and blinding. Nothing was questioned. All they would utter was 'Yes, gaffer!' or 'No, gaffer!' and get on with following the order. (I hate that word – it sounds like language from the industrial revolution.)

In the rugby environment I was used to, in our final team meeting on the eve of a Test match, the players would lead the conversation, reminding us of our key focus points in each discipline of our play. The difference at Southampton was stark. The coaches stood up at the front of the room and worked through the points, line by line, like the worst kind of unimaginative 'chalk-and-talk' teacher. The players were not engaged or involved – some of them were not even listening.

Harnessing technology

Early on at Southampton, I quickly realised that nobody was using the available technology properly. They had ProZone – they had bought it because Arsenal had it – but, to my disbelief, nobody really knew how to use it. After settling in for a few weeks, I decided it was time to speak up. I put together a presentation based on possession statistics and ProZone data. It fundamentally challenged the way Southampton were playing. The essential question was obvious: why are we kicking the ball forward all the time and losing possession? Why don't we keep possession? Why can't we keep the ball for more than five passes?

I remember the last slide: 'There is a reason we are losing games. We don't practise possession and passing!'

I wanted us to learn to pass the ball out from the goalkeeper forwards and manage the game and the score that way. My audience were unconvinced and the meeting ended pretty quickly but, on reflection, I was trying to promote a style of football that has since become widely adopted by the top teams in the modern game. The most expensive goalkeepers in the world are valued now on the quality and accuracy of their distribution. It is why Liverpool broke a seventeen-year transfer record for a goalkeeper in 2018 and paid Roma a world-record £66.8 million for Alisson Becker. In his debut season, he kept twenty-one clean sheets (the most by any Premier League goalkeeper in a debut season by some distance), won the Golden Glove and kept a clean sheet (and made eight saves) in a victorious Champions League final.

He was, it turns out, a decent investment.

Innovation in football

There were two problems I noticed early on when coaching young professional footballers. The first is how much is at stake: a lucky break here or a piece of misfortune there can literally define the quality of the rest of your life and, often with minimal fall-back options, the disparity between making it or not as a professional footballer is bleak. The second problem is the huge influence that a first manager can have on a player's career, a situation that encourages the sense of subservience. Nobody will challenge the manager because they are desperate to break into the first team and terrified of jeopardising their selection.

In fact, I would say the only tangible difference between a young Gareth Bale and a young Jonny Wilkinson would be a willingness to challenge and to question. Jonny wanted to know why we were doing something, he wanted to understand the process, and if it did not make sense to him, he sought clarification. A sixteen-year-old Bale did not question anything he was told, but nor was he encouraged to. It does so much damage to a culture if someone does not want to speak up for fear of ridicule.

I also noticed one other reason why so many football managers are so conservative in their outlook – and that is that they are such a protected group. Nobody really gets fired properly; they just rotate to a different club in an endless game of musical chairs. At the outset of the 2019–20 season, eleven managers had taken charge of three or more Premier League clubs. The top four most prolific had a total of twenty-three managerial stints in the Premier League between them. Steve Bruce, taking charge of Newcastle at the start of the 2019–20 Premier League season, was taking up his eleventh managerial post. Just imagine if that were true of business. Eleven stints as a CEO! It simply would not happen.

A change of atmosphere

There was another key difference between rugby and football: the fans. Two particular moments early on in that first season at Southampton crystallised this for me.

The first was my very first game.

I had just flown back from the Lions tour of New Zealand and I was more than ready for a fresh challenge and to move on. Jumping straight into football as soon as possible felt partly mad and partly perfect. I was dressed in one of my best suits and ready for my first home game with Southampton. Jayne and I were given tickets located just alongside the executive box, where chairman Rupert Lowe – the man who had hired me – was in his seat, ready to watch the game.

The whistle blew for kick-off and instantly – without even so much as glancing at the football match beneath them – a handful of raucous Southampton supporters sitting directly beneath the directors' box started chanting, to a familiar melody: 'Stand up if you want Lowe out! Stand up if you want Lowe out!'

Within thirty seconds, there were about 25,000 Southampton supporters on their feet screaming for his head. They were frustrated by the relegation to the Championship and – as every football fan in the country tends to feel around late August – angry that the team had not spent more money on summer signings.

I turned to Jayne and said: 'Whatever you do, Jayne, don't stand up.'

She looked at me and said: 'It's a bit different from Twickenham, isn't it!'

Jayne is a life-long Derby fan and no stranger to football, but we both realised the intensity of sitting in the firing line that day.

Up close and personal

Later on that season I had my first taste of getting up close and personal with the most impassioned fans and had one of those moments in life when you wonder what the hell you are doing.

It was two years to the day since England's World Cup victory in Sydney and I had been sitting in a freezing KC Stadium watching Harry Redknapp's Southampton side earn a dull 1–1 draw at Hull City on a Tuesday night. After the game, the first-team bus pulled up twenty yards from the door of the away changing room. This was a different culture from the one I was used to, one in which you tend not to give supporters any chance to get close to the team.

The players got safely on to the bus and I walked out last with Harry. He was getting all sorts of abuse, the kind of vitriolic, personalised nastiness that I was simply not used to hearing – and certainly never in this context. These were fans who had paid a fortune to travel from Southampton to Hull for a midweek Championship fixture, and yet they were staying behind to speak to their manager like that! I quickly learned that the most loyal and zealous of fans often feel entitled to behave in the worst way.

While I was becoming a little rattled by the growing swathes of people hurling abuse at the man walking alongside me, Harry seemed completely unfazed. Because of his history with local rivals Portsmouth, they were calling him 'Pompey scum' and all manner of four-letter words and anatomical phrases. Rugby does not have to deal with fans whose passion manifests itself in such violent fury and it was a real eye-opener for me.

We got to the door of the bus and Harry paused. 'After you, Clive,' he said, and I thought nothing of it.

But the moment I got on, Harry turned around and launched himself at these guys! It was dark now outside the stadium and he grabbed hold of these blokes by the scruff of their necks and told them exactly what he thought of the things they had said.

As soon as Harry got back on the bus, I asked him what he was doing and why he reacted like that. His response was emphatic.

'Whatever happens in this game, Clive,' he said as he turned to me, 'you never let guys like that get the better of you.'

'But you didn't seem remotely bothered, Harry,' I replied.

'Of course I was – I just wanted to get you safely on the bus first.'

Lesson from Japan: Utilising technology

The influence of technology on sport is inescapable and its continuing impact inevitable. As an example, Scotland estimate that the weight of their team freight has doubled in tonnage in the four years since the 2015 World Cup simply because of the amount of new technology, hardware and supplies they now use for training. It is not only the laptops and cameras that have been familiar features of the professional game for twenty years; now it is training drones and GPS tracking systems, too.

Teams like England and Japan are using GPS data in training, tracking the speed of players getting off the floor and either competing for the ball at the breakdown or returning to the defensive line. They can even measure the number of accelerations a player makes in a session. Precision is everywhere: a giant digital clock on the side of training constantly updates to define how much time the next drill will take. With England especially, the data being accrued during training by the performance-tracking software STATSports even measures the impact of collisions and the stress on each foot while running.

With Wales, Gatland's more recent metric of performance for his players involves high-speed metres, not just the general mileage but distances covered at a particularly intense work rate. He and his coaching team use this as a judge of a player's efficacy in training, replicating the kind of target-setting that has been used to judge match performances, but bringing the same methodology into training sessions.

However, the continual harnessing of sports science and technology has the potential to lead to a player-welfare issue. Today's coaches, including Jones, view rugby as a twenty-three-man game. He has rebranded 'replacements' as 'finishers' and he picks a squad for a match, making the personnel on the bench a core influence on his tactical preparation. For the quarter-final against Australia, he switched Owen Farrell to 10 and moved George Ford to the bench, but with a plan to involve Ford as kicking strategist in the final quarter.

This squad approach works within the current parameters of the game and, if anything, gives an even bigger advantage to teams with greater depth and richer resources. But it could end up having unforeseen consequences. If you start designing players to play for sixty minutes, or even produce specialist thirty-minute 'finishers', then you are going to make impacts and collisions even more severe. In light of this, the idea of a 'load-passport', measuring the collisions and stresses a player endures over a set period of time, is an interesting one for the future, designed to combat long-term burnout or damage.

Finally, there is a tactical consequence here, too. If I can look at a twenty-three-man squad and predict with almost 100 per cent confidence that a team is going to make one or two key changes on the hour mark, my preparation will in turn include a tactical switch on the hour mark, targeted precisely to deal with this scenario.

CHAPTER X

FLY-HALF

How do you want to be remembered?

'I am not afraid of an army of lions led by a sheep;
I am afraid of an army of sheep led by a lion.'

Alexander the Great

Winning behaviours: The fly-half is the conductor on the pitch and the chief executive in the boardroom. The business does not function without the fly-half and the team cannot cope without one. In an organisation of meticulous professionals, this is the player who continues to push the boundaries and raise the standards in every facet of the operation. Their knowledge and preparation ensure flawless performance under the most extreme of high-pressure scenarios. Their motivation is absolute and obsessive, as is their continuing drive to learn and improve. It is this singular devotion to greater performance that drives great teams to glory.

'Genius' and 'obsession' are misused words in sport and business. 'Genius' is a name given to people who have trained themselves to a higher ability than anyone else. 'Obsession' is not a dirty word.

Jonny Wilkinson is celebrated for his obsession with kicking; people forget that he tackled with a ferocity that endangered the longevity of his career and that we had to place him in a protective bib in training to remove the contact element because he simply would not moderate his standards of training. He was always quick to discard the bib – he would literally throw it to the ground if you were not watching.

When I have come into conflict with backwards-looking people in a professional context, the conversation always goes the same way: 'Calm down! You're getting a bit obsessed with this.' *Of course I'm obsessed – and if you deserve a seat at this table, then you should be too.* As a coach, there is nothing worse than waking up to the discovery that one of your rivals has thought of something you have not.

Obsession is one of the key characteristics I look for in any high-performing individual in sport or business. If you look up the word 'obsession' in the dictionary the definition will be something like 'an idea or thought that continually preoccupies or intrudes on a person's mind'. What is so wrong with that? I pride myself on being obsessive, but that does not mean working crazy hours every week or sending emails at midnight. It means being obsessive about detail and about beating the competition: working smart as distinct from working long.

Energisers versus energy sappers

Here is a crucial – and very simple – binary to consider as you think through the members of your organisation or team. Who are energisers and who are energy sappers?

ENERGY SAPPERS

sap (*v*) bleed, deplete, devitalise, drain, erode, exhaust, undermine, weaken, wear down.

ENERGISERS

energy (*n*) drive, efficiency, exertion, fire, force, intensity, power, spirit, stamina, strength.

The competence of your team derives not only from the combined skills of the group, but from their personalities, too. One wrong team player, one wrong personality, can sap all the energy from an otherwise highly functioning team. Quality is not an act; it is a habit.

Olympic obsession

Dave Brailsford is someone who is driven by performance and perfection. His legacy for British cycling is immeasurable. One moment from the 2008 Olympic Games in Beijing sums up his attitude towards every detail of performance.

One thing people do not realise about the Olympics is that, unlike in a rugby or football team, you do not all get on the plane together and arrive as a unified group. The Olympics are a staggered affair and it is a disparate, drip-feed arrival process. The British competitors fly in from training camps all over the world on different days across a huge time scale and, from their perspective, it can feel like quite a fragmented, and fragmenting, experience.

The 2008 Olympics was my first Summer Games and I still had plenty to learn. For starters, the triathlon team were placed on the same floor and corridor as the British track cycling team. The accommodation had always been organised in this way and it was widely assumed (and never challenged) that the notion of 'cyclists with cyclists' made sense. But unbeknown to me, while the track cyclists were all ensconced in the Olympic Park and settled in their rooms ahead of their first morning of competition, the triathlon team – with their event still days away – arrived in the middle of the night.

At this point there was a frenetic, angry banging at my door. I opened it to find Brailsford, still in his GB kit, and he was fuming. He started shouting, literally shouting in my face, in the corridor of the fifth floor of this apartment block in the Olympic Village. In the midst of his rage, I quickly gathered that one of the triathletes had landed from England and he had a bit of fever, possibly flu. Brailsford was now screaming at me that I had to get this guy out of the Village that night.

By the time I arrived on the third floor, where the cycling team were staying, Brailsford had his entire management team out cleaning the corridors. Bike technicians, video analysts, nutritionists – they were all there on their hands and knees, wiping down the banisters with disinfectant and cleaning products for fear of contagion. At the time, I might have dismissed it as one of his famed eccentricities, but four years later we made sure to have a team doctor at the entrance of the park and no British athlete could get into the Village before passing a brief medical. Brailsford was obsessed with speed on the track – and sometimes that obsession with perfection meant grabbing a J-cloth and wiping down a staircase at three in the morning!

When it comes to obsession, I remember a conversation with Sir Ben Ainslie, a four-time Olympic champion and one of the most successful sailors of all time, who embodies the pursuit of flawless training: 'A lot of people in sport talk about their performance and from what I've seen they are kidding themselves. They fall by the wayside by not training hard enough or being properly prepared. Preparation is everything to me.'

The margins between madness and obsession

The few days before a big event are often the most stressful of all. Once an Olympic event or a World Cup final begins, you just click into your processes. Muscle memory and training take over. But in the days before, you can often catastrophise, working through every conceivable scenario that might go wrong and how to resolve that issue. Brailsford is well known for his 'marginal gains' mantra, and after many years of working together, I know him well – but he still keeps you on your toes.

It was three days before the Olympic opening ceremony in 2012 and Brailsford was at the velodrome with his cycling team. 'The Pringle', as it had reluctantly become known, was a state-of-the-art £105 million facility and one of the most expensive builds of the Games. The track itself was designed by Ron Webb, the man behind the Sydney and Athens velodromes. It was an extraordinary, award-winning feat of structural engineering, the fastest track in the world (based on geometry, temperature and environmental conditions), as well as being ecologically designed, with a 250-metre circuit track built of thirty-five miles of the finest sustainably sourced pine from Siberia. But it wasn't good enough for Dave Brailsford!

In the final days before the opening ceremony, I was navigating around the Olympic Park, visiting the key venues and trying to ensure that there was no member of Team GB who was not entirely comfortable with the way their preparation was going. I entered the velodrome and came over to the track, to find the team in the middle of a tapering training session. A few were warming down on the stationary bikes; others were whizzing around the track, hitting top speeds, which was breathtaking to watch. Up close, these tracks seem almost vertical, almost gravity-defying as the velocity needed to hold your line propels you round the track. It is one of the finest sights of any Games.

Brailsford saw me from a distance and stopped his team talk mid-sentence. He started waving me over furiously.

'You're here. Good. Follow me.'

He turned away and started walking. I was not entirely sure what this was about, but I certainly knew that it was best to follow his instructions when he was in this particular frame of mind. We walked down some stairs at the side of the track and down a long corridor. At the end was a door that was slightly ajar.

'This door could cost us a gold medal. If this door is open and a draught comes through, it will change the atmospheric conditions upstairs and on the track.'

My instinctive reaction was to say: 'David, stop talking such bollocks!' But I sensed this was not the time to challenge him. He was understandably on edge as we were so close to the start of the Games. He seemed adamant and remained so as we found ourselves locked in a staring competition. Finally, he broke, slammed the door shut and told me that under no circumstances was this door to be opened. He said that he had trackside readings that would prove to me this door in the bowels of the velodrome was costing his riders vital split-seconds on their lap times.

To this day I still do not know if he was being serious or whether this was an elaborate hoax and he was testing me for a laugh. He certainly has a sense of humour. But the very fact that he *could* have been serious only serves to highlight the all-encompassing obsession of his pursuit of performance. The fact that his cycling team have won the Tour de France in six of the seven years since that Olympic summer is an extraordinary and quite unprecedented achievement in the sport.

On the eve of the first track event, *L'Équipe* were scenting a scandal prompted by the French team's cycling boss, Isabelle Gautheron, who was claiming foul play because of how much faster the speeds of Team GB were, even though they were supposed to be using the same Mavic wheels as the French. When asked at the ensuing press conference about the secret of these 'magic' wheels by a journalist from *L'Équipe*, Brailsford answered curtly and briefly: 'The secret? They are round.'

As for the door in the basement of the velodrome, put it this way: it stayed locked for the duration of the Games.

Invention and legacy

Years ago, on a research mission about sports coaching and culture, I visited three football clubs in Brazil, as well as the head-quarters of the national team. I spent time with Santos, where the legendary Pelé played, as well as São Paulo FC and the Corinthians FC. For much of the twentieth century, Brazil had been the best team in the world. Consequently, in order to continue to improve, the ethos imprinted in their culture was geared towards getting better against their own standards of performance, avoiding complacency and striving to go **'beyond number one'**.

Beyond number one: Never settling for being the best but always striving to find ways to improve at what you do and set new standards.

There were a number of things about that trip that really struck me. The first was the coaching philosophy. The convention among football fans is that certain teams play certain ways. The German football side, for example, are revered for their organisation and tactical regimentation. The Brazilian sides are frequently celebrated for their technical virtuosity, and there is a lazy and ill-informed assumption, based upon damaging stereotypes, that Brazilians are born with some kind of genetic talent for ball control and English players are not. But this has nothing to do with a freak accident of birth or a mythical land of baby Pelés and Neymars; this is a reflection of an institutional attitude that is geared towards coaching skills. Children are actively taught ball skills and they are drilled in repetitive pressurised environments.

Coincidentally, in the same season that England won the Rugby World Cup, Arsène Wenger's 2003–04 'Invincibles' side went a season unbeaten in the Premier League, an achievement unmatched in the top flight before or since. Wenger had noticed that Arsenal's training sessions were dragging on with minimal net gain, so he brought a stopwatch along to prevent lengthy drills with little purpose and refused to allow sessions that focused solely on building stamina and replicating fatigue. Training became shorter and sharper, allowing more time for meetings and tactics. Initially, the team felt under-prepared, but they soon recognised they had more energy and were peaking on match days. He employed osteopaths and acupuncturists to help prevent long injury lay-offs. He notoriously stopped the players eating Mars Bars before games and prevented the club canteen from serving burgers and chips, replacing them with fish or chicken, mashed potatoes and steamed vegetables. Instead of wasting millions on established stars, he searched for young talent that he could buy cheaply and mould into his own style of play, to suit his methodology and playing principles. Nicolas Anelka was bought at seventeen, Thierry Henry at twenty-two.

But of particular interest to me was that Arsène Wenger was

prepared to adjust the dimensions of the pitch to suit the training session. So the squad often trained on a narrow pitch, to focus on ball retention, or different-shaped pitches with different options to create space in tight configurations and to buy time, the most precious commodity in sport. Players had to learn to keep possession under a huge amount of pressure, so that when it came to match days, they suddenly felt a sense of composure on the ball.

Watching Brazilian kids in the favelas playing *futebol de salão*, their particular variation of five-a-side, made me want to invent our own equivalent in English rugby – a skill-centric game taught in schools and at rugby clubs up and down the country that would produce a generation of players with fast footwork and immaculate ball skills. The game would be played at incredibly high speed on an indoor court – avoiding the disturbing factors of wind and rain on such a skills-focused activity – and with a smaller, heavier ball. The game's emphasis would be on footwork, passing technique (accuracy and distance with this heavier ball), hand-eye coordination, fitness and fun. Crucially, there would be no contact at all – no attritional injuries or risk of concussion – and no kids would lose time in their skill development because they had spent an hour in the freezing cold on an old-fashioned tackling drill.

Lesson from Japan: Handling the conditions

Humidity can make a rugby ball feel 'sweaty' and the conditions in Japan caused more handling errors than normal, especially in the earlier stages of the tournament. The moisture on a ball from humid weather feels markedly different from a wet ball on a rainy December day. It is actually greasier and more slippery to handle. The teams prepared for this in different ways: while England filled water buckets with washing-up liquid and placed them at the side of training sessions, Wales experimented with using baby oil to grease up the ball – and even taped it up in places to lessen the grip. Again, the theory is that by replicating match-day conditions – or even exaggerating those conditions to accelerate a player's adaptation – players are put under less stress in competition.

Similarly, bodies have to adapt: to dehydration, to an increase in core body temperature and, sometimes, to a shift in energy production, in which your body starts to use its muscle energy more rapidly. This means that sustaining body weight over an extended period – in training and in a tournament – requires very careful nutrition. Test match rugby players can lose up to 8 per cent of their body weight in a single game.

The Olympic sports have led the way in acclimatisation research over the past twenty years and Jones sent members of his coaching team to the British Olympic Association to ensure England were working with the most up-to-date science. England's pre-tournament training camps were designed very precisely to recreate the conditions of Japan: hooker Jamie George would do lineout drills without using a towel to dry the ball, or even further test his control by wearing boxing gloves; they trained in the intense heat of northern Italy and Miami; they used not only bespoke tackle shields for separate elements of the game, but bespoke 19-stone mannequins as props when practising technique at the breakdown.

Some England players, including replacement scrum-half Willi Heinz, experimented with taping up the ends of their fingers to try to manage the challenging handling conditions, learning the technique from a Japanese scrum-half, Genki Okoshi, whom Jones invited to train with the squad. The installation of a heating system at an indoor training centre to generate sauna-like conditions before the summer tour to South Africa in 2018 encapsulates Jones's obsessive attention to detail. Ahead of this World Cup, England wrapped their players in plastic to increase waste sweat production, a practice England had begun in 2003 when preparing for the possible Sydney heat.

Wales worked with a martial arts expert to use their body weight effectively in close contact. Other Home Nations similarly sought to replicate Japan's heat ahead of the tournament: Ireland went to the Algarve, Scotland to Portugal, Wales to Switzerland and Turkey.

While training with a slippery ball three months out will mitigate the surprise, it will not necessarily imprint that skill set under pressure situations. I would be interested in asking Gilbert to design a training ball with fewer dimples to really challenge the players' handling skills.

CHAPTER XI

SCRUM-HALF
Never stop asking why

'A genuine leader is not a searcher for consensus but a moulder of consensus.'

Martin Luther King

Winning behaviours: The scrum-half is a persistent and insistent questioner, whose natural intellectual curiosity is matched by a natural skill and ability to read a game in the heat of battle. He or she possesses a dose of healthy cynicism and an intrinsic confidence that means they are always willing to challenge norms and question why. This player exposes any organisation to relentless inquisition and scrutiny; always questioning methodology and process in an insistent but respectful way and always thinking outside the box. As a leader, you should not take offence at this approach but embrace its enquiry. Ask yourself: are we doing it this way because we always have, or are we sure this is the right way?

Hannibal won his wars by doing exactly the opposite of what his enemies thought and tradition had always dictated.

History is littered with people who will say what people want to hear. The history of business is the same. Speaking out on risky topics, or trying to deliver ambitious targets, can hinder personal and political ambition. A great leader should operate by a very simple principle: if you do not agree with me, then stand up and scream and shout about it. Every successful team or organisation needs a wasp: the person who is willing to challenge everything in a professional manner and ask: 'Are we sure this is right?'

Inherited thinking is one of the most insidious, invasive and damaging diseases in any culture or organisation. The same is true of unconscious bias, which is any detectable bias in our attitudes or behaviour that operates outside of our awareness: a tendency to continue to follow an inept or inefficient operational model because that is how you have always behaved. It is an absolute impediment to any sense of innovation or ingenuity.

So often we can be blind to our own errors and if anybody disagrees with us, we assume they are ignorant. Our attachment to our own sense of being right means we tend to be suspicious of good ideas from other people. The education system in the UK has a lot to answer for here. When I went to school it was drilled into me that mistakes were wrong - people who made them were either lazy or stupid. Such flawed logic can haunt you in your professional life unless you consciously shift that narrative. Mistakes are often the consequence of the most inventive and innovative minds in the world.

Unexpected benefits of asking why

In my first two years as England coach we lost plenty of players who could not work in that style of operation. This is where Lawrence Dallaglio and Martin Johnson – along with several other leading players – stood out for me. Supporters saw them as warriors on the pitch, but they were warriors in the team room, too: challenging, engaging, dynamic, creative, open-minded. They were leaders in every way: they were without question the best players in their position; the standards they set exceeded everybody else's and their behaviour was beyond reproach and scrutiny; they were masters of T-CUP in the toughest of environments; they were aligned with me as coach in recognising the need to work together and to keep respectful conflicts behind closed doors; they had the experience necessary to lead. Scrum-half Matt Dawson was a consummate communicator who would challenge referees constantly – but in the right way.

An important incentive for always challenging is the simple truth that you never know where an answer will lead or what the collateral gains of a good idea might be. Collateral damage from an experiment can be absorbed within a good business; the collateral gains from an unexpected idea are priceless. Pursuing an idea can open up extraordinary – and completely unforeseen – opportunities.

One of my favourite origin stories in sport is the beginnings of the Tour de France. In 1902, the story goes, a French journalist named Géo Lefèvre was struggling to sell newspapers. Not enough people were buying his daily sports newspaper, *L'Auto*, and he knew something needed to be done. So he thought outside the box. He invented a fanciful, impossible race as a stunt to boost his circulation figures. He avoided the mountains for his own sake, as the Alps would prove too hard to navigate as a journalist, but drew on a map a 1,500-mile loop of the country, travelling clockwise from Paris to Lyons, Marseilles, Toulouse, Bordeaux and Nantes and back to the capital.

A marathon, multi-stage race meant nobody could keep up to date with the leaders and drama without buying his newspaper. The first event, in 1903, brought sixty men together, professionals and amateurs, and he decided to introduce a few rest days to spread out the race to lengthen the duration of paper sales.

According to folklore, some amateur riders fell so far behind they were navigating by moonlight, while others were drinking swigs of red wine as a presumed performance enhancer. Whatever the truth, something was lit in the imagination of his readership. By the time the leader, Maurice Garin, arrived in Paris (with an as-yet-unsurpassed three-hour lead) there were 20,000 supporters lining the streets and the most gruelling, exciting and dramatic endurance race in history was born.

The *intended* consequence was good business: during that first tour his sales went up six-fold. The *unintended* consequence, the collateral gain, was that a struggling journalist inadvertently launched one of the most lucrative and popular endurance events on the planet. All because he wanted to shift a few extra copies of his failing newspaper.

Asking different questions

Sometimes the most effective leadership is about asking the right questions, not just handing out answers.

After England had lost in the 1999 World Cup quarter-final to South Africa – and notably five consecutive successful drop goals from Jannie de Beer – I wanted not only to get the players thinking about scanning for and defending against the drop goal, but also to weaponise it when the time was right.

I asked Mike Catt and Will Greenwood to stay behind after a team meeting. They looked suspicious.

'I've got a question I want to ask you both. Suppose for a second that the whole game of rugby is geared around scoring drop goals. How many can we score in a single game?'

Catt immediately started to laugh. I knew what he was thinking: *Here we go again! Clive's got another hare-brained idea.*

'I'm serious,' I continued. 'What is a realistic target?'

Catt said: 'I don't know . . . If Jonny's on a hot streak, I guess nine or ten?'

'No,' piped up Greenwood, 'we can score twelve.'

'Interesting,' I said, happy that they had provided precisely the answer I was hoping for. 'And how many teams are going to score thirty points against this England defence?'

They looked at each other, eyes widening.

'Something to think about, no?'

A lesson from big business

A few weeks before the opening ceremony of the 2012 Olympic Games, I was approached by the chief executive of a major Olympic sponsor and invited to speak to the senior board about our reciprocal vision for using their branding with Team GB during the Games. This was nothing out of the ordinary and I was expecting it to run like a typical meeting and prepared accordingly. Partnership is a crucial aspect of a successful culture and the brands that put enormous amounts of money into the Olympics are understandably keen to ensure they receive appropriate and proportional recompense from their sizeable investments.

I walked into the room to see a typical sight: twelve executives in leather seats around a mahogany table. I had been given twenty minutes to speak and had planned it carefully. I wanted to ensure their time was not wasted and that the information I provided was sufficiently detailed where relevant, but sufficiently concise where it was not.

As I began my presentation, in my peripheral vision I caught one of the men looking down at his BlackBerry. Then I heard what was unquestionably the sound of him tapping away at the keys. I did not miss a beat of my presentation but I quickly glanced to my left to check that what I thought was happening really was the case. Then I made a decision: I would give him thirty seconds to finish that email or whatever he was writing – but then I was going to have to stop.

Thirty seconds passed and he did not even look up once. That did it.

BANG! I was using a heavy remote to operate the slideshow behind me and it resonated with an almighty crack as it landed on the dark wood from a great height. The man with the phone almost jumped out of his suit, then he looked up at me, both furious and bewildered.

'Excuse me,' I said, trying to defuse the situation while being assertive. 'I'm sorry, but I'm not going to continue with my presentation until you stop typing away on your phone.'

Silence. Nobody spoke.

The chief executive, the man who had originally invited me there to speak, started to go bright red with the collective embarrassment in the room and – finally – interrupted the silence.

'Clive, I am going to ask you to leave the room for a second. Can you please wait outside?'

Here was a guy in the senior boardroom of one of the biggest brands on the planet – and neither he nor his colleagues were used to being spoken to like that. None of them were used to being challenged. I was not rude. I did not insult him. But I was assertive in demanding the same basic standards of courtesy I would give anybody else.

After five minutes, during which time I was beginning to wonder whether a security team was coming upstairs to escort me out of the building, I was invited back into the room.

'Clive, is there anything you want to say?'

I think they were expecting an apology.

'Yes, there is actually,' I began, being very careful to state this calmly and without making accusations. 'Does anyone think it is acceptable to ignore me when I am speaking to you? You have an external guest in this room and this is my very first impression of your company and, therefore, of your values. Does anyone think it is acceptable conduct for the culture of this company to be such that you can tap away on your phones while an invited guest is speaking to you?'

I certainly got them thinking!

In fact, a few months after the Games in 2012, much to my surprise, I was invited back for the debrief. As soon as I walked in, I could tell something was up. There was a sense of smugness about the room. And then I clocked it: sitting in the middle of that giant mahogany table was a 12-inch-high model of the iconic red British phone box. As the chief executive called an opening to the meeting, every member of the board suddenly leant forwards and placed their mobile phone in the box.

'Right, Clive, you have our full attention. You can begin!'

It was brilliant.

Olympic Teamship

In my role as director of sport for the BOA, while I was in charge of Team GB's operations in Whistler during the 2010 Games, I was also observing how the Canadians hosted a Winter Games. It was eye-opening to see such a shift in focus in an alien sporting environment and an equally unfamiliar climate. For starters, the Canadian ice hockey team, a bunch of players I had never heard of, were national icons who operated under the same pressure and scrutiny as the Brazilian football team.

One abiding memory was, bizarrely, a pair of gloves. The

Canadian organisers had produced red winter mittens with a white maple leaf in the middle of the palm. They were branded with the Games logo and stamped with the date. Something so simple became a cherished iconic symbol of the Games for so many Canadians. I realised then the complexities of merchandising an Olympics and, more importantly, the essential role of equipping our athletes properly. From the point of view of Adidas, our manufacturers, they had twenty-six sports to kit out – and multiple events within those sports – which each required bespoke equipment, from high-spec swimwear that might offer a nanosecond advantage in the pool, to an ergonomically engineered helmet on the track. There were more than 3,000 athletes, and Adidas were generating 170,000 units of kit. Any mistakes would be unacceptable. Can you imagine waking up on the morning of your 400 metre Olympic heat to find your shorts are the wrong size? That kind of logistical detail may seem unglamorous, but I can assure you it is not unimportant.

The other key lesson was to do with infectious bacteria.

There are 15,000 people in the Olympic Village at a modern summer Games. In London there were 10,768 athletes and about a third of that again in coaches and management staff. You arrive in the Village a few days before your event in an alien environment. Whether you are a canoeist or a triple jumper, this is an event that – if you have a genuine shot at gold, at least – you have devoted your adult life towards and around which every waking hour of your last four years has been designed. But every athlete you walk past is carrying around 100 trillion microbes of bacteria. Some are essential for human survival, some are good bacteria from which your body benefits greatly. But some are bad bacteria that could affect your basic level of cognitive or physiological functioning tomorrow – and tomorrow you compete for gold.

Your hands are the biggest source of transfer of germs in day-to-day human interaction. What do people do in an Olympic Village? Everyone is shaking hands and giving high fives! There is a celebratory atmosphere that can feel at times like a carnival or a festival and you are suddenly exposed to germs brought by athletes from more than 200 countries around the world, many of whom are sleeping in the same building and all of whom are eating in the same canteen.

In Beijing in 2008 such odds were left to fate, but I was not going to allow that to happen in London. I knew we had to establish Teamship rules, or what we called 'winning behaviours' in an Olympic context. We put antibacterial-liquid-gel dispensers all around the Village. In fact, one of our first Teamship winning behaviours, under the value of responsibility, was a very simple action: *Nobody in Team GB – player or coach – is allowed to walk past a gel dispenser without using it first.* And every athlete did it. I could not get from my bedroom to the athletes' canteen without cleaning my hands five times.

And it worked. We did not have a single British athlete fall unwell or underperform through sickness during the seventeen days of competition. I employed five very expensive doctors in case of illness and they spent twenty-one days filling up hand-gel machines. The two isolation rooms that we had kept on standby for any health scares were empty and redundant for the duration.

Meticulous in every way

There is no point being meticulous in one facet of health and negligent in another. During the Games, athletes were not allowed to use their own branded bottles. We all had to use Team GB bottles. But bottles end up being discarded before, during and after play. They get thrown on to the grass, shared around all the players in a team, left unattended on the side of a swimming pool, or handled by trainers in the boxing ring. I knew we had to combat this, so right outside the residential block where the bulk of GB athletes were staying, we set up a sterilisation unit. Here was another early winning behaviour to which every single one of our 542 athletes committed: *Every morning you hand in your two sports bottles from yesterday, and receive two new bottles back.* Because of the sign-in, sign-out accreditation rules, we knew at any given point exactly who was in the Olympic Village. Every athlete and every coach switched two bottles every morning without complaint. Nobody missed an appointment.

A wonderful knock-on benefit from this Teamship rule was the mingling and networking in that medical room. It was like the dormitory of a youth camp. You would walk in to see cyclists talking to long-jumpers talking to footballers; Rebecca Adlington discussing the canoe slalom with Ryan Giggs. In the context of the Olympics, even the likes of Roger Federer are brought down to earth. My one regret is that David Beckham should have been in that team: Beckham as captain would have been inspirational.

The critical non-essentials were just as valuable to Team GB's Olympic success as they had been to English rugby: ensuring family and friends had good seats to watch their loved ones compete; making sure the athletes knew where their families were sitting so as not to be distracted searching the crowd before competing; even building a space in Stratford within walking distance of the park that was just for immediate family and friends. It was a place to unwind with a tea or coffee and a bit of food after competing.

As always, I wanted to make sure athletes were supporting other athletes, but this time on a much bigger scale. Within our new Teamship culture, they became so much more emotionally invested and suddenly intrinsically motivated to do so as part of a cohesive team. British athletes who had finished competing – successfully or not – did not want to leave the Village and party but stay and support their compatriots and team-mates, still following Teamship rules. We organised tickets and in no time athletes were swapping ideas and sharing training methods. We planned their whole 'journey' from arrival to departure. It was important to me to be there to meet each team as they arrived for their Olympic experience so they could focus on performance.

The operation had to be flawless. Every sport had its idiosyn-crasies and the days leading up to the Games were a series of complex puzzles to resolve: taekwondo needed clarity on the scoring system; boxing needed different food provision; fencing had concerns about equipment control; archery needed more targets on the practice ranges; the position of the medical room was a problem in handball; temperature control was integral to world records being made in the cycling. Stressors adversely affect cognitive performance (decision-making, attention, concentration etc.), cardiovascular performance (VO2 and heart rate), endocrine and immune function (increasing the risk of infectious illness) – and my job was to ensure there were none.

Ensuring everyone understands your basics

One of the most influential people in the development of this management strategy – and in England's World Cup victory – was a man in the Israeli armed forces who had never watched a game of rugby before in his life. His name was Yehuda Shinar, and back in early 2000 he was an accomplished graphologist I had never heard of before. From his research and comprehensive study of more than 3,000 competitive individuals, from elite athletes to military squadrons and corporate executives, he had compiled a database of common characteristics in psychological conditioning. I was very interested to hear more.

An old business associate and friend of mine, someone to whom I had leased computers in a former business venture, called me out of the blue: 'Clive, I've heard about this guy in Israel. I reckon he's cracked the secret code to winners.'

The secret code to winners sounded like too good an opportunity to miss. Had an Israeli scientist really found the Holy Grail?

His background was in handwriting analysis, but he had since developed a computer program that could assess an individual's ability to perform under high levels of pressure and stress. It was based on all manner of performance-related measurements, from mental acuity and agility to psychological make-up. But what I was most excited about was the idea of a program that could train my players to increase their awareness and skill in a collection of key areas of competitive behaviour.

I found myself on a flight to Tel Aviv to meet someone I would not even recognise. It was utterly surreal but genuinely life-changing. On arrival in the airport, this man walked up to me, dressed all in black as if he was an Israeli spy, and started speaking. I knew he was involved in high performance because, like so many of the top athletes I have had the privilege of working with, he did not bother to make any small talk.

'What are the basics in rugby?' was his opening question.

'Well, that depends,' I responded, hot, flustered and feeling slightly pounced upon. I had not even stretched the flight out of my legs. 'I'm not sure exactly what you mean by that.'

'I can't believe you don't understand the question.'

He seemed genuinely frustrated and bewildered. It was not a great start and I was beginning to wonder if the five-hour flight had been a complete waste of time.

He took a sip of coffee and tried again. 'What are the non-negotiables? What are the things you have to get right? And if you cannot answer that, then the first thing you have to do is go back home and get all your coaches together. Each of you needs to come up with the basic things that you need to get right in a game of rugby to win the match.'

So that is exactly what I did. And the short version is they all came up with different answers. I felt embarrassed and elated. Embarrassed that I had not yet clocked this, but elated that we had identified a fundamental flaw in our system. How were we going to win a World Cup when the coaching team – when pushed to extract what they felt were the highest-priority indicators of success in a Test match – all came up with different responses? Of course there was overlap, sometimes significant, but fundamentally the coaches were working from a handful of different blueprints for success.

After a huge amount of consultation and research, we filleted down the complicated game of rugby to a few simple mathematical fundamentals. This data included some other fascinating revelations. We never lost a game if we could field our first-choice team minus up to three players. A fourth injury or issue over fitness jeopardised the statistical probability of England winning by an astonishing amount, which only reinforced our commitment to strength and conditioning and nutrition. I found some extraordinary clarity because of a man who was asking different questions.

His other point was equally transforming and will be explained in the next chapter. . .

Lesson from Japan: Wasting talent

There is a difference between panic and flexibility. While France's endless team rotations suggested a leaderless culture lacking direction, New Zealand approached the Japan tournament by experimenting and reshaping their selection to ensure they had their best players on the pitch. With Beauden Barrett playing full-back, they had a talented playmaker who could pounce on turnover ball from deep and target tired forwards, while fly-half Richie Mo'unga could act as lead orchestrator of the attack. New Zealand's selection showed strategy. France's selection showed desperate hope. Although, when push came to shove, New Zealand were, of course, thoroughly outclassed by an outstanding England team who were more skilful and more powerful.

Let's be clear: France have players as good as those in any other side in the world. Better still, they are a young squad, rich with talent and depth. But in their administration, coaching and fitness they are currently just too far behind the best teams. They waste their talent.

France won the Under-20 World Rugby Championship a few months before the Japan tournament and, as hosts of the 2023 Rugby World Cup, they will need to find a way to stop shooting themselves in the foot. They pose a huge danger in a one-off fixture – and put together some of the most destructive twenty-minute spells in the World Cup – but they are not in a position to win a tournament. Their implosion against Wales was entirely self-inflicted because there was no cohesion and no foundation of trust and leadership in that group. For starters, it is very basic coaching to protect your scrum if you are down to fourteen players: you pack down with eight and go to a six-man back division. Such mistakes are condemning of their leadership.

The best leaders spot and harness talent; they never waste it. An example of that comes from one of those summer tours that occur every four years while the eyes of the world are on the British and Irish Lions. They provide the perfect platform for coaches to seek out and test new talent, to explore ideas and experiment with personnel. In 2017, while most eyes were on the Lions tour to New Zealand, the outstanding young pairing of Sam Underhill and Tom Curry were making their England debuts in Argentina.

CHAPTER XII

NO 8

Thinking correctly under pressure

'When the effective leader is finished with his work,
the people say it happened naturally.'

Lao Tzu

Winning behaviours: The No 8 is the kind of Warrior who
thrives in a pressurised environment: physically uncompromising and mentally agile. This is no place for a rookie, but an
experienced, seasoned general, with a compelling personality
and a standard-setting attitude to hard graft in training, who
can make the right tactical decisions in the most extreme
scenarios and situations and is quite rightly admired for it.
Decision-making is an art that can be learned through training
and, having worked in a range of elite professional environments, there is nothing more profoundly powerful as a training
methodology than T-CUP: Thinking Correctly Under Pressure.

Your individual skill set is only as valuable to the team as the psychological strength you possess to utilise it under pressure. Pressure and time management in a sporting context were two of the key conundrums I was trying to grapple with when I first met Yehuda. He was approaching the same problems from a different angle.

In my time with Yehuda, I was especially fascinated by a concept he called CTUP, 'correctly thinking under pressure', which he regarded as the key to performing, or even excelling, in pressured situations. This was precisely how I wanted the England team to perform in the cauldron of a Test match. Amidst the fatigue, the noise, the emotion, the pressure, it fundamentally came down to making instant correct decisions at every moment.

Consider for a second how many decisions rugby players have to make in a minute of a game, depending on such things as how close they are to the ball, which team has possession, their playing position and the area of the pitch. Every decision made then opens up a cascade of subsequent decisions, too. Worse still, decision-making in the second half gets corrupted by an unconscious bias based upon the events of the game up to that point: judgement gets clouded and players think incorrectly and make bad decisions. Furthermore, it is remarkable how often an individual error is backed up by a second successive error in a panicked attempt to fix the initial flawed action, compounding the team's problems.

Yehuda asked me to list the factors that make the difference between a winning and a losing team.

'Well, it's a combination of preparation, fitness, skills and mindset.'

'Ah, yes, mindset,' he said. 'Thinking. That is the difference. Your mind controls your behaviours. Control your mind under the most intense pressure and you control the game.'

In his detailed and complex research, he had compiled a database of common characteristics in psychological conditioning. He used this data to identify key patterns of thinking, and then worked out a way to develop and train these key patterns of thinking in three key settings: military, elite athletic performance and corporate executives. The results were strikingly consistent. When patterns of thinking were expertly developed, personal performance increased in every circumstance. These winning behaviours covered identifying opportunities, pressuring your opponents, decisiveness, time management, momentum, self-control and one-on-one situations.

It remains one of the most remarkable assessments of the competitive situation I have ever heard or seen – and it was as applicable to running a commercial business successfully as it was to a Test match scrum-half. I had never heard anyone articulate so crisply and clearly the essential components of winning in a competitive environment. After identifying our critical areas of performance and applying his developed training in performing under pressure, I immediately recognised England had a new edge in our preparation for the world's biggest stage.

In the end, my England players spent hours on his simulator, the bespoke software he had spent years developing, which helped both identify and enhance their strengths and weaknesses when forced to make quick, incisive, wide-ranging and mutually affecting decisions. Imagine working through increasingly difficult levels on a computer game that was simultaneously making you demonstrably better at performing under pressure.

It also informed and influenced my coaching. As a team, we had always used the vocabulary of pressure, but now we were able to design and run specific coaching sessions on how to manage momentum, self-control and pressure. This could be measured, controlled and specifically coached. Yehuda's research and software was the single most significant factor in developing my ability to coach pressure in a team environment and prepare individuals to make the right decisions. Suddenly, players were learning to respond to any context, quickly and accurately, precise in their response to different stimuli. That mental flexibility was transforming our ability to manage the last twenty minutes of Test matches.

There was one thing Yehuda and I could not agree on, however. He was horrified when I changed the order to 'thinking correctly under pressure'. I had to put my own bent on it, after all, and in that moment the very English acronym **T-CUP** was born. There remains for me a sense of poetic justice in that I was mocked mercilessly back in my playing days in Sydney for having a cup of tea in the changing room at the end of a game. Twenty years later and it was England's T-CUP that would prove their undoing in a World Cup final!

Think about this: extra time does not normally feature much in rugby union. Nobody in that England team had experienced it as a player, and yet in the 2003 final we played twenty minutes of rugby in uncharted territory, making consistently good decisions when the pressure was at its greatest.

Training for T-CUP

Yehuda showed that mental toughness is a state of mind that you can train like a muscle. Intuitively, I had always believed that, but for the first time I had access to the science to prove that between stimulus and response there is a space for choice.

Can you calm your heart rate and hit double top on a dartboard? Let's assume you have the basic skill set: the hand-eye coordination, the muscle memory accrued through repetitive practice and so on. The likelihood of you doing so in a room by yourself is significantly higher than if you have, say, three friends watching. In fact, with every discernible raising of the stakes - a financial reward on offer, an additional emotional investment or an increase in the number of people watching - so the statistical likelihood of you making the shot decreases. Unless, of course, you train for that precise scenario, teaching body and mind to deal with both the psychological and the physiological factors.

For the England rugby team, after working with Yehuda, I designated a War Room everywhere we went, on every tour and inside every team hotel. Inside that room I always had two props available and a final stimulus: a scoreboard, a clock and a unique scenario. I would describe a specific context in a game at a moment's notice and randomly select players to come up with a solution within seconds to the set of circumstances laid before them. 'There is a minute left on the clock, you are 10-12 down, the play is stretched and you have the opportunity to take a quick lineout, with one of your wingers down receiving medical treatment. What do you do?'

Most pressure situations in sport have a clear time constraint. These moments could be fun – they would inevitably provoke all manner of abuse and banter from the floor – but we would then talk through the scenario as a vital process of education. I remember once interrupting the middle of a team dinner out at a restaurant one night. Everyone was expecting some down time at the end of a long week of training, and just as they were about to dive into a juicy red steak, I stood up and tapped a glass as if I was about to give a speech. The players stared at me, bewildered and more than a little irritated, no doubt fearing the beginning of some tub-thumping address. Nobody knew what I was up to.

'I'm sorry to interrupt your dinner, but I want to run through our "Zigzag" drop-goal routine.'

They thought I was joking but I was absolutely serious. And so we did, jumping from table to table, with each relevant player taking over the script to outline the key components of their role. It was cohesive, confident, unwavering and fluent. I was not done there, however. We talked through our 'Freebie' counter-attack, then our 'Donkey' mismatch routine, finally our 'Jackshit' routine if caught behind the gain line. Each work-through was quicker and slicker than the last. Finally, they could relax and enjoy their dinner!

Pinpoint your pressure

There was method to my madness. I was continually trying to find ways to use Yehuda's science. When events occur in the real world, events which you have already thought through and successfully navigated as a hypothetical pressure situation, the chances are you will make the right decision when it matters. If you have not already experienced it – conceived of the issue and worked through its resolutions under strict, incentivised time pressures – the chances are you will fail. England's ability in the Rugby World Cup final to create the platform for Jonny Wilkinson to score that iconic drop goal was nothing to do with luck. Every single member of that team knew what they were doing. It was the final embodiment of perfect T-CUP synergy from one to fifteen: a philosophy we had been quietly mastering for years.

I have outlined the genetic make-up of the Warrior in an earlier chapter, on the DNA of a Champion but there is an essential final distinction: someone who performs under pressure. And, it is worth repeating, nobody is born with the pressure gene – you train for it. Nothing embodies that necessity more than elite sport. It comes down to a single moment in time during which you know you will not get a second chance: an Olympic event that lasts a few seconds, a penalty shoot-out that comes down to one single strike of the ball. Consider the pressure involved in Usain Bolt's 100 metres final at the Rio Olympics to complete his unprecedented gold-medal sprint hat-trick, Sergio Agüero's composure in his title-winning goal against QPR in 2012, Muhammad Ali's ice-cool calculation in his eighth-round victory in the 1974 Rumble in the Jungle against George Foreman after seven rounds of rope-a-dope. American sports fans revere single moments remembered simply by their signifier: 'The Shot' (Michael Jordan's buzzer shot in Game 5 of the 1989 NBA Eastern Conference in one of the most celebrated moments in the history of basketball); 'The Catch' (Dwight Clark's end-zone catch from Joe Montana for the San Francisco 49ers in the 1981 NFC Championship Game); or 'The Drive' (a monumental five-minute American Football drive from the Denver Broncos spanning fifteen plays in the 1986 AFC Championship Game). Time and again, sport at the highest level comes down to decision-making and execution in a single moment.

Identify what pressure looks like in your world. Is it a client whose portfolio you need to win or an awkward meeting to navigate? Do you frequently find yourself being called on to make a presentation to an important external contact with little warning and less preparation? If you have not worked through that process, your chances of success, by any discernible measurement, are horrendous. There should not be a single type of pressure situation you have not thought through, carefully documenting how you would proceed. Even if you cannot conceive of every possible scenario, the very training of working through pressure situations rationally and practically gives you a significantly higher chance of making the right decision. You have thought through and –

better still – problem-solved processes like this before. If you think about it, such a philosophy lies at the heart of both education and parenting: you try to train children to make the right decisions in difficult contexts because you cannot always be there.

A lesson from the Olympics

No moment has captured for me with greater clarity the power of the T-CUP model to transform performance than one single event at the Olympic Games in Athens in 2004. Less than a year after England's victory in the World Cup final, I found myself watching a diving event that will forever be cemented in my memory.

The Men's Synchronised 3 metre springboard event requires five dives from each team and, unlike other events at the Olympics, the score from every dive counts towards your final total. The Chinese pair of Peng Bo and Wang Kenan were the superstars of world diving. Imagine a two-man football event in which Lionel Messi and Cristiano Ronaldo were on the same side at the peak of their powers. The Chinese duo were untouchable and had never been beaten in competition. After four dives they were way ahead, leading the American brothers Justin and Troy Dumais 283.89 to 271.41. In the context of Olympic diving, overturning a 12.48-point deficit is inconceivable, all but impossible. To really capture the extent of this lead, consider the following: the second- to fourth-placed pairs were separated by a total of 1.71 points.

What happened next is one of the most astonishing examples

of pressure inhibiting performance I have ever witnessed. The Chinese leaders came out and failed their dive in the most spectacular fashion imaginable. The two best divers on the planet looked as if they had never dived before, let alone dived together. One splash-landed on his back, the other on his front in different twisted and contorted shapes and they were awarded zero points.

But the drama did not end there. The Russian team – highly experienced and highly regarded, but not enjoying their best competition – were down in fifth place and were suddenly handed a chance to climb up the standings with their fifth and final dive. In Olympic diving, competitors confirm with the judges their set dive before beginning, and the Russians' dive – because of its complexity – had the potential to score highly and secure them an unexpected gold. But Dmitri Sautin failed to clear properly on take-off and caught the edge of the board with his feet halfway through a descending somersault. Another spectacular splash and fail.

Next up, the American pair. They were in second place and suddenly in with a shot of winning gold after the Chinese pair's implosion. They also choked, earning shockingly low scores from the judges by all but bomb-diving on entry. The team left? The unfancied home nation, who had qualified not on merit but because they were the home nation. Thomas Bimis and Nikolaos Siranidis had already taken their final dive, unaware of the spectacular drama that was to follow, and – out of absolutely nowhere – found themselves Olympic champions. They had secured their final dive free from the looming pressure that it might ultimately win them gold.

So what had happened? Certainly, this was the biggest moment of their sporting lives – especially so if you consider that in a sport like diving, the Olympics is the absolute blue-riband event – but these world-class divers had handled pressure before. So what was different? Something unforeseen happened, something for which they had not prepared.

After the Greeks had taken their final dive, and with the Chinese, Russians and Americans still to complete their set, an idiotic and over-excited fan in a tutu had jumped over the hoardings and climbed the steps to the 3-metre board, jumping up and down and causing pandemonium. In Olympic terms, this was a major security breach and so the event was delayed to ensure the safety of all athletes and spectators. It meant the routines and rhythms upon which the divers, like all athletes, relied were completely disrupted. The head judge sent them back to the changing room for an unspecified and unknowable amount of time, which turned out to be two and a half hours. They found themselves in new territory under the most intense pressure. They had to try to stay mentally focused and physically limber and then return to complete the final dive. These athletes simply sat in the changing room and did not know how to handle the situation.

I watched these events unfold and knew one thing: I had to see the press conference. I am glad I did because I could not believe what I heard. Both they and the world's media were blaming the bloke in the pink tutu, saying he was the reason they did not win gold. I do not accept that. They failed to win gold because they did not practise T-CUP. They were not prepared. Of course, you would have to think pretty laterally to prepare for a pool invader in a tutu, but you strategise and you work through possibilities. One key possibility is some sort of emergency or delay: a pollutant in the water, a fire alarm, a drunk supporter, a fight in the stands, a terrorist alert, a bomb scare. You train yourself to deal with that possibility.

I used this example to help Team GB prepare for the London Games. High-performing athletes at the very top of their game had not thought through these scenarios properly. In Olympic sport, it is hundreds of unprepared athletes; in the business world, it is millions. I have often been surprised at the number of business people I encounter who work on the basis that there will be a second chance. Unlike for an Olympic diver, there will be another meeting on Monday. But if you want to be great at what you do, you have to forget that and take your chance.

A team of Warriors

The true definition of a Warrior is the person who thinks correctly when pressure is at its greatest.

Minutes into the World Cup final, Jason Robinson scored a scintillating try with burning pace in the corner – and then he immediately started to organise players into positions for the restart.

The lineout that ultimately won England a World Cup was in that position on the pitch because of the Warrior spirit shown by Lewis Moody as he tried to charge down a clearance kick. Australian Mat Rogers had a left foot that could kick the ball ninety yards-plus, but under pressure he ended up slicing it into the stands. That lineout should have been back on our own 22; instead we had an attacking platform for one last manoeuvre.

Twenty-two million people watched Wilkinson's drop goal. There were twenty-nine seconds left in extra time of the World Cup final. And he took it with his wrong foot.

But there was one moment when T-Cup failed us. After the drop goal sailed over, we failed to line up properly for the restart. Trevor Woodman was meant to be thirty yards to his right and was instead in the centre of the field on the 10-metre line. They chipped it to him and – thank God – he leaped up like a salmon and caught the ball.

Dave Alred has a great line on this: 'Everyone's a champion when no one else is looking.'

A lesson from Brazil

Anybody who watched the spectacular Brazil–Germany semi-final at the 2014 Football World Cup will remember the remarkable drama of the occasion. The eviscerating 7–1 scoreline marked one of the most extraordinary games in World Cup history and the most spectacular implosion from a host nation when the pressure was at its greatest (a warning England so sadly failed to heed as host nation of the 2015 Rugby World Cup as they unravelled despite all their advantages).

What you may not remember from that evening at the Estádio Mineirão in Belo Horizonte is the behaviour of the Brazil team during the national anthems before kick-off. I do – because I could not believe what I was seeing.

The build-up to the game had been fragmented and disruptive for the host nation. Neymar, the face of the tournament, Brazil's striker, talisman and national icon, had been injured in the quarter-final against Colombia. Injuries happen in sport; they are setbacks that a winning culture can absorb. But fast-forward to a week after Neymar's injury and the starting line-up for the World Cup semi-final looked as if they were still in a state of national mourning. As the camera moved from one player to the next, zooming in dramatically on their tormented, furrowed faces, they were sobbing. While the German side looked controlled and focused, the Brazilian players were so upset that they were simply unable to focus on the processes. I knew they were far too emotional to perform and I knew they were going to lose. I cannot, however, claim to have predicted the score . . .

Neymar watched the semi-final at home with his mother – and, according to Brazilian folklore, he switched off the TV some time during the second half because it was too painful to watch. Terrified, anguished, fearful. They were history-makers for the very worst reason: the first Brazil side to lose a World Cup semi-final for seventy-six years; the first Brazil side to lose at home in any competitive fixture for thirty-nine years; it was the country's most emphatic defeat of any kind for nearly a century; in the history of the World Cup, the only other teams to be five goals down at half-time are Zaire (to Yugoslavia in 1974) and Haiti (to Poland in the same year).

Sir Alex Ferguson's hairdryer

In seven years with England, there was only one time I decided to tap into the emotional charge in the changing room. I did borrow Sir Alex Ferguson's infamous hairdryer just once – and even that was a conscious, strategic decision to inject necessary emotion into the occasion. It was the 2003 World Cup quarter-final against Wales. I felt like an emergency paramedic with a defibrillator in my hands and one chance to inject life into our World Cup campaign. We were playing badly and losing at half-time and I let rip in somewhat colourful (and certainly uncharacteristic) fashion, culminating in a very simple ultimatum: 'If we don't sort our shit out, we're going home.'

Suffice to say, we came out in the second half and immediately sorted our shit out. If you do not use emotion all the time, then it can be weaponised as a persuasive and formidable tool. You would be amazed how quickly players become numbed to a coach who spends a training session shouting and swearing. I have seen it: it has no power. Worse still, you very quickly lose any sense of command.

You become the red-faced leader who everyone can hear but nobody respects.

Lesson from Japan: Controlling emotions

'Early in our history we ran away from pressure. These days we acknowledge it's there.'

These words, spoken by New Zealand coach Steve Hansen in

Japan, capture one reason how and why the All Blacks sustained their dominance of the game over the past decade. Judging by England's preparation and performances in Japan, they have the opportunity to match this dominance over the next decade.

But pressure can manifest itself in so many ways – and one of the most distracting is in emotional behaviour. Ahead of their opening pool match against France, Argentina's players were going berserk in the changing rooms. The replacements were screaming at them and thumping their chests in the tunnel, and their leaders were sobbing during the anthems. These images were broadcast around the world. You do not win a World Cup for singing your national anthem.

By contrast, Wales were the picture of composure ahead of their pool match against Australia, and Owen Farrell was actively calming his players down at the end of their quarter-final victory. At kick-off, New Zealand are a clinically ruthless team, not hot-headed individuals. In modern professional sport even the haka is a performance – and England's response to it before their resounding semi-final victory was perfect: respectful but defiant. The changing room is a place to think. You cannot sustain an eighty-minute performance running on emotion.

Some teams start out rational and composed, only for tension and emotion to creep into their game, especially in the knockout stages of a tournament. One way to manage that is to control the scoreboard. The drop goal remains one of the most under-valued weapons of rugby. It requires rational preparation and precise skill in execution. Any good team can set up eight to ten drop-goal attempts, and how many teams are going to score 30 points against you? It should not be seen as a last-ditch tactical scrabble for points when chasing a lead but as a platform to accumulate scores throughout a game.

Steve Hansen is a calm and unruffled operator, but at half-time against Namibia he gave what his players called a '10/10 team talk'. It was effective because it was shocking. Emotion has a place, but it must be controlled.

France failed to use T-CUP thinking and it cost them a place in the World Cup semi-final. They were comfortably dominating against Wales, when Sébastien Vahaamahina elbowed Aaron Wainwright in the chin in front of the referee, the 40,000 in the stadium and the millions watching at home. He was sent off and France were forced to play for more than half an hour with 14 men.

CHAPTER XIII

OPENSIDE FLANKER
How do we do it better than anybody else?

'We are what we repeatedly do. Excellence, then,
is not an act, but a habit.'

Aristotle

Winning behaviours: In rugby you need the ball and in business you need possession of the product. The openside flanker secures possession – or disrupts your biggest competitors – and, crucially, he or she knows the nuances and complexities of the laws better than anyone else, as well as modelling the courage to risk everything in the team's best interest, with no sense of self-protection or self-preservation. The openside flanker will help any coach tap into and utilise the expertise of every asset in a unified team, and best share that institutional knowledge. Their diligence and work ethic makes them the most reliable engine: quicker, stronger, fitter, faster. In a business sense, this might be the customer-facing, cold-calling engine of your operation.

It was 12.49 p.m. on 6 July 2005, and IOC President Jacques Rogge was about to make an announcement from Singapore that nobody had seen coming. Paris, widely expected to host the 2012 Olympic Games, had just lost out to London by fifty-four votes to fifty and we were hosting the Olympics.

Soon afterwards, I received a phone call at home. It was Lord Colin Moynihan, chairman of the BOA. Fate works in mysterious ways, because the last time I had spoken to him was 35,000 feet above the surface of the earth on the plane back from Australia in 2003 – and to say that journey was lively would be putting it mildly. He believed Team GB would need to raise its game for a home Olympics and he wanted to beef up the BOA in terms of performance. Given the complex and multifaceted nature of the BOA's operations – involved in both sponsorship and performance – he felt my background in business and sport would be a useful skill set for London 2012.

At the time, I had just earned my UEFA coaching licence and I was on the brink of becoming a full-time football coach. I found myself sitting at home with two options on the kitchen table and a difficult decision to make. On the one hand, I had my first professional football coaching offers. I had received a great offer from Pete Winkelman to take over the MK Dons as first-team manager. While considering that offer, I had gone to speak to

Steve Hayes, who was the owner of rugby club London Wasps, but he was also the owner of my local team in High Wycombe. I asked for his advice and he offered me a different job – taking over the Wycombe Wanderers first team. He said he would take a lot of heat from football fans, but that he was willing to take that risk. I even had my coaching team sorted out to cut my teeth at a lower level of professional football.

While I was hugely excited by the idea of proving myself in football, on the other hand, there was a six-year contract with Team GB and I did not know what to do.

Jayne looked at me from across the kitchen table and asked me one simple question: 'Are we really having this conversation? The Games in London . . . it's a once-in-a-lifetime opportunity.'

Uniting Team GB

I took the Olympic job. I couldn't turn down the chance to be part of a London Games, and I thought it would be a lot of fun. But to be brutally honest, the Beijing Olympics in 2008 – my first experience of the Village – turned out to be hugely illuminating. First and foremost, there was a prevailing culture of individualism and hardly any sense of a collective. Olympic sports are known to be traditionalist in their outlook and the institutional set-up of their funding is not conducive to a sharing culture. The different sports are direct competitors.

Just consider for a second the range and breadth of skills, talents, personalities to be found in the aquatic sports (diving, marathon swimming, swimming, synchronised swimming, water polo), cycling (BMX racing, mountain biking, road cycling, track cycling), gymnastics (artistic, rhythmic, trampoline), equestrianism (dressage, eventing, jumping), volleyball (beach, indoor). And then comes the archery, athletics (I won't list all the events here!), basketball, badminton, boxing, fencing, hockey, football, golf, handball, judo, modern pentathlon, rowing, rugby sevens, sailing, shooting, table tennis, taekwondo, tennis, triathlon, weightlifting. That constitutes more than twenty world governing bodies, each with their own operational standards and mechanisms.

When I started in 2006, Dave Brailsford was just embarking upon his quest of transformation with the British cycling team. But the interesting thing was that the very first phone call I got – the morning after the news of my post was made public – was from him. It was a breath of fresh air because, unlike some of the other team leaders from Olympic sports, he saw me as zero threat. Quite the opposite, in fact. I think a few felt threatened by me in my new role, as if I was there to disrupt their operation or to challenge their funding, but Brailsford invited me to the cycling training facility in Manchester. He wanted to show me everything they were doing. That is the attitude of a leader.

Interestingly, when I was given the post at Southampton Football Club, Arsène Wenger and Alan Pardew had responded in precisely the same way. They offered to do anything to help and invited me to tour their training grounds. Their attitude was exemplary: you come with a reputation and a different skill set – we're fascinated to see what you can do.

Silo culture

As regards my preparation for the Olympics, for the summer games alone there were twenty-six different sports, all operating as separate businesses, yet collectively branded under one logo and supposedly acting as one team. It was the most complicated web of competitive relationships and the most complex operation I have ever been involved in. The world of Olympic sport is multifaceted and political, made of innumerable moving parts (funding, personnel, direction, priorities), and it took me some time to observe it and understand it.

> **Silo culture:** An organisation operating in separate cut-off groups and not unified by communicating or sharing best practice.

In the context of Olympic sports, the funding kitty is limited, so sports within the collective of Team GB are competing with each other for their share. There is absolutely no incentive to help each other; in fact, when I first arrived the entire structure was anathema to this model of Teamship. After every Olympics, UK Sport allocate their finite funds based on gold medals won, so if you help another sport win more medals, you are very likely to diminish your own share of the pot.

With the London Games fast approaching, we had hundreds of separate events, 542 athletes, 450 coaches and 300 volunteers within the operations of the BOA. The sports were existing as twenty-six completely distinct silos of operation, with minimal communication and no cohesion between them, and my job was to unite them all. The cyclists were obsessed by systems, while the athletes operated as free spirits – and they were in danger of undermining each other.

We would all be under huge pressure and scrutiny because it was a home Games, with the potential for great distraction.

One thing I absolutely valued about that environment was that nobody was in it for the money. There are some mercenary personnel who have corrupted other professional sports, but Olympic athletes are competing out of a genuine and pure sense of love of their sport and a desire to win. They are competing for a gold medal, not a pot of gold.

In any successful operation, you must hire people who can seamlessly slip into other positions in the company or team, who understand more than the functioning of their immediate expertise, so that you are not just stuck in a silo. In fact, one revelation in the chaotic wake of the devastating 2008 global financial crisis was the degree of segregation within big banks. There were armies of 'silos' who were specialised teams in optimising risk, but they only had access to their piece of the jigsaw and not the big picture of a potentially catastrophic whole. Here is a perfect example: in 2009, the US government launched a federal programme to try to incentivise banks to lower their monthly mortgage payments and give homeowners, who were stuck in the sinking sand of the sub-prime crisis, a chance to make partial repayments. But while the arm of the bank in charge of this specialised mortgage-lending saw the beginnings of lower repayments, another part of the bank in charge of foreclosures noticed these homeowners were suddenly paying less, declared them in default of their financial obligations and seized their homes. A government adviser went on record later to say: 'No one imagined silos like that inside banks.' Too much individual specialism can lead to a collective meltdown.

Another convincing reason to avoid any organisation operating in silos is the essential truth that you want your most talented, committed, motivated people working alongside each other. And if not together, then at least side by side, observing each operation, learning from a general pool of winning behaviours. Consider the two best employees in your company – by whatever matrix of measurement you see fit – and now imagine if they swapped ideas every day on what they were doing and how they were doing it.

I could not believe much of what I saw at the Beijing Games in 2008 and I knew that, if we were going to excel in London as we all wanted to, there had to be institutional transformation in our operational culture. How can you measure the value of Teamship? UK Sport gave us a realistic target of at least forty-eight medals at the London Olympic Games. In the end, Team GB won sixty-five in total – twenty-nine of which were gold.

Breaking down the silos

We got some things wrong in 2008, but we got away with it at the time for two reasons: Beijing and Brailsford. The Beijing factor was the distance away. Competing more than 5,000 miles from Great Britain helped dilute expectation. The Brailsford factor was our cycling success, securing eight golds.

Despite a successful haul of medals, I recognised the operation would not survive the intensity and scrutiny of a home Games. It is often assumed that home advantage is a huge plus, but it can act as home disadvantage thanks to the enormous pressures placed on any team trying to perform at home. I knew there had to be a massive step change over the next four years or we would have a major problem. First and foremost, the team for a home Games would grow to three times the size with an increasing investment and so many places available to the host nation. That also meant that the British media would be all over us.

Some of the things we got wrong in Beijing did not take place in the stadiums. Walking around the Olympic Village where the athletes lived on the last few days of the Games, I could not believe my eyes. I took photographs to capture the terrible state of the rooms that British athletes left behind. In terms of off-field behaviour, my last frame of reference was an English rugby team who had not only committed in writing to litter-picking around the team hotel as part of our Teamship rules, but had even vowed to offer to help out Dave 'Reg' Tennison, a former Marine who had become our kit man, at the end of every training session.

This was not an issue restricted to the British team, but it did show the manner in which Olympic athletes operated in the Village. Far too many had no sense whatsoever of the greater good or of the team around them. By the time 2012 came around, not only had our athletes subscribed to tidying their rooms and leaving them respectable, but on arrival they were greeted by rooms which they had partly helped design. This created a buy-in and ownership of their part of the Village. I believe that respect for the environment in which you operate is paramount to an elite performance.

There were other issues in Beijing. There was such a disparity in professionalism and culture between different sports. While Dave Brailsford was investing in new technology and skin suits, and even borrowing pillows designed for the Royal Ballet for both hygiene and ergonomic reasons, other athletes were far removed from this. While some sports were meticulous in their preparation and professional focus – if you wear the wrong socks for Brailsford, then you are on the first plane home – others took a much more relaxed approach. One athlete decided to take a walk around the Village in full view of the world's cameras in a T-shirt with a giant Nike tick emblazoned across his chest. Nike had been an incredible partner for the England rugby team, and remain a deeply impressive company, but the problem was that the Great Britain Olympic team had an exclusive sponsorship deal with Adidas! It was hugely embarrassing and had the potential to destroy one of our key partnership relationships. It was also a very selfish act. An athlete promoting their own sponsor to the detriment of everyone else.

I sensed there was the potential for conflict everywhere, within the team and within the park. The swimming is an early event at the Olympics and always the first major sport to finish. When the swimming ended in Beijing, there were seven days of competition left. What happened next was apparently what had always happened at a summer Games. Swimmers from all over the world descended on downtown Beijing for the biggest celebration of their lives. The potential for chaos and

Assume nothing: Question everything and operate on the assumption that nothing is too obvious to be forgotten.

upset was obvious. In the carnage and pandemonium, many athletes in the Village were woken up and their preparation unforgivably disrupted.

It reinforced the necessity of assuming nothing in sport and business. As a distant observer, you might look at the Olympic Games and assume it is the absolute paradigm of elite sport, but a two-week scratch beneath the surface and I realised that there was a big gap to fill between the top sports and those that would be new to the Games, from handball to BMX racing.

New Olympic standards

It was after Beijing that I knew one crystallised truth: for Team GB to enjoy any meaningful success in London, we were going to have to introduce Teamship rules. I decided to face the problem head on. I arranged for the twenty-six performance directors to meet in a single room and implored them to listen to my idea. When they walked in, the first slide projected in giant writing on the wall was a single, emphatic sentence:

THE AIM OF THIS ESTABLISHMENT IS TO CREATE AN ENVIRONMENT WHERE CHAMPIONS ARE INEVITABLE.

One response stands out. Dave Brailsford was so focused on the success of his cycling team he did not want to worry about the rowing team. He knew he could deliver eight more gold medals and wanted to be left to his own devices. I knew I had to try another strategy.

By 2008, social media was really beginning to kick in as a major force in the interaction between supporters and sportsmen and sportswomen, and I knew managing this platform sensibly was essential to our potential to excel. I was able to persuade Dave by explaining how someone from another team could actually take down his own team from within. Quite easily, in fact. A daft, thoughtless post on Twitter from an athlete, or a positive drugs test in any team, might seem to have no immediate bearing on the cycling team, but it could have a very damaging and direct impact on the team's preparation if it all kicked off the day before an important race. As a head coach or director of sport, the very last thing you want to do is to walk into a press conference in front of flashing bulbs and a horizon full of microphones and have to discuss or defend the actions of somebody else.

Over the next few months and years we wrote a Teamship model for Team GB that we called our '**values**'. I did not produce a Black Book as I had for England, but instead we used the symbol of the Olympic Games, the five multi-coloured, interlinking rings. Those discussions were confidential forums behind closed doors, but I remember especially that Ben Ainslie, Rebecca Adlington, Katherine Grainger and Chris Hoy drove the culture with their brilliant ideas. Andy Murray also spoke very powerfully about being unprepared for the Olympic experience and how being wrapped up in too much distraction had tainted his performance in Beijing. He was haunted by the memory of returning to the Village and walking past the Team GB table, mounted on the wall, that is continually updated with the names of who has, and who has not, won medals.

This process was entirely spearheaded by the leading athletes, many of whom became the successful role models and heroes of the 2012 games. By driving it themselves, they gained complete buy-in to this cultural shift from their own team-mates. These winning behaviours then filtered down through each of the sports and were ultimately disseminated through the whole of Team GB by athletes talking to each other.

There were five Olympic rings and five fundamental values to which we committed to subscribe: Performance (blue), Pride (yellow), Responsibility (black), Unity (green), Respect (red). Here is the framework that the athletes produced ahead of the Games:

Performance

Performance first is central to One Team GB culture and beliefs
- Professional
- 100% me
- Health

Responsibility

Every member of Team GB has a responsibility to inspire the nation
- Role Model
- Time
- Accommodation

Unity

Team GB is the team of teams. We support each other to achieve the best for all
- Team
- Ideas
- Communication

Pride

We are unique and proud to be representing our country at a home games

- Kit
- Friends and Family
- Welcome

Respect

We respect ourselves, fellow athletes and our nation

- Social Media
- Language
- Noise

Managing social media

As predicted, London became the first Social media games. To some teams who had not fully prepared for that phenomenon, it became a nightmare. Two Australian swimmers, Nick D'Arcy and Kenrick Monk, posed for pictures holding rifles at a gun shop in the United States, where members of the Australian Olympic swimming team had been training ahead of the Games. They were sent home in disgrace as soon as their events were over and banned by the Australian Olympic Committee from using Facebook or Twitter.

At the 2008 Games, Australian swimmers won six golds, six silvers and eight bronze medals. At the 2012 Games, Australian swimmers won one gold, six silvers and three bronze medals. That extraordinary downfall surprised everyone but me. The Facebook photo scandal was emblematic of an endemic culture that was rotten in terms of the standards of behaviour it accepted. There was plenty of warning. Four years previously, D'Arcy had been ejected from the Australian Olympic team for punching another swimmer in a bar, while Monk had previously lied to the police about a hit-and-run accident.

In contrast, well ahead of the Games, the 500-plus athletes from Team GB had collaboratively come up with – and committed to – the following winning behaviours in their use of social media:

DO . . .
- Show your personality
- Remember everyone can see you
- Be responsible
- Share your performances and achievements
- Answer people's questions with 'real' life stories

DON'T. . .
- Talk negatively about other competitors, officials, countries, organisations or brands
- Forget your rivals may be reading
- Swear
- Assume anything you delete will completely disappear
- Give out any personal information or encourage a user to do so

These rules are simple and based on common sense, but their clarity prevents incidents like the one the Australian team suffered and the distraction caused by having to fire-fight the consequences of unpredicted, but completely predictable, stupidity. Their culture was reactive and ours was controlled.

The London Games were as successful off the field of play as they were on the field of play – or track.

Dividing into disciplines

When dealing with such a vast and complicated operation, you have to compartmentalise it into functioning constituent parts. Our entire Olympic operation was divided into eight key functions, some of which were adapted from my experience with England rugby: Code of Conduct, Coaching, Fitness and Nutrition, IT, Media, Legal, Admin, Medical.

Setting aside the mental strain, physiologically, sport is about peaking. With contemporary sports science you can plan that workload in meticulous detail, bespoke to the needs of that athlete. You do not train non-stop for twelve months or you will fatigue to the point of exhaustion or breakdown. And training methods should always be challenged. The world's top cyclists are now training with batteries on their bikes so they have complete control over their periodisation (structuring sports training into periods of work and recovery), concentrating the stresses and overload periods specifically for that session's purpose.

Another essential asset in any team is identifying the skill sets in your team and harnessing those talents to their absolute capacity. The positions laid out in this book capture that very notion, but in business terms within the structures of a single team that might mean approvers, influencers, coaches, gatekeepers, evaluators, decision-makers, innovators.

Fixing an underperforming culture requires one of two things: either absolute authority or an overwhelming strength in numbers. The Olympic experience taught me that only the latter cements lasting institutional change in any organisational system.

Establishing ground rules

Finally, fixing an underperforming culture also means first establishing ground rules. As an England team, we generated essential rules that covered how we wanted our culture to operate. They were as follows:

- Be open and encourage openness in others.
- No clichés or mumbo jumbo.
- Have your say.
- Ensure you spend time on self-analysis.
- Have and show respect for other team members.
- Keep it in the team.
- Agree to disagree in a non-confrontational way.
- Have loyalty to each other.
- Encourage a 'no blame' culture.
- No excuses.
- 'Beyond Number One' in everything we do.
- Committed to progressing 'From Good to Great'.

In the context of business, looking after employees can involve more than ping-pong tables, bean bags and free beer on a Friday. American car manufacturers Chevron show they care about the well-being and welfare of their employees by providing health-and-fitness centres in their biggest offices or through health-club membership. The company's own working policy insists on regular breaks and offers personal training. It is no surprise their culture is thriving.

Similarly, the company REI is an American outdoor-lifestyle supplier and again they immerse their employees in the value of what they sell. Their own staff can win equipment through 'challenge grants' by submitting a proposal for a suitable outdoor adventure, and the company also host regular town-hall style meetings in which employees can submit anonymous questions to ensure management understand the concerns of the company. Employees are embedded in the cultural evolution of the company.

Lesson from Japan: Control and contingency

First and foremost, it must be acknowledged that the consequences of a rugby tournament pale into insignificance in the context of the lost life and the trauma that Typhoon Hagibis caused the people of Japan. It was a violent and dramatic storm. While the weather may have affected a few days of World Cup rugby, its aftermath will resonate long after the final whistle of the tournament.

From a rugby and a leadership perspective, it was about preparing properly for any contingency.

England's players were intentionally put through unpredictable scenarios ahead of the tournament. Before facing Ireland in their summer warm-up match, Jones ensured the team coach arrived late at Twickenham, just to see how the players might cope and adapt to a curtailed warm-up and the disruption to their routines. The best leaders expose their team to dislocated expectations to ensure they can adapt.

Strangely enough, this scenario actually happened to England before the World Cup final. They arrived late. We will never know if this affected their preparation and start to the game.

While recognising the wider disruption it caused and the significance to the country, within the camp England were philosophical about the typhoon. Jones even used a Japanese saying that week: '*shikata ga nai*' ('nothing can be helped'). It is not dissimilar to the more familiar sentiment of 'control the controllables': identify what is and what is not within your agency and therefore what to focus on. When England landed in Japan for the tournament, they ended up playing eight hours of cricket on the tarmac outside the airport terminal, because of the disruption of an earlier typhoon. They were not stressed by the circumstances.

From a conditioning point of view, the disruption certainly benefited New Zealand and England, with Jones's squad flying to Miyazaki – the familiar location of their pre-tournament training camp – within three hours of the announcement of the cancellation of their last pool match, and they arrived to beat Australia in the quarter-final in fine form.

In the face of that catastrophic typhoon, the people of Japan were brave, dignified and pragmatic.

As for World Rugby's response, more on that later . . .

CHAPTER XIV

BLINDSIDE FLANKER

Learning the value of self-control: dislocated expectations

'I have been impressed with the urgency of doing. Knowing is not enough; we must apply. Being willing is not enough; we must do.'

Leonardo da Vinci

Winning behaviours: The blindside is your pit bull who plays on the edge, but does so knowing the laws and without ever seeking praise or attention. This player, a born competitor, refuses to operate in an 'if only' culture and will push everyone's capacity to its limits. The rest of the team are grateful for his or her presence and follow the example. But this also requires immense self-discipline, self-control and self-awareness. There is no point being the most physical and aggressive defender on the pitch if you give away ten penalties in every match. Such recklessness will always come at a cost. Discipline is key.

In the late 1990s, Humphrey Walters completed the BT Global Challenge, dubbed 'the world's toughest round-the-world yacht race', as an amateur sailor. He is an engaging and inspirational man, who spent eleven months sailing the wrong way around the world, having never sailed before in his life. A unique and extraordinary experience: the fate of your life dependent on the next weather report, urgently fixing a leak while trying not to burn your exposed skin to the point of risking infection, operating in extreme temperatures at optimum levels while sleep deprived.

I invited him to spend some time in the England camp and I remember him very vividly telling me: 'You're trying to fire a cannon out of a canoe!' Lack of foundation and stability was not helping the intended precision of our operation. He helped clarify this with his insistence on a 'no if only' culture.

There is a poisonous trend in analysing performance, whether on the pitch or in the stock market, that comes down to two insidious words: *if only*. 'If only we had done this, if only we had a better bunch of players, if only we had better training facilities, if only we hadn't decided on that.'

No more 'if only'

Walters helped us to create a 'no if only' culture. In fact, the phrase was immediately banned. I saw my role as leader in very simple terms: to get the team to number one in the world in the whole way we operated. If we were to achieve that, there was no room for excuses. As a team, we could deal with losing, but we could not deal with losing if we had not tried something. There was to be no sense of 'if only' in the aftermath of any failure. That philosophy drilled right down to, and included, our game plan, in

'No if only' culture: An organisation that is meticulous in its preparation to ensure there is no possibility of looking back and thinking 'if only'.

which I wanted us always to play an open, ambitious, aggressive brand of rugby that would get Twickenham on its feet.

When England were preparing for the 1999 Rugby World Cup, we were still existing in a 'fingers crossed' environment – the opposite of a 'no if only' approach. We were hoping that, through a combination of good fortune and good will, circumstances would work out in our favour and we would progress to the final. No one would conceive of running a business like that – especially one upon which their livelihood might depend – so I was not going to prepare for a major tournament in that way again.

You challenge the systems and you make sure there are no excuses. Success in high-pressure environments could always be attributed to how the team worked together under pressure, how they understood the importance of teamwork and loyalty, and how they were willing to do 100 things just 1 per cent better.

I ramped up my planning. The players would travel to the stadium the day before a match so they were prepared for the journey – when to take on food, liquids, what landmarks were on the way, how much time was left. You want to know the route and the traffic pinch points. We used to know where we would all sit on the England coach, what music would be played, track by track. We even selected the Eminem song 'Lose Yourself' to come on two minutes before we turned into the stadium drive (*Look, if you had one shot, or one opportunity / To seize everything you ever wanted, in one moment / Would you capture it, or just let it slip?*).

I would sit in the front left seat and shake everybody's hand as they got off the coach. You might say one or two words to the less experienced or more nervous players, but it is not a time to get emotional. With experienced players no words are needed – just eye-to-eye contact and a firm handshake.

Half-time thinking

One of Humphrey's biggest impacts was on our 'half-time thinking'. He made the point that England ran out for the start of big games in crisp, white shirts for the national anthems, looking like a million dollars and ready for a high-octane performance. But we ran out for the second half bloodied and muddied and slightly dishevelled. As he was telling me this, I remember thinking: *Where exactly is he going with this?* His answer surprised me.

'Clive, it's simple: you should change your shirts at half-time.'

My instinctive response was *We don't have time*. But my instinctive response was wrong. Of course we did. If an idea is good enough, if the reasons are compelling enough, you make time. We also began personalising the shirts for each of the players at this time. The date, caps and fixture were all embroidered. It is now common practice for all teams to personalise their shirts. No England shirt was left lying around a changing room again.

In fact, over the next few months we completely transformed our half-time routine and it became a meticulous, military operation. The whole point was to recreate the feel of the start of the game, and no matter what the score was, it was the mindset of a 0–0 scoreline.

One coach went to the changing room just before half-time. We would make three key points – no more. Sometimes these were minimal, sometimes they were major. On entry, nobody said a word. In the first instants the players changed their shirts and shorts, took on any liquids and fuel, and the medical team got to work. Everyone took a moment to think and looked at the three points on the board. I spoke quietly to the captain and made sure we were agreed on the key points. For the next three minutes I was on my feet with the other coaches and we went through the key points. Then we split into forwards and backs for a few moments, before coming back together with the captain, who had the final word.

How it broke down:

- 0–2 mins
  Absolute silence. Think about performance. Shirts off. Towel down. New kit. 0–0 on the scoreboard.
- 2–5 mins
  Coaches' Assessment. Take on food and fluids.

- 5–8 mins

  Captain/Coach final word. Take on food and fluids.
- 8–10 mins

  Absolute silence. 0–0 on the scoreboard. Visualise kick-off.

Especially effective was the absolute silence. Changing rooms in the middle of a Test match were cacophonous and chaotic affairs when I first took over the England rugby team. How could players be expected to return to the field in the right mindset of focused endeavour and calm execution if their half-time refuge was a place of swearing, shouting and conflicted messages? We ultimately filtered this all down to three key messages on a whiteboard, and a period of silence to reflect and process.

It worked wonders.

Pressure with pressure

This was another mantra that came out of my time with Yehuda. In a normal game of rugby, if one team has been defending for phase after phase in their own 22 or, more typically even, on their own 5-metre line, throwing bodies on the line as a last-ditch desperate defence, watch what happens if the whistle blows and the referee awards the defending team a penalty. The attitude of the weak team is *Thank God we survived that!* They will slow down the game, reach out a hand and help

> **Pressure with pressure:** Transforming a moment of perceived weakness or vulnerability into an opportunity to attack.

each other up, get their breath back, and then there will be high fives before the fly-half kicks the leather off the ball, desperately trying to steal every yard from the kick. But a top team will tap and go. A team that backs itself to be relentlessly and ruthlessly fitter and faster will see that there are opportunities to strike in front of a disorganised and fatigued opposition. There is no better turnover in international rugby than inside your own 22, as the full-back will be up in the line of attack, the attacking team will be compressed and there will be oceans of space once you break the first tackle.

There is one moment that defined this mentality for me. We had started slowly in a Six Nations match against Scotland in 2001 and we were gutsily defending our line at Twickenham. Tackle after tackle after tackle, and you could see even the attacking team were starting to run out of puff as Scotland's attacking shape became shallower and the ball slowed down. But suddenly – ping! – the referee awarded us a penalty at the breakdown and everyone stopped. The Scottish team all but took a knee to suck in some air and catch their breath, but Jason Leonard looked up and saw the space. It was on. He tapped the ball and launched an immediate counter-attack. It is moments like that which reveal the ambitions of an organisation and measure the quality of a culture.

Good businesses are made of good people

There is one little-noticed moment immediately after the final whistle in Sydney in 2003. Everyone remembers Will Greenwood

223

and Jonny Wilkinson bouncing around the turf, hugging and shouting two very obvious words on repeat: *World Cup!* But amidst that wave of euphoria, there was one brief gesture that, for me, summed up our Teamship principles and our fundamental standards of being good people.

Seconds after the final whistle, having won the biggest game of his life, in the most dramatic circumstances that anyone could imagine, Ben Kay takes a moment to perform one simple action. Before embracing a team-mate in a wild frenzy of celebration, before he has even raised his fist in tribute to the sheer awe of the moment, he puts his arm on the shoulder of the referee and thanks him. It is fleeting – but it is everything.

It is a testament to the culture we built that, no matter the agony or the ecstasy, we would operate with courtesy, responsibility and grace in the face of whatever might befall us.

Dislocated expectations

About a decade ago, New Zealand's culture, by their own admission, was unrecognisable from what it is today. By 2011, they were able to win the World Cup with their fourth-choice fly-half. One of the most iconic shirts in world sport – the All Black No 10 – was worn by a guy who had spent the early stages of the tournament on a beer-and-whitebaiting holiday on the Waikato River on the North Island.

After not being picked in the New Zealand squad for the World Cup, Stephen Donald had done his best to ignore the tournament – he had even deleted the coach from his phone contacts. He thought he was having a good day when he hauled in 11 kg of whitebait. When he switched his phone back on he had a number of missed calls from an unknown number and a voicemail from New Zealand coach Graham Henry.

Days later, Donald was squeezing his off-season bulk into a skintight black jersey. Thirty-five minutes into the final and third-choice fly-half Aaron Cruden went down injured and suddenly Donald was running on to the pitch of a World Cup final at Auckland's Eden Park for his first taste of the tournament. With scrum-half Piri Weepu having a nightmare in front of goal, Donald ended up landing the penalty kick that won the game – and the World Cup for New Zealand on home soil. Extraordinarily, if you consider their historical dominance of the world game, it was their first World Cup victory since 1987.

This story for me illustrates the necessity of embracing '**dislocated expectations**'. It was a methodology I had learned several years before watching this World Cup final, when I decided that England players should experience what it was like training with the Royal Marines. What I learned from that adventure changed our entire training ethos.

> **Dislocated expectations:**
> Constantly changing and challenging the way you think and train so that you are prepared for the unexpected.

The week had included some extraordinary experiences. The players were pushed into zip-wire rides at phenomenal heights and speeds (and through extremely tight and precarious spaces) and, as soon as they landed, were suddenly given psychometric and memory tests without warning. After a frenzied physical assault course, they were given twenty seconds to remember as many objects on a tray

as possible. They had to go through a crash procedure and evacuate a helicopter underwater. Again, once they had resurfaced,
and once they were elated at having completed the mission, the
Marines immediately plunged them back under the water – and
this time they had to evacuate in the pitch-black darkness. It was
a stimulating, challenging, revelatory week – and its impact was
long-lasting.

On my return from Lympstone in Devon, I realised that something I had always considered one of my absolute coaching
strengths could actually handicap my team. I was as detailed as
anybody in terms of my preparation – but counterintuitively that
was not helping my team prepare for battle. I remember Brigadier
Pillar speaking to me at the end of the week.

'The one thing we picked up about you, Clive, is that your
planning is immaculate.'

Great news, I think! Does that mean my team is ready for war?
I assume – briefly – this is a compliment.

'The problem is it's almost too good. You need to throw in a
few curveballs; you need to keep your team guessing. Your meticulous planning makes it all predictable. War is not predictable
and I imagine international rugby is the same. It never happens
the way you planned. The enemy will do things you do not expect.'

'OK . . . that makes sense. But what do I do?'

'Our training is about dislocated expectations. We put our
soldiers on the edge in training and we keep them there. You
need to start doing the same. Change your training. Change your
routine. Everyone in the England camp goes to bed thinking
training is starting at 10 a.m. and – lo and behold – training

begins at 10 a.m. Wake them up and start training at 6 a.m. - and do something you never have before.'

He was absolutely right, of course. When the players cross the white line on to the turf, we think we know what will happen, but we don't. The opposition will do things, try things, push you. Then there's the weather conditions, the referee and all manner of unpredictable events. Furthermore, if you play the way the opposition think you are going to play, you are already on the back foot. If you shock them with your unpredictability, however, you unravel their preparations. The same is true in beating your rivals to win customers in business.

The Brigadier was enjoying this speech now. He could see I was taking it in - really engaging with what he had to say - and then he went for the jugular.

'I hate to say it, Clive, but I'm going to be honest. These guys are simply not thinking for themselves. And you are in danger of turning them into a one-dimensional team.'

He could see I was fazed. I was not sure what he meant. How could he say I had a dull team? He saw my face turn.

'Let me explain what I mean by that. Look, they are clearly phenomenal athletes - and clearly have the potential to be phenomenal men - but right now they cannot cope with variables. You have to start training in a different way.'

Changing the routine

We brought that learning into our culture. We started to change the timetable, vary the way we trained, break up our routines.

We played football to work on our kicking skills, American football to help us visualise space on the pitch ahead of us (not just looking to pass the ball backwards). We used balls of different sizes and shapes to develop our handling and passing skills, changed sleeping patterns and training schedules. We briefed referees to referee badly to see how people responded. Would they throw their toys out of the pram or would they adapt their play to beat the game?

Of course, none of this stuff should be done just to be gimmicky or because it makes a good photo opportunity for your website. You have to consider the training value and the purpose – and then you experiment.

The 2017 Six Nations match between England and Italy was a timely reminder of the importance of being prepared for the unexpected. Italy deployed tactics to avoid committing any players to the ruck at all and therefore – within the IRB laws at the time – remove the offside line from play altogether. Suddenly blue shirts were swarming around the England scrum-half before he even had his hands anywhere near the ball. Provided they did not touch him, they were doing nothing in contravention of the laws of the game.

England were perplexed. They could not understand or cope. They could not problem-solve. At one point, when the Italian scrum-half Edoardo Gori was down receiving treatment on his head injury, there was a brief conversation between flanker James Haskell (a role that requires specialism at the breakdown), England captain Dylan Hartley and referee Romain Poite. The exchange was picked up by the microphone on the referee's collar and broadcast on live TV around the world.

Haskell asks: 'We just wanted to know what the rule was, what the exact rule is?'

Poite replies: 'If there is no ruck, there is just an area around the tackle on the ground making an offside line that is not set.'

Quizzed further by Haskell and Hartley, Poite reminds them: 'I am the referee, I'm not the coach.'

England had no concept of dislocated expectations, had not used any critical reflections in training and had not prepared to problem-solve. Poite knew the tactic was coming ahead of the game, but he told his assistant referees that the English team would find a solution after ten minutes.

One final irony was that the nefarious tactic was invented by Italy's defence coach, Brendan Venter – the man who had learned his trade under England's Eddie Jones at Saracens a decade previously. Venter knew he could unsettle England. And he knew he could give his Italian team belief if the plan worked. And it did.

There were two further telling comments afterwards.

Jones: 'We sent messages down on the field. But you just can't change as quickly as that. We don't have players who are naturally pick-and-go players.'

Venter: 'The reason it worked so well is because we already knew what England were going to do next. You don't just make the plan, you think about how the opposition will react. And we knew the only thing they could do was start to pick and go. So we had prepared for that.'

There is nothing easier to beat than predictability.

Learning when to say no

The British and Irish Lions have a magical romance about them; they are a cherished artefact from a different time and provide wonderful stories, precious in rugby folklore, from the annals of the amateur era.

As a player, I loved my time in South Africa with the Lions. The tour in 1980 was an enriching, eye-opening experience. The New Zealand tour in 1983 was less enjoyable. As a country, I love New Zealand, but as a touring destination there is no tougher place. I knew that as both a player and a coach.

However, as an England coach, the Lions are a challenging distraction that gets in the way of your successful business. It is a drain, physically and emotionally, that exposes your players to fatigue and exhaustion. In 2001, most of England's starting players were picked for the trip to Australia. It was a difficult tour for a lot of them and, on their return, some said they would not be prepared to play for the Lions again. Looking at it simply from the perspective of injury, it is a huge risk. Nearly half of the most recent Lions squad - nineteen out of forty-one - suffered a significant injury (three weeks or longer out of the game, often considerably longer) in the season after the 2017 tour to New Zealand.

My heart wanted to coach the Lions in 2005, but my head said no. The pragmatist in me wanted to turn down the job. A tour to New Zealand, of all places, and against one of rugby's great sides, with players like Dan Carter, Tana Umaga, Richie McCaw, Conrad Smith, Sitiveni Sivivatu all at the peak of their powers. In the end, I made a decision based on my heart. I remember having a conversation with Jayne. She said to me: 'Only do this if you know you can go down there with a full-strength side and win.' When I took the job on, I absolutely believed that. But we never got the chance to prove ourselves. By the end of the 2004-05 season, the England players especially had played far too much rugby and were suffering.

A few months out, I had my Lions team picked in my head. Our first team could have made history, but by the time we arrived in Christchurch for the first Test, about a third of the team were no longer fit. It is the one place where you simply have to have your best players fit to win. If you were to bring together the best players of New Zealand, South Africa and Australia into a scratch team and play against the 2003 England team at Twickenham, that SANZAR team would have been well beaten. Travelling there was the same scenario in reverse.

I tried to shortcut a lot of the Teamship process and we came up short against an exceptionally gifted New Zealand side. We did not have time to establish a culture that ensured cohesion or to fully empower the players in the way I wanted. However, one of the highlights of that trip was having a brief opportunity to get to know some outstanding players from Wales, Ireland and Scotland. At the end of the tour, Gareth 'Alfie' Thomas slipped a note under the door of my hotel room that said it best: 'You did everything you could.' It was a classy touch, greatly appreciated, and it speaks volumes of him as a bloke.

The big, painful lesson here is to learn when to say yes and when to say no. Success in business, just like in professional sport, is about learning how to make those decisions: when to listen to your heart, and when to listen to your head. There were too many 'if onlys' on that tour, and everything was with fingers crossed.

The journey home was the longest in my life. If the last time I had flown home from that part of the world had been one of the happiest and most memorable flights, for all the right reasons, this was its absolute antithesis. I got home and – for the second time in my life – went straight to the bedroom, shut the door and switched off the lights, to grieve in silence and darkness. I had done this once before, after England lost to South Africa at the 1999 World Cup, and for me it is an important coping mechanism, an important part of the process. You shut the door and you lie in bed for three days. You have to tap into that emotion, you have to grieve; you have to come to terms with what has happened. But then, at some point, you have to get back up.

The best way to move on from a setback is to analyse what happened – what went wrong, why did it go wrong, could you have done anything better? And then come to terms with it and move on. I worked out my answers to each of those questions, and I got out of bed.

Lesson from Japan: Adapting to survive

The High Tackle Sanction framework exposed certain leadership cultures during the tournament because they did not adapt in time. The new directive was first employed at the World Rugby Under-20 Championship in June in a bid to enforce lower tackle technique. At that tournament – just as it did in Japan – it produced a flurry of red cards for the teams who were too slow to respond.

First and foremost, World Rugby had a duty to act. Nothing is more important than player safety. If we do not protect the players, we cannot protect the game. Four young men died in France last season. The ethical imperative is clear – but there is also a financial incentive. The National Football League, the organisation that runs American football, is now dealing with a $1.25 billion concussion settlement. The latest research on concussion in football – published in the week of the semi-finals – established that former players were two and a half times more likely to suffer from dementia.

Successful cultures adapt. Farrell's tackle technique came under serious scrutiny during the 2018 autumn Tests. In response, he worked one-on-one with John Carrington, assistant in defence to England's John Mitchell, to ensure his technical precision was spot on. He managed to adjust his tackle technique and ended up becoming a target – rather than the agent – of controversially high tackles in the first few weeks of the tournament.

Teams like England and New Zealand made sure to 'underload' and 'overload' numbers in training, so that they could adapt to potentially being reduced to thirteen or fourteen men, or finding themselves scrambling in defence facing a two-man overlap.

Decisions over red cards are made on merit, taking into account mitigating factors (such as the body position of the ball carrier), but not all nations adapted well. Within the first four weeks of the tournament we saw five red cards – surpassing any previous records for an entire tournament. To place that in a wider context, there had been only one red card in a year of Test rugby until Japan.

The caveat here is that when you go in low for a tackle the defender is still in danger. Hitting at hip height or catching a knee can still bring serious injury. The focus needs to be on technique. Some players are tackling high for their own protection because of the angle of impact with the ball-carrier. There is a natural instinct to protect yourself during the tackle and we must ensure that the laws are not adjusted to the point of making it easier for an attacker to get an opponent sent off. Forwards especially – given their typically bigger frames – had to practise lowering body height and targeting the hips before the tournament. My simple rule was always to tackle below the ball: you guarantee your tackle is legal and you have a chance to dislodge the ball.

While it has always been illegal to tackle around head height, the complication in the modern game is that defence coaches have put a premium on big hits. World Rugby must continue to distinguish between contact around the chest that slides up to the head, and initial contact with the chin or above. Players must also learn to be meticulously careful with footwork into the tackle. The focus on defensive line speed can lead to uncontrolled collisions, while planting feet too early can bring wild tackles as players overstretch to make contact. Size disparity must also be considered in mitigation.

You can often detect the severity of an illegal tackle from the reaction of players. Compare how the England players responded to John Quill's hit on Owen Farrell in the pool game against the

USA with how Samoa's players reacted to Ireland centre Bundee Aki's tackle on UJ Seuteni. Punishing both those infractions with the same sanction is something that needs to be properly examined. In an ideal world, the game would have two clear seasons to prepare in which everyone is playing by the same rules.

CHAPTER XV

SECOND ROW
What makes a great individual?

'It is better to lead from behind and to put others in front, especially when you celebrate victory. You take the front line when there is danger. Then people will appreciate your leadership.'

Nelson Mandela

Winning behaviours: The Warrior, the tough guy, the enforcer. This is the kind of team player who leads by example in every element of their professional and personal life: work ethic, strength and conditioning, nutrition, behaviour, appearance and the way they look after everyone else. They will be the first player to step into the line of fire to protect a team-mate, and also the first player to step away from the limelight off the field, especially when things go right. But for all their generous spirit, 'in battle' they are ferocious and intimidating. These great individuals ask 'How can we help you?' not 'What is in it for me?'

In team games, as in business, you need a variety of skills and personalities to thrive. You need key people who can make decisions, but also key people to lead the charge. Martin Johnson was a born leader, but that does not mean he was a master tactician capable of making the key decision in the middle of a Test match. If anything, he was often too busy sorting life out at the bottom of a ruck or looking after his own!

I am often asked about whether I would be prepared to select the fabled 'unmanageable' personalities. Those athletes and players who, rightly or wrongly, have a reputation for being impossibly challenging. My answer is always the same: of course I would. Do you think the England team of 2003 were a bunch of gentle snowflakes? I want the best talent, which means I would relish the challenge. Leaders want to hire the most talented, skilful, challenging athletes of a generation: Eric Cantona, Kevin Pietersen, Danny Cipriani, Paul Pogba. Those outside of elite sporting environments tend to make the false supposition that these players are only interested in their own success. All you need to do is to ensure they know that your only mission objective is to make them better players.

Cantona understood Ferguson's culture and revelled in it. Do you think he could have played with that sustained level of passion and craft if he had not been wholeheartedly committed to the culture that Ferguson built at Old Trafford? Seven different coaches worked under Sir Alex Ferguson: Archie Knox (1986–91), Brian Kidd (1991–98), Steve McClaren (1999–2001), Jimmy Ryan (1998, 2001–02), Carlos Queiroz (2002–03, 2004–08), Walter Smith (2004) and Mike Phelan (2008–13). That is a staggering range of tactical diversity, style and knowledge. Every time Ferguson hired a new coach, United's playing style evolved in subtle but discernible ways, but the one constant was the institutional standards Ferguson demanded of anyone in a United shirt. Cantona understood that. I am not suggesting that kung-fu-kicking a supporter was Cantona subscribing to that culture, but one rash moment of rage does not mean he was disloyal to Ferguson or the winning ethos at Old Trafford.

Embracing the difference

The beauty of sport is that every coach is different. There is an art to picking players you can get on with. In that sense, it really is no different from business. You have to pick the personalities that will work in your team, embrace your team cultures and champion your team values. When it comes to the maverick players – whether it is Eric Cantona under Alex Ferguson or Cipriani under Eddie Jones – there is no right and wrong as long as you win. If you lose, you live with question marks. I did not leave Austin Healey out of the England 2003 World Cup squad for any other reason than his fitness to play – I loved that spark. He brought a mercurial energy and levity to training for which we were all grateful. He was left behind because he was not fully fit.

A winning culture does not put people in handcuffs; it actually provides an environment in which personalities can flourish. A strong culture allows gifted players more freedom to play because they know where the line is and that if they cross it, they are gone. You manage these personalities by immersing them in the winning culture and securing their involvement. If you say I cannot teach Kevin Pietersen to hit a four or Cantona to hit a volley, then you do not understand the process of coaching. Coaching and teaching share a huge range of common functions here: you can still teach a virtuoso how to play the violin. Do you think Dave Alred can kick a rugby ball like Jonny Wilkinson or sink a 15 ft putt like Francesco Molinari? Earlier, I described the genetic make-up of the DNA of a Champion, and the same necessities are absolutely true of a Champion coach. A relentless attitude to learning and improvement must be a core part of that. The athletes push boundaries but the coach stays in charge.

But Ferguson also understood where the line is. Never underestimate the damage that one personality can do to a culture. Consider some of the most high-profile departures of Ferguson's astonishing reign: David Beckham, Jaap Stam, Cristiano Ronaldo. People kept saying the United team were past their best, that they would fold in the face of fresh investment from Chelsea, then Manchester City, that it was the end of a dynasty – but every time the team became stronger.

Long before I became performance director at Southampton Football Club, I visited their training ground to see what I could learn from a different sporting culture. There was one footballer who stood out. Matt Le Tissier had an image as a lazy maverick. Unquestionably, he was a gifted technical footballer, but he had a reputation for not working hard enough in training. The first time I saw him he was by himself on the training ground. What was he doing? If you followed Premier League football in the 1990s I do not need to tell you: practising penalties. It is almost too clichéd to be worth saying, but I continue to find it utterly mystifying that the England football team failed to practise penalties for so many major tournaments, as if being led by superstition rather than common sense and reason. But just like Jonny Wilkinson, Le Tissier was out by himself perfecting his technique with targeted, deliberate practice. He remains the most efficient and clinical converter of penalties in top-flight English football (ignore those who have taken only a handful).

Astonishingly, he converted forty-seven of his forty-eight penalties while at Southampton – the one that got away being saved by Nottingham Forest's Mark Crossley in 1993. That was neither magic nor innate talent alone: it was a professional practising his craft long after the car park had emptied – until he was a Champion.

Test of character

During a tournament like a World Cup or an Olympics, how you manage your time off depends on a range of contexts, especially the length of the tournament and its down time. If I ever felt I needed to worry about how a player might behave, then he had clearly failed to subscribe to our culture and he no longer had the right to a place in the squad. The All Blacks have their famous 'no dickheads' policy that is part of rugby folklore, and even Netflix have followed suit with their company-wide 'no brilliant jerks' policy. No matter your technical brilliance, innovative creations or financial nous – if you do not abide by a community's essential standards of conduct, there is no place for you.

When England went training with the Royal Marines, I was given an envelope with the names of a few players at the end.

'My men have been listening to everything over the past few days. These are the players who we wouldn't expect to make a Royal Marine.'

Interestingly, the vast majority of players picked for the World Cup squad in 2003 had excelled during these days of Marine training, surpassing the incredible standards of dress, conduct and behaviour.

England's Teamship rules on coaching and player standards

In the Black Book we came up with eight coaching standards that championed precisely these kinds of values. These standards were about sustaining certain levels of behaviour and promoting attributes of character that would help us in our quest to be the best team in the world. There were simple things policed by the players – ensuring that everyone helped tidy up and clear up rubbish around the pitch, being positive and energising in training when things were not going to plan – and there were expectations from the coaches concerning the planning, quality and objective from every session.

We also, as a group, established eleven players' standards, which were written to protect the highest principles of attitudes and behaviours from everyone in the group, regardless of whether we were arriving at the team hotel or sitting on the team bus to Twickenham. Nothing was 'off the table' in terms of honest and open discussion, but any problems had to be raised in the confidence of the War Room. Simple expectations regarding language and dress ensured that the professionalism of our winning environment was never undermined. Finally, we were operating in a no-moaning culture. If anyone had an issue, they were encouraged to discuss it face-to-face with me or Martin.

The value of charm

There is an essential attribute to leadership that is so often overlooked: charm. I have yet to meet an inspirational leader at the very top of sport or business who was not charming.

There are three key qualities that encompass the idea of charm: engagement, enjoyment and collaboration. Successful leaders need to embody these qualities to take the board with them, to convince people to follow, to engender loyalty in their army. This is also part of managing upwards and is especially vital in a field like sales in which you are not just dealing with a company.

Ask yourself: do you know how to be charming? To what extent do you prioritise or value these attributes? Simply put, people like doing business with charming people.

Lesson from Japan: Breaking the rules

The circumstances regarding the typhoon required common sense and open communication. Worst-case scenario from the tournament's perspective? You wait twenty-four hours until Monday, hire two jumbo jets and play the game in Hong Kong if that is what it takes.

Weather forecasting is phenomenally accurate these days and the country hosting the tournament was in the shoulder of typhoon season. Its magnitude was severe, but the possibility did not come as a surprise. In its planning phase, the tournament needed to work through contingencies and come up with flexible, credible options should a typhoon strike.

In the last round of pool matches, there were still three teams who could mathematically have qualified for the quarter-finals: Italy, Scotland and Japan. Supposing there were only two games that could have been played over that weekend, then New Zealand versus Italy and Japan versus Scotland were the two games that simply had to be played.

It would have been a logistical challenge, financially profligate and disruptive to players and supporters – but you do whatever it takes to protect the integrity of the competition. The Olympic Games are coming to Tokyo in the middle of typhoon season and they must learn from this.

I was surprised by the decision to call the games off so soon, because once you have formally cancelled a fixture, there is no going back. Meanwhile, tournament officials on the ground slept in the stadium overnight as the typhoon was roaring outside, just so they might assess – and resolve – any damage as soon as possible. They started pumping water out of the dressing room at dawn.

Although Scotland had every right to feel enraged, they pushed the button too soon in their furious recriminations against World Rugby, hypothetically arguing against the supposed cancellation of a fixture that ultimately went ahead as planned.

Italy hooker Leonardo Ghiraldini broke down in tears when his last Test match was cancelled, while Sergio Parisse – a majestic player in his pomp but already playing one tournament too far – publicly declared that the game would not have been cancelled if it was New Zealand who needed the points. It was an ugly few days for the tournament, but World Rugby did not make the decision lightly.

Through lost ticket sales, commercial deals and compensation to broadcasters, the cancellation cost them around £30 million. But that means nothing compared to the cost of human life.

CHAPTER XVI

SECOND ROW
The Hive Learning model: digitising the process

'Innovation distinguishes between a leader and a follower.'

Steve Jobs

Winning behaviours: The student. The second row who operates the lineout – one of the most essential but technically complex elements of the game – is passionate, informed and obssessed by the idea of providing the rest of the team with the perfect platform for success. They will demonstrate an unending academic curiosity in the minutiae of every element of the discipline and an unending willingness to discover more to enhance their expertise. They will embrace new technology, not as a fashionable gimmick, but to exploit its functionality in a way that benefits the shared goals of the entire operation.

Between the last two Rugby World Cups, data surpassed oil as the most precious commodity on earth. The quality and detail of that data will evolve as digital technology continues to evolve, but the theory and value behind its application will not.

While England coach, I heard about a new cutting-edge technology that was being used by Arsène Wenger at Arsenal. I swallowed my pride as a life-long Chelsea supporter and arranged for a tour as soon as possible. In all my time working in elite sporting environments, that experience at Arsenal's training ground, playing around with this new technology, was one of the most exhilarating, cherished and eye-opening experiences in my career.

At the time, ProZone cameras were at the forefront of digital innovation. When I took over the England team, I had never heard of the software, but soon – within a matter of months of intense development, in fact – we had bolted twenty incredible high-tech cameras onto the rafters of Twickenham Stadium, each capable of picking features of every individual player. Better still, we were the only rugby team on the planet using the technology. Nowadays, England players wear microchips sewn into the back of their shirts and have tablets in the changing room providing bespoke clips and data on key details or set pieces at half-time. But although the technology has evolved, the essential idea is exactly the same.

Retiring Irish captain Rory Best cannot stop New Zealand's Aaron Smith from crossing the line in a crushing quarter-final defeat.

England flanker Sam Underhill – one of the most prolific tacklers in the tournament – eyes up Australia scrum-half Will Genia during the quarter-final victory.

Wales's Aaron Wainwright makes a clean break against France on his way to a try.

France's Sébastien Vahaamahina was sent off for elbowing Wainwright in the quarter-final and retired from Test rugby the following day.

Captain Owen Farrell steps round New Zealand captain Kieran Read in England's pulsating 19-7 semi-final victory.

The England team form a 'V' to wrap up the All Black pre-match haka as a clear signal of intent.

Manu Tuilagi forces his way through New Zealand players to score England's first try.

England lock Maro Itoje towers over the All Black lineout in a commanding semi-final performance that saw him take charge of the vital set piece.

A bloodied and bruised leader, Kieran Read reflects on a semi-final exit at the hands of England.

South Africa scrum-half Faf de Klerk and Wales second row Jake Ball exchange a word or two during their semi-final.

South Africa centre Damian de Allende breaks three tackles while powering over the line.

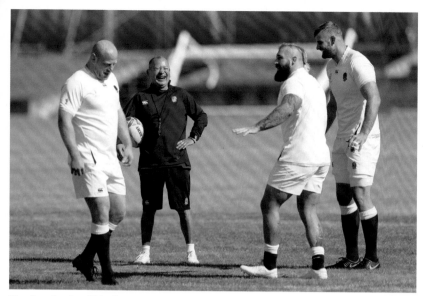

The close bonds within the England camp are clear to see as Eddie Jones shares a joke with Dan Cole, Joe Marler and George Kruis.

A bloodied Billy Vunipola takes a moment to reflect on England's performance in the final.

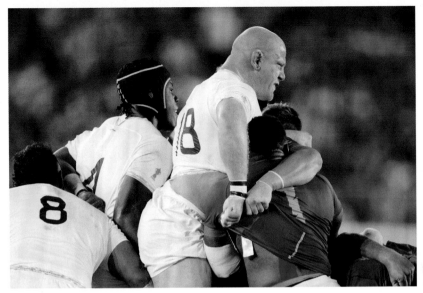

Dan Cole and the England front row concede another scrum penalty under the pressure of Tendai Mtawarira.

Wing Makazole Mapimpi scores South Africa's first try in a World Cup final to extend the Springboks' lead.

Two outstanding leaders, South Africa coach Rassie Erasmus and captain Siya Kolisi, worked together to mastermind the victory.

Kolisi becomes South Africa's first black captain to lift the Webb Ellis Cup and sparks emotional celebrations across the country.

A whole new perspective

The data that ProZone provided us with was, and this is no exaggeration, a complete game-changer. For both coaches and players, it meant we could see the game from an entirely new dimension and perspective. The screen might have looked like a *Championship Manager* simulation but this was not a toy or a kid's game. The information had a demonstrable impact on how we coached and how England played. While the technology has changed since, the principles have not. During the 2019 Champions League final, Tottenham manager Mauricio Pochettino was nervously parading the touchline, clutching a tablet that provided him with live data-based analysis and footage about every single player.

After the very first game using ProZone, I realised I had been coaching the game from the perspective of a TV screen. Suddenly I was able to see the game from the perspective of a map, looking down without any misleading angles and with a consistent view of the entire pitch. The technology immediately supplied us with an abundance of meaningful data which could be unpacked and excavated for fascinating revelations about our style of play and the nature of the game itself. It also meant I could know, the evening after a game, who was running furthest and fastest, who was being lazy, who was cheating at the offside line – essentially who was and was not doing their job properly.

When I first showed it to the England rugby team there was total silence in the room. From their perspective, this was not a good week to play for England: there was nowhere to hide! I started calling it 'Big Brother Plus', in homage to Orwell, as we began collating reams of data from the twenty cameras that, at the time, nobody knew we had.

This was not just data for coaches and leaders, though. Champion players owned this data: recognising the insight it provided them in bettering their performance, they consumed it.

Initially, I was providing players with CD-ROMs to take home and review over the weekend before coming back to give a presentation on their performance and the performance of their opponents. But it soon completely changed the dynamics of how we coached and how we managed. Email also meant we could quickly ping discovered data to each other as coaches and players – even between filmed training sessions. The intricacies of analysis meant the quality of our one-on-one player-review meetings went up another level. No longer were our conversations – and subsequent analysis and decision-making – based on subjective, emotional memory but on hard, empirical data instead.

'Competitive intelligence' is defined as the information collected by a company about rival businesses and markets, which may then be analysed to create more effective business strategies. In that regard, this ProZone data was an extraordinary 'CI' asset – as is the abundance of statistical data and video available to coaches at the 2019 World Cup.

There were three swift unforeseen and revelatory impacts of this new technology.

1. The first impact was a crucial psychological consequence: it demystified the All Blacks. Instantly, fifteen blokes in a New Zealand rugby shirt were reduced to dots and data on a projected

screen. They were no longer the imperious, domineering, fabled men in black: they were statistics. To this end, I stopped calling them the All Blacks and referred to them only as New Zealand. Language and technology were not the reason we beat them, but they helped nibble away at this narrative the rugby world likes to project of their immortal, unbeatable status.

2. The second impact tested our Teamship principles, but the strength of our culture was such that we had the foundations in place to cope. In short: team meetings got pretty lively. The England set-up is a tough and unforgiving place, and it could be an aggressive place, too. We had big arguments, but when they were over everyone shook hands. The data proved how hard everyone was working at the weekend, and it made accountability a mathematical truth. Test-match animals do not like to lose and they will let you know if you have let somebody down. I can never speak highly enough of players like Martin Johnson, Lawrence Dallaglio and Phil Vickery, players whose knowledge and understanding of the game grew weekly because of their analysis of the data and whose perform-ances consequently improved exponentially.

There was nothing worse in the team-review meeting than a pointed finger and a question: 'What the f--- were you doing?' There was one particular meeting that really kicked off. We had played poorly in an autumn international in 2002 and our restarts had been especially chaotic. At that time our kick-off routines were run by forwards, but our back three were furious. Jason Robinson, Dan Luger and Josh Lewsey started really taking it to them, laying into Ben Kay, Martin Johnson and Lawrence Dallaglio. We decided there and then to change it. Why not put the wingers in charge of restarts? They were so animated and invested that it made sense for them to take sole responsibility for that part of the game. Our revised target was 100 per cent ball retention on kick-off receipt and a 25 per cent win rate on tapping back our kick-offs and securing possession. It was an excellent team meeting with an outstanding outcome.

3. The third impact provided a sense of vindication about my philosophy of coaching rugby and my ambition for the team. When I first took the job, I was staggered by the influx of experts who told me that the professional game is tougher and stronger than anything I could understand as a player from the amateur era. Everyone told me that defences were on top and would remain so, and that there was simply no space on the pitch in the modern game. Ten seconds of ProZone data proved beyond any reasonable doubt that this was complete and utter nonsense. The images below are taken from the kick-off against France in April 2001 and they are staggering. They remain some of the most amazing images I have seen in twenty years of working in professional sport. It looks like a bad Under-5s football match. The French are swarming to the ball as if they have never played the game before.

For England's team meeting on the following Monday I turned this screen grab (Fig. 2) into the world's biggest poster, hanging it on the wall of the meeting room ahead of everyone's arrival. On the poster I had printed, in the biggest letters that would fit the wall, 'THE SPACE IS THE GREEN STUFF.'

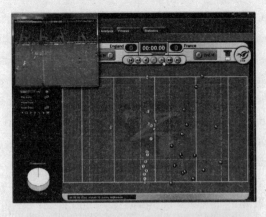

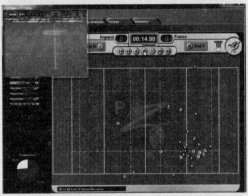

Leaders use the data

Professional or not, 120 kg players or not, there was still loads of space on a rugby pitch – you just had to see it. In the context of sport, Formula One has always led innovation in technology. It is a sport in which races can be won or lost on fractional errors of micro-engineering or nanotechnology. But that is where leaders pay attention.

When I work in the corporate sector, the first thing an executive always seems to want to do is show me some new technology, software or data. The first question I ask is: 'So, who uses this data?' Almost without fail, the reply is the same, as I am proudly told: 'It's not my job any more.' Inevitably, there is some bright young thing in the tech team who does the number-crunching on behalf of the boss. Worse still, this seems to be regarded as some misguided badge of honour.

This a fatal mistake. If you are that person, then you are already drifting towards complacency and disconnect from the very essence of a winning culture. If you are delegating the front line of analysis and reflection – the insight that should direct your actions – to a bunch of people who may well have profound intelligence but who lack your experience and your analytical eye, your business or your team is in trouble.

Hive Learning software and social learning

After leaving England, I saw an opportunity to develop software that used modern technology to help communicate and evolve my coaching philosophies. I wanted to use the power of mobile technology to help teams deliver continuous high performance. Hive Learning is a mobile-first learning platform that enables a modern social learning experience. In 2003, England's seven winning disciplines were illustrated with graphics; Hive Learning represents the digital evolution of that process. While England players and coaches sat in a room together, sharing their knowledge in longhand before capturing the key details,

Hive Learning is an online tool, capturing and sharing knowledge for both sport and business.

Hive Learning is a bespoke peer learning online platform that is built on the principle that it is the connections across any given network that can revolutionise and innovate the way in which everyone operates. The platform combines technology, content and expertise to catalyse precisely the principles of learning that have been laid out here. The software offers a radically faster route to driving inclusion, collaboration and innovation inside an organisation. It is currently used by more than fifty leading organisations, including Barclays, Deloitte, Dow Jones, Pepsico, Jaguar, Land Rover and Sky. The FA have been using it with around 30,000 coaches, sharing collected knowledge and disseminating the information efficiently and engagingly.

In the chapter on the Inside Centre, I explained the process of 3D Learning: Discover, Distil, Do. In the world in which we now exist and compete, we can add a fourth dimension: Digital. The Hive Learning model means that learning can be downloaded into a shared resource. Do not let somebody leave your company and take years of institutional knowledge with them. You now have the technology to capture that intellectual property and harness the information on a shared platform. Not only that, but with Hive Learning you can actually measure the extent of collaboration.

The Hive Learning model is built on four key pillars:

1. **Mobile:** Our mobile-first platform goes where employee attention is and can be accessed at every moment.

2. **Intelligent content:** Our intelligent content tools stay relevant by adapting to learners' ever-changing needs.

3. **Group-centred social experience:** Our platform enables collaborative learning that encourages practice and keeps motivation levels up.

4. **Daily action:** Our powerful nudges and notifications encourage daily action to embed real behaviour change.

Digital learning and innovation

Learning is the pathway to innovation. According to a report published by Deloitte on technology and the workplace, technological progress has contributed to the loss of more than 800,000 low-skilled jobs over the last few years. That element is unsurprising. It makes intuitive sense that scientific progress will increasingly replicate the mechanism of typical low-skilled jobs. In 2018, a burger-flipping robot received global attention after it cooked more than 300 burger patties in its first shift. More interesting, however, was the Deloitte report's other key finding: in the same time frame, technology has led to the creation of 3.5 million new, higher-skilled jobs. On further consideration, technology should not be seen as jeopardising the future of employment; instead, harnessing technology can actually be the catalyst for better productivity, efficiency and performance.

The Hive allows you to share valuable knowledge and relevant learning with employees across the world, and across time zones, at any given moment.

On an average day, a working person (probably an employee

of yours?) will unlock his or her smartphone nine times an hour. Why not make that a learning opportunity? The learning content needs to be relevant, purposeful and bite-sized: designed to be consumed in short, manageable chunks. Half of learning and collaboration on the Hive Learning app happens outside office hours and 65 per cent of usage is mobile. How many companies improve the quality of their team's daily output during the dead time of their commute?

Innovation as rugby's future

More than anything, the England team of 2015 failed to adapt. England appeared to use the same blueprint for every game without grasping one of the essential facts of international rugby: every opposition plays differently. Everything down to your kick-chase has to be different for each top-class team. For example, New Zealand tend to look to pass the ball twice off a deep kick, moving the ball the full width of the pitch to shift the point of attack, so any kick-chase must have full-pitch coverage. Australia, on the other hand, tend to rely on the footwork and change of pace of their back three to beat the first defender and buy a small pocket of time for their back row to hit the breakdown and secure the ball.

Why are certain factions of the rugby community so terrified of football? In Premiership Rugby's leaked 2011 World Cup review, it was even written: 'There is a real culture of expectation from the players and a fear that rugby union is following a "football mentality".' Fear of what, exactly?

Commercialism is not a dirty word. Rugby turned professional in 1995 but so much of it is still lost in an amateur era. Professional sportsmen and sportswomen navigate a world of image rights, multiple endorsements and social media. Football is tapping into urban culture and social media has changed the landscape – and business – of the sport. Football is building its links to fashion and music. Street football is growing as a game. The consequences of all this are what we saw in the Champions League in 2019, with four English teams in the semi-finals of arguably the highest-quality tournament on the planet, World Cup included. Meanwhile, for the best part of a decade, any English success at the top level of rugby has been mostly reliant on Saracens.

French football freestylers, who are merging gravity-defying ball skills with breakdancing and contemporary dance, get more than 50 million views on YouTube. Meanwhile, 'Football+' is an emerging community of projects, tapping into football's existing relationships with music, fashion, gaming and its notions of social mobility and equality. It is an authentic symbiotic relationship in which football connects players and fans with other interests, particularly on a youth level.

I cannot see a football coach going into rugby, because it is a complicated game that evolves in accordance with the styles of the domestic league and local interpretations of the law. Rugby is a game of chess in which you have to outwit your opponent, not with brute strength but with imaginative guile. The reason football is the biggest game in the world is its fundamental simplicity. Every fan in the world thinks they understand the game better than anyone else in the stadium!

Where is 'rugby+'? It is time that its guardians had the vision and aspiration to expand the sport. It is not a truly contemporary or global game right now.

The future of the English game

Eddie Jones is absolutely right to probe the essential question: *Are we creating a generation of Manus and not enough Messis?* When he spoke those words he was in no way criticising Tuilagi. In fact, England's wrecking-ball outside centre was one of the outstanding players of the World Cup, matching his power with skill in attack and intelligence in defence. But what Jones wanted to probe was our priorities at the developmental level of the game. By that he means are our development programmes and all our coaching at grass-roots level focused on muscle and power, trying to reproduce the muscle mass of a seventeen-year-old Manu Tuilagi, or are we also creating players with flexibility and guile and skill, epitomised by Lionel Messi? Put another way, the infrastructure of the RFU needs to continue to nurture talent for the next generation of England's World Cup athletes. The current team are a wonderfully talented group of individuals, but there are fewer people playing the game. This World Cup marks a profound opportunity to focus on the development of rugby in England.

Hundreds and thousands of boys and girls up and down the country have just witnessed an England team string together enthralling, exhilarating performances based on world-class skill and a foundational freedom to play. Yet, since the 2011 World

Cup, government figures suggest participation among young people has dropped from its 23 per cent peak to around 14 per cent last year. That is deeply concerning for the future of the game. It is imperative that more state secondary schools begin to play the game and that the gender division between children taking up the sport all but dissipates.

From a financial perspective, the World Cup year (in a non-host cycle) is always the most challenging for the RFU – and its more than 550 full-time employees – because of the lack of autumn internationals at Twickenham and the subsequent loss of ticket sales, sponsorship and broadcast rights. In the four-year cycle up to the 2007 World Cup, after England's victory in 2003, the RFU's investment in rugby was £179 million. In the last four years that figure has become £400 million, yet England's community players are not seeing the benefits of that investment. The RFU made approximately £30 million profit from hosting the Rugby World Cup in 2015 and they own their key asset – Twickenham Stadium.

Off the back of Japan, we must also revolutionise the role of education and what is happening in schools. An Ofsted report took a survey of players in the top flight. While 94 per cent of English players playing in football's Premier League were educated in the state sector, only 39 per cent of rugby's Premiership players were. The other 61 per cent were educated privately. Now consider that the independent sector only educates around 7 per cent of children in England, and you get a sense of how skewed those figures are, how disproportionately privileged and elitist the game's roots appear to a wider society and how much more work rugby has to do to open its doors properly in England and balance that out.

Even briefly putting aside any sense of moral or social responsibility, from a purely performance perspective at the very highest level, can you imagine the pool of talent that is being missed? Jason Leonard, the most-capped prop in the history of Test match rugby, only took up the sport when a new teacher happened to join his school, Warren Comprehensive in Chadwell Heath, and added rugby to the curriculum. It was pure chance that his new PE teacher happened to be Welsh.

It is not just a problem exclusive to rugby. According to a 2019 study by the University of Bath, nearly two in three (64 per cent) of children from the highest-income households take part in sport, compared to 46 per cent of young people from families on the lowest incomes. In certain areas, there are access difficulties as schools do not (or financially cannot) provide these activities, and youth provision has been cut back by councils. But sometimes young people from disadvantaged backgrounds do not take part because they lack confidence, or fear they will not fit in. Rugby – above almost any other sport – has the power to combat this. It is the ultimate democratising force as it is the sport that welcomes every shape and size, any demographic.

There are some initiatives out there. The All Schools programme targets clusters of state schools so that they can play local, well-matched fixtures without spreading the net too thinly, and Premiership Rugby has launched other initiatives to target inner-city children, as well as reaching more ethnic minorities and women and girls to take up the game. But that progress is reliant upon a few inspirational individuals operating with one hand tied behind their back, and the RFU need to invest and commit more seriously.

Furthermore, the RFU need to continue to champion more innovative, progressive and exciting coaching methodologies. One example is CARDS, which stands for Creativity, Awareness, Resilience, Decision-making and Self-organisation. The objective is simple: if you can create a generation of players who match their talent with a capacity to problem-solve and react to the game around them, without any traditional, prescriptive shackles of how the game 'should' be played, then you will soon consistently produce the best players in the world.

Why only train your fly-half to kick-pass to a winger? Imagine the danger of fifteen players with an entirely versatile skill set. The coaching methodology is dynamic and exciting, the focus on game-playing and pushing players out of their comfort zone and challenging their expectations: play full-contact rugby in a circle and you rethink how to create space; prevent the fly-half from being allowed to kick and someone else has to step in at first receiver; tell your winger he has to pass after taking ten steps or it is an automatic turnover and suddenly the half-backs are incentivised to follow their pass and work harder in support. By manipulating training environments and changing the conditions of a game, you can highlight character flaws and technical weaknesses in your players. This is something Eddie Jones has utilised at the highest end of the game, but now is the time to filter down that progressive coaching ethos through to rugby's grassroots.

SECOND ROW

There are undoubtedly players and coaches who are interested in promoting the game to expand beyond its conservative and traditional means. But there have been failings in the infrastructure of the sport that is not giving them the platform to express this. One individual who does seem to have the spine to challenge conventional thinking is Ben Ryan, and he continues to experiment with seven-a-side and five-a-side versions of rugby. At the O2 Arena in the autumn, a five-a-side version of rugby called Rugby X experimented with the game – speeding up and simplifying rugby with a model closely following Twenty20 cricket.

Even the advent of gaming has been widely ignored by the rugby community. Why not sell out Twickenham for an e-games event that promotes the sport? Can you imagine even trying to explain to those in a real position to influence the game what this is all about? While the England team are opening doors to a new future, too many people are trying to protect a history that does not need protecting, when in truth the sport needs to explode out into new opportunities. England's performances in Japan have given us that chance. I would hate to see us waste it.

Lesson from Japan: Standards of conduct

Wales found themselves in an extremely difficult position on the eve of the tournament. Rob Howley, Gatland's trusted assistant coach for more than a decade, was accused of an alleged breach of sports-betting rules. Howley flew home immediately and shut himself off from the world for the duration of the tournament. It was a nightmare situation after four years of meticulous preparation, but Wales and Gatland handled it brilliantly. You make the tough call quickly and communicate honestly.

In short: front up and move on.

Gatland offered one press conference in which he said everything on the matter that he was prepared to say and sat in the glare of the spotlight until every question was answered – then he, and the team, focused on their rugby.

The flip side of that was Howley's own role. There was complete radio silence until the tournament was over. This behaviour from all parties shows a private cohesion even in the face of such a public separation. Under the most trying circumstances, when players and coaches could have ranted and raved, nobody in the Wales camp was going to jeopardise their World Cup.

Similarly, Jones built so much of England's culture around the idea of social cohesion, intent on improving player relationships, but still ruthless in making decisions if he felt anyone endangered that or breached protocol. Before his very first meeting with the England squad, Jones had the team room redecorated so it felt like the start of a new culture, something which he could build and something of which he had complete ownership. There were signs of Jones's clear thinking in this area ahead of the tournament. Whatever it was that happened between Ben Te'o and Mike Brown during the summer training camp, Jones did not hesitate to act swiftly in removing them for what he decided was the good of the culture.

CHAPTER XVII

TIGHTHEAD PROP
The power of sponges and rocks

'I've learned that people will forget what you said, people will forget what you did, but people will never forget how you made them feel.'

Maya Angelou

Winning behaviours: The tighthead is the foundation of your core unit, who provides the stability and support to an organisation. He or she is the anchor of the scrum and the rock of the team, but mentally he or she is a sponge, keen to absorb as much knowledge as possible to enhance their performance. If the tighthead breaks down in a game, you have no chance. Identifying weak characters in an organisation or team is an essential part of leadership, and how you deal with them will define the success of your whole operation. Weak links will bring about failure and destroy trust. It is what you learn after you think you know it all that makes the ultimate difference.

Two words capture Jonny Wilkinson: *relentless learning.* Learning demands exposure and practice as a regular part of your professional daily life and nobody personifies that attitude better. There was the obsession of the professional, and then there was the way in which Wilkinson trained.

He knew how and precisely where to strike the stitching of each new model of rugby ball. He knew the yardage of his kicking distances depending on the balance of fatigue and adrenaline he might feel on any given day of a training week. He forgot about aiming between the posts and started picking out smaller and smaller targets. At first it was an area of seats behind the post, then it became an imaginary old lady called Doris in the stands, then the newspaper she was reading, then her can of Coke. Finally he was aiming to knock the single scoop of vanilla ice cream off the cone she was holding.

'**Sponges**' continue to absorb knowledge throughout their career, constantly inputting that information into the systems in which they work. Imagine a beating heart that is pumping fresh oxygen around the body with every beat. '**Rocks**',

Sponges: People always willing to absorb new information and learn new skills.

Rocks: People reluctant to absorb new information or learn new skills.

by contrast, will destroy a culture and hinder the growth of any business. Their brains are barren, infertile deserts and they have reached their maximum cognitive load, through either intellectual incompetence or intransigence.

When Carles Puyol moved from a small town in the Pyrenees to Barcelona's talent school, La Masia, as one of forty boys sharing four rooms for two years, there was a reason he emerged as the most heralded player: not his talent, but his drive. He was a sponge, not a rock. He might have had skill, control and agility dripping from his boots, but it was his desire to learn the game that set him apart from his rivals in the dormitory.

Training, like business, can be hard – but it does not always have to be serious. Forcing your body to endure sprint cycles when the lactic acid is burning in your quads is not a pleasant feeling; enduring a twenty-hour day while poring over the minutiae of a complex contract is not pleasant either. But your general culture can have room for fun, and learning can be enjoyable. The best teachers love their job because they enjoy their time in the classroom. The same is true of coaches and the same should be true of business leaders. If nobody in your office or team smiles or laughs during the working day, then the business is not going to last very long – or at least it is not going to succeed for very long. What is the incentive to return? What is the incentive for investing the time and energy to make the difference?

The research is clear: interactive learning increases retention rates by up to ten times. Passive learning – lectures, reading, demonstration – typically results in a retention rate of somewhere between 5 per cent and 30 per cent, contingent on all manner of contextual factors, including the subject and the subject's familiarity with the topic. But that statistic jumps when learning involves 'doing' – discussion groups, evaluation exercises or teaching others. Suddenly the retention rate sits around 50–80 per cent. That is an extraordinary disparity, one that is controlled entirely by the manner and methods in which learning takes place.

The most successful people in the world, from Barack Obama to Bill Gates, are evangelical about the power of learning, dedicating at least one hour a day to it. They celebrate the intrinsic value of knowledge for its own sake, as well as remaining conscious of its other personal and professional benefits. The knowledge economy is becoming an increasingly familiar refrain in modern commerce. As billionaire Paul Tudor Jones puts it: 'Intellectual capital will always trump financial capital.'

A team of learners

Let me give you another example from the world of rugby. One of the first things I did was to insist that every England player should be given a laptop computer. For some of the players it was the first time they had operated one. My mantra in business was that whoever wins in IT tends to win – and I remain convinced that sport is no different.

The laptop was not a trap. We trained them. This was a financial and personal investment in the players and their success. I brought in the very best IT Specialists to offer every help to them and along the way there were some casualties. But the process helped me instantly identify the rocks (I remember one player crossing his arms and calling it bullshit) and the sponges, diving into this new world of high-performance analysis and better lines of communication. Technology is only valuable if it enhances performance. This technology was not a gimmick – I knew it would instigate phenomenal changes in our ability to self-assess and improve. But I remember being challenged by a few of the old guard at the RFU, who seemed to think analysing data was an unnecessary expense and a little far-fetched in a game when you are smashing people.

It probably goes without saying that my friends in the media had a field day. The headline writers certainly enjoyed the fun. One of my favourites – a cut-out I have kept – carried a picture of Martin Johnson walking into the England camp with a laptop tucked under his right arm and the headline 'WHY ISN'T HE GIVING THEM MORE RED MEAT?'

One of my most cherished memories is a picture of three England front-row players – Richard Cockerill, Graham Rowntree and Darren Garforth – some of the toughest players in the England set-up, all hunched over their respective laptops, studying footage and data between training sessions on tour. They were not concerned with the headlines or conventional thinking; they were students of the game, only interested in learning more and getting better.

It is too easy to suggest that the ability to learn is inherent and there is nothing much that can be done about it. 'I'm just built that way.' 'I'll never understand it.' 'Numbers aren't my thing.' Such an attitude is a cop-out. Individuals change and can be taught. In fact, many people start out as a sponge, eager to learn and to better themselves, but over time they become a rock, resistant to new ideas, set in their ways, suspicious of change and therefore unable to create sustained success. If you have a rock in your company, you are more likely to sink. Managers have to identify anyone within their team who has succumbed to a rock mentality and do all they can to turn them into a sponge once again. That is a key management role. If you have a group of sponges within your team, collectively you will achieve extraordinary things.

Sponges are also competitive beasts. English sport typically resides in a warm bubble of celebrating participation more than victory and shying away from the harsh truths of competition and hierarchy. In my first job at Xerox as a young, aspiring professional, I still remember the feeling of walking into the office and seeing the league table, which ranked the sales of every employee in the country. It was a hell of a motivator and it certainly focused the learning of new staff. I loved that competitive edge: the scoreboard tells the truth.

How to coach knowledge

This is a coaching model that is widely applicable to business and sport. Knowledge can be broken down in five ways, regardless of the subject matter:

Background

The origins and accumulation of information that underpin and support the body of evidence of a particular subject.

Variations

A list of all the workable methods that differ even slightly from the model protocol.

Model

An example of the most common, or simplest, protocol for performing a certain movement or skill.

Winning Moves

A list of certain technical aspects of the subject that MUST be performed regardless of which method is implemented.

Losing Moves

A list of certain technical aspects of the subject that MUST NOT be performed regardless of which method is implemented.

You could generate this table for your company tomorrow.

Nothing is uncoachable

Another important contribution that Yehuda Shinar made to the England team was the use of video games. Not FIFA-style fun exactly, but a joystick that assessed your ability to function, to rationalise, to make decisions under increasing pressure. This was not just about pressure and T-CUP, but also about training your brain to absorb live information quickly. The game play may sound relatively arbitrary – essentially using a joystick to follow a dot around the screen with increasing variation in speed and movement – but the results were anything but. They were transformative and illuminating. It changed our mentality and educated us about both pressure and learning.

I remember one player new to the England squad who arrived at a training session and was astonished to find the front row standing on medicine balls and wearing eyepatches, the back row throwing 100 passes off their weak hand while standing on wobble boards, and the second rows using a slip-catching cradle. They were doing visual fitness training. I had first heard of Dr Sherylle Calder as a visual performance skills consultant who had helped the world-beating Australian cricket team in 2000. I was convinced that an athlete with good visual memory always seemed to be in the right place at the right time, and that nothing happens in sport until the eye tells the body what to do. When it comes to achieving elite performance, vision coaching is just as important as every other aspect of coaching. It became an essential element of our 'working ahead of the ball', ensuring we were anticipating play, not reacting to it.

By this stage in our evolution as a culture, we had begun to properly institutionalise the coaching systems that would ultimately win the World Cup. Even our visual coaching ensured our players had now improved their speed of scanning defences quickly, the speed of responding to information received in their peripheral vision, the speed of focusing on small targets, and the speed and accuracy of their eye–hand coordination.

It is important to realise that rugby, like business, is a game without rules. There are laws – and the laws must be obeyed – but aside from that you can utterly reinvent the way in which you operate by harvesting every idea you can gather and rethinking how you play the game. When I first started coaching rugby at Henley, we drank tea in the changing room, played loud music during training and never kicked the ball. We broke every rule going, but we never broke the law!

How learning can change the game

Here are perhaps the most revelatory statistics I saw as England head coach, based on the laws being refereed at the time, but certainly applicable in their sentiment to today's game:

England's chances of scoring

Slow ball	Chance of scoring
1 phase slow ball	8%
2 phases slow ball	6%
3 phases slow ball	5%

Fast ball	Chance of scoring
1 phase fast ball	17%
2 phases fast ball	45%
3 phases fast ball	60%
4 phases fast ball	75%
5 phases fast ball	85%

The power of these numbers was transforming. They defined the targets of our entire operation and made sense of everything we were looking to achieve. Instead of seeking to play fast-paced rugby just because the idea had some magical quality or made intuitive sense, here were mathematical statistics that proved we would win if we won fast ball.

Add to this the fact that 85 per cent of Test matches were being won by the team who scored the most tries, and suddenly our blueprint game plan – and our entire collective ambition within our Teamship culture – made perfect empirical sense.

Lesson from Japan: Learning cultures

'Success isn't always about winning competitions. Success is about over-achieving. What drives me is an insatiable appetite for knowledge. Every time the players come in to a camp or a new campaign, we've done something to the environment so they can see that we're not staying still, that we're still striving.'

Warren Gatland spoke these words just before Wales flew out to Japan and they sum up a real leader's attitude to learning. The best leaders and the best coaches will forever seek new knowledge.

Furthermore, this 'insatiable appetite for knowledge' is contagious: players recognise its value and pursue it for themselves. Wales scrum-half Gareth Davies's eye-catching interceptions against Australia in their fascinating pool-stage encounter were neither miraculous nor fortunate: he trained for them. He learned a new skill, and for this he credits Dr Sherylle Calder, the eye coach England used in our preparation for the 2003 World Cup. She taught him to improve his peripheral vision and, by doing so, helped him learn to time his acceleration on to the pass. He then worked with the conditioning coaches to improve his change of pace.

Such compulsion to learn and develop manifests itself in different ways. Consider the flexibility in selection shown by Jones, the absence of emotion and sentiment in his decisions, and the relative tactical diversity. Then consider England's predictable 2015 campaign. In the four years up to Japan, Jones picked 129 different players in his England squads, so he spent time identifying his best players. England were operating in a learning culture.

CHAPTER XVIII

HOOKER
Operational culture: checklists not to-do lists

'A leader takes people where they want to go. A great leader takes people where they don't necessarily want to go, but ought to be.'

Rosalynn Carter

Winning behaviours: The hooker is the glue that binds the team together; the most headstrong and unflappable member of an organisation; a magnetic blend of skill, mobility and power. Just consider the vulnerability of the hooker in the scrum and their complete trust in the two team-mates on either side: their arms are wrapped around those two players while their neck, head and shoulders are completely exposed to what is a combined total force of around 7,000 newtons that pulses through a Test match scrum. This trust is built and earned by the day-to-day operations of a culture.

I read a fascinating book by Atul Gawande entitled *The Checklist Manifesto: How to Get Things Right*. The research he produces is compelling and indisputable: no matter the level of your expertise or experience, no matter how much repetition and time you have invested in training, the single most impactful change you can make involves one common practice – well-designed checklists.

Gawande makes a crucial distinction that crystallised for me something I had always sensed but never articulated with such clarity. He distinguishes between 'errors of ignorance' (the mistakes we make for the simple reason that we do not know enough about the given subject matter) and 'errors of ineptitude' (the mistakes we make because we fail to make proper use of what we already know). This is behaviour you can manage, professional habits within your control.

I was convinced – and remain so – that our failures on a rugby pitch as an England team were the consequence of the second type: errors of ineptitude. I am sure that the same is almost always true in businesses. A surgeon by profession, Gawande offers stark evidence about the processes followed ahead of successful, or unsuccessful, operations. Simply put, taking into consideration experience, expertise, training and complexity of procedure, the only discernible consistent difference was whether a checklist had been written and followed properly. The more complex the operation, the greater the need for a checklist to ensure high performance and, in this context, avert fatal catastrophe.

Things go wrong when someone, especially someone under intense pressure, forgets to do something simple, something they have done thousands of times before. They assume the process has been internalised and normalised, but this reliance on habit cannot be trusted in such high-stakes environments.

One of the strengths of England's seven disciplines, examined in the chapter on the Inside Centre, is that despite their simplicity – in both procedure and language – they allowed the team to deal with the increasing complexity of their responsibilities, especially in the heat and chaos of a Test match. The graphical illustrations then provided the distilled checklist for our team meetings.

Success from Setbacks

It is essential to face the idea of failure. It remains just about the only inevitability of a successful career in either sport or business. A career of avoiding failure simply means that at some point along the way you have begun to accept mediocrity, consciously or not.

I regularly talk to teams about losing. Business or sport, you sit in the team room or your meeting room, and you strategise worst-case scenarios. *What if? What will happen on Saturday if we lose this game? What do you tell your agent if you aren't picked? How are we going to behave? How will a team member respond to being overlooked for a promotion? How do we manage our response? Are there rules in place?* You start to conceptualise the issues and you start to document the necessary outcomes. To that end, in the build-up to the 2003 World Cup, I even hung the picture of every rival international coach in my office. I was always of the mindset that they would be watching my every move – so I might as well have them staring over me! If they knew what we were doing, then we had to do it better.

You cannot spend enough time analysing your opponent, but this needs to create respect and not fear. The difference between respect and fear is fundamental to your preparation as a team. One is rational and informative; the other is emotional and self-destructive. Of equal importance is a confident sense of your own strengths, and identifying areas that

> **Success from Setbacks:**
> Using the most challenging or difficult experiences as learning opportunities to inform future success.

will set you apart from your opponent. During my time with England, I formalised a strategy of '**Success from Setbacks**'. Many competent leaders build on success, but all too frequently setbacks are swept under the carpet (often to mask disappointing results from inquisitive shareholders) or forgotten as quickly as possible because they are costly and upsetting. There was never any need to lay into my players after a defeat – they were just as gutted on an emotional, human level as I was. But my job was to rationalise and intellectualise our defeat, to identify the links between our behaviour and the unwanted result. That is real leadership.

Facing the idea of failure

At the London Olympics, there was a moment that captured this perfectly. Australian swimmer Emily Seebohm was the comfortable favourite for the 100 metre backstroke and had swum the fastest heat at a canter, but in the final she lost to America's Missy Franklin by 0.35 of a second. After the race, weeping in front of the world's media at the press conference, she said: 'I don't know, I just felt like I didn't really get off social media and get into my own head. Maybe I just started believing that and just thought I'd already won by the time I had swum and I hadn't even swum yet. I guess when you swim that fast in the heat, then people put pressure and more pressure on you, saying: "Oh, you're going to get the gold." When people tell you a thousand times "You'll get the gold", somewhere in your mind you are going to say "you've done it".'

The next day's headlines wrote themselves: *Seebohm blames Facebook and Twitter for failure to win gold.*

She had failed to face the idea of failure. Not only does this help you deal with the worst-case scenario in advance, but better still, if you actively explore these possibilities, the realities of failure hit home and make that disastrous outcome less likely. In essence, conceptualising the nightmare outcome is a phenomenal motivator and incentivises you to work with an enhanced level of focus and scrutiny.

Inverting the question

Once you have faced the idea of failure, you strategise your plan for success. With England I identified seven elements of the peak state of winning:

1. More points on the scoreboard.
2. A performance of world-class standard in the core areas of your game – all measurable.
3. A team that really clicks in the heat of the match – not measurable.
4. An experience off the pitch that is enjoyable and inspires the whole organisation.
5. Playing and beating teams you know can beat you.
6. 75,000* people on their feet going nuts – a performance your supporters wildly applaud.
7. Knowing you can do it on a consistent basis.

Many coaches and leaders go about the question of winning in the wrong direction. They start with where they are and ask the question *How do we get to the position we want to be from here?* What I did was begin with the end in mind and then work out what it takes to get you there.

I can remember sitting in my office late one night and writing a longer version of the following. I split up the necessary factors and made a list of what needed to happen, and who we needed to achieve it.

1. **Coaching the basic skills:** We needed full-time specialists to lead the development of our game in every key area: attack, defence, kicking, scrummaging, lineouts etc. I not only needed specialists with the necessary expertise, but they also had to possess a shared approach in terms of their philosophy of how the game should be played. My team of coaches had to invest

---

* I should point out that when I wrote this, 75,000 was a sell-out at Twickenham, rather than the 82,000 it is today.

wholeheartedly in the Teamship winning culture we were building.

2. **Fitness/nutrition:** I needed a full-time fitness coach and I needed more than just running, weights and ice baths. I wanted personal training programmes for England to become the fittest and most powerful team in world rugby. I cannot believe in the years since 2003 it is Wales who have taken this further, exploring recovery technologies such as post-match cryotherapy treatment in the car park to maximise their recovery. It does, therefore, fit that Wales have won the Six Nations Grand Slam four times to England's one in that time frame.

3. **Psychology:** I wrote down at the time – and my words were eerily prescient – that a single kick can determine the closest games when everything is at stake. Jonny Wilkinson's parents had funded his training with Dave Alred from the age of thirteen and it is England's gain that they were forward-thinking enough to recognise the technical and psychological elements of the game. I felt mental and personal preparation was a completely untapped area of professional rugby. It was from this initial reflection and the ensuing investigation that the beginnings of T-CUP were formed.

4. **Medical/Recovery:** We had investment in this area already, but I was concerned that the focus was almost entirely on emergencies and injuries. I needed full-time specialists committed to preventing injuries – as far as is possible in such an impact-focused, attritional sport. The work that the RFU's Headcase programme is now doing with schools to treat and prevent concussion is a perfect example of revolutionising the way teams warm up and prepare, and, furthermore, in educating school coaches and rugby clubs around the country.

5. **Analysis/IT:** The digital landscape has evolved dramatically,

but my ambition in this area remains as relevant as ever. I wanted to scrutinise our game in as much detail as technology could allow to inform our future training and preparation. By the same token, I wanted as much competitive intelligence on our rivals as was possible within the technological restrictions of the early 2000s. I needed a team of analysts to break down *all* of the Test matches played, not just our own.

6. **Management:** As well as my coaching role, I was determined to ensure that I took responsibility to remove any possible distraction or handicap from our operation to ensure every player was at their absolute peak on a playing day. I would manage the operation off the pitch to maximise our potential and create an environment in which the only thing in a player's mind was performing to the absolute best of their ability. This involved logistics, timings, facilities, equipment – anything that had the potential to corrupt or influence the match-day experience. This ultimately became 'Transforming the Experience – Driveway to Driveway.' In 2000 I appointed Louise Ramsay as England team manager, who was vastly experienced in logistics after working with Team GB, and she was instrumental in ensuring we were the best-run rugby team of that era.

7. **Leadership:** This area, working alongside my captain and other key leadership players, was essential if England were going to achieve their aims and maintain the necessary standards along the way to do so. Ultimately, we would develop a team of leaders who would all share this level of responsibility and self-police a culture that only accepted the very highest standards of behaviour and performance, with accountability and consequences at every turn for those underperforming. It would be fully supportive but completely uncompromising.

Maintaining operational culture

In the run-up to the World Cup, England had a Senior Leadership Team within their playing squad consisting of George Ford, Owen Farrell, Maro Itoje, Elliot Daly, Ben Youngs and Billy Vunipola. Eddie Jones had also hired a head of high performance in former Australian Football League coach Neil Craig. His brief was primarily focused on improving player leadership and developing England's coaches and players. I liked the language of Jones on his appointment: 'We want the environment to be the best in the world and, to do that, we continually have to bring in people who have got more knowledge than we've got.'

England's senior players would regularly meet with Craig for a formal meeting and update on the health of the squad, but they were also able to speak to him outside of those set times. The conversations were not structured, but Craig would ask them about things they might have noticed at dinner time – if a player did not seem happy or quite himself. The Senior Leadership Team took on more responsibility than they had before. Aside from organising fun distractions – games of dodgeball and external day trips – one of their primary responsibilities was to take care of the players, ensuring that everyone was being looked out for. The SLT did not have direct involvement in selection, but if someone was struggling mentally or lacking in confidence and it might affect their performance, then the SLT was empowered to make that known. England players shared bedrooms again on tour and were encouraged to mix up their room-mates. For dinner socials, the names of three separate restaurants were put in a hat and players picked out a name. You turned up at the restaurant whose name you had pulled and sat with whoever happened to be there.

Initiatives of this kind are the reason the culture of that group matured so quickly. This operational culture really does make a difference to the heart of the team when they are most under the pump and under pressure.

England's Teamship rules on day-to-day organisation

While social media was yet to saturate the communications industry, even in 2003 I could see how mobile-phone use could threaten our Teamship culture if not properly managed. We had a set of 'day-to-day' rules that covered simple expectations of behaviour in and around the camp. I wanted the team to bond, to be a socially cohesive unit. Mobile phones were not allowed in team meetings, at training or in areas of the team hotel aside from bedrooms and team rooms. Players were not allowed to walk around the hotel talking on their phones.

Another important 'day-to-day' rule in our culture concerned disciplinary issues. The rule was that these would be dealt with by me, but that Martin Johnson would always be involved in any issue concerning a player. The final rule was that if the disciplinary issue involved me or Martin, then we were all in deep shit!

Lesson from Japan: Setting targets

Calibration is an essential part of target-setting in sport.

To use an example from golf: I cannot beat Rory McIlroy in match play (as much as I would love to!). However, I am a five-handicap golfer and if I compete against another five-handicap golfer, my target is very simple: beat my opponent.

Sometimes you have to set realistic targets because chasing after dreams does not achieve anything. After qualifying for a quarter-final for the first time, Japan now need to use the 2019 tournament as a springboard for the next World Cup and revise that target. Rugby is currently the fourth most popular sport in Japan and their team has not yet been invited to join one of the major annual rugby tournaments. Their players, meanwhile, are being paid around $100 per day. Put bluntly, they do not yet have the resources or support to win the World Cup – so setting that target would be ridiculous. Instead, Japan coach Jamie Joseph targeted winning their pool and they did that. Compare their resources and their performance and you can see they massively over-achieved at this World Cup.

For England and Wales, the aspiration was different: win the World Cup. To continue to support the growth of northern-hemisphere rugby, I would implore the Six Nations to concentrate the structure of that tournament. The Six Nations is currently five games and I would champion its distillation into five games over consecutive weekends. It would replicate a World Cup campaign and ensure coaches and players are used to managing rotation for tournament competition – and it would certainly support the necessary growth of the Premiership club game.

Setting realistic targets provides vital steps to building a winning culture. Wales lost every game in the 2003 Six Nations under Steve Hansen, but he was intent on using that experience as an opportunity for learning and he revamped their playing style, changed his selection and recalibrated their target in time for the World Cup that year. The result was that his Wales team very nearly beat England in the quarter-final! From that learning experience, he ended up coaching the first team to retain the Webb Ellis trophy when New Zealand won the World Cup in 2015.

CHAPTER XIX

LOOSEHEAD PROP
Moving beyond number one

'Leadership is about making others better as a result of your presence and making sure that impact lasts in your absence.'

Sheryl Sandberg

Winning behaviours: The loosehead is a strategic disrupter, striving to challenge and undermine the competitive advantages of any rival and exploit their weaknesses. In corporate terms, that means always seeking to innovate, whether that is through industrial espionage, experimental methodology or market research. A winning culture is never satisfied and is always looking to improve. The future of any business – and any great team – relies on the assumption that you never stand still. Performance, like profit margins, is never good enough.

The art of managing people is fundamental to building any high-performance team. But the art of managing people is relatively simple and self-evident. You can hold people to any standard you set, provided (1) you involve them; (2) you are consistent and fair.

If you are new, you ensure you study the culture, the operation, the tides of an organisation before you barge in with big ideas. You must get the foundations of the team culture right before you build up new thinking and new strategies. Too much change at once can destabilise an entire team or company.

After all my experiences in the corporate sector, it does not surprise me that the companies that have best utilised this Teamship model are either creatives in advertising or service-industry types committed to enhancing and improving the quality of their customer experience.

I was often told that creative types do not like working in a team, and so my philosophy would be rendered useless to an advertising company. 'Zero value,' was how one obstinate executive put it. Then I spoke to a group of open-minded, driven creatives at Grey London and they have now become a blueprint for capturing these Teamship principles in a business context. As part of their Teamship strategy and remodelling, they produced a series of postcards that set out their principles, displayed at the entrance to the office for all customers and visitors to see.

This transparency ensures they remain absolutely accountable to the standards they espouse.

When they started discussing their culture, they recognised their biggest professional flaw as a company with unanimous agreement: they all hated meetings. I knew what they meant. When you run your own small company with ten people, no HR and no lines of management (as I once did!), you do not hold a meeting unless it is going to be demonstrably productive. I understood that completely. But you also have to recognise that there can be value in that face-to-face interaction. The problem at Grey was slightly different. Rather than being used properly to generate ideas or problem-solve, meetings constantly ran over or were bulldozed by one or two people, or decisions were not made and there were no consequent measurable actions or targets. Does this sound familiar to you?

They changed all that by collaboratively generating their own winning behaviours as an organisation. Here are some examples of the operating standard that they built:

Ambition meeting: Agreeing a cultural ambition, for all our brands, is business-critical. Getting to a cultural ambition is an audacious goal from one meeting. So we get the right people, round the right table with the right energy to find the new, push for better and land brilliance.

Collision chair: All Grey meetings have a dedicated chair, literally. One of their jobs is to ensure everyone gets involved. It means different perspectives and different opinions. And difference is good, that's where we find great ideas.

Do great meeting: Every meeting at Grey should be as crafted and creative as the work we produce. Please tell us how your meeting went today.

Flight mode: A great meeting is a focused one. We respect everyone's time in the meeting. So we drop the phones and get in flight mode. Literally.

ABCD awards: Above and Beyond the Call of Duty awards. Monthly awards. Anyone can nominate anyone. These people are legends.

It is amazing how uncomfortable modern professionals feel without their mobile phones for a forty-minute meeting. Is your to-do list that day so urgent that you cannot spare 10 per cent of your working day on maximising your company's efficiency? Grey London built one final rule that captured how much this progressive mindset can be embedded in the very psyche of the company: you are not allowed to get your phone out in the lift. You must speak to whoever gets in with you. Suddenly the leader on the Volvo account is chatting to the head of marketing at Lucozade and new ideas are formed – and new exciting partnerships are made – between the first and fifth floor.

Mandarin Oriental

Equally impressive has been the Mandarin Oriental Hotel Group, a luxury hotel brand devoted to providing the very best customer experience in a highly competitive and challenging market. They used the Teamship process to bring to life their five guiding principles and, for each, came up with two associated winning behaviours:

1. Delighting our guests (Welcome, Phone Free).
2. Delighting our colleagues (Time Out, MyMO).
3. Becoming the best (MO Time, Red Flag).
4. Working together (10@10, MO Mindful).
5. Acting with responsibility (Doing More, Email-Free Friday).

They then used the software available on the Hive to turn these principles into an interactive forum of tangible actions. As a company, they now have the ability to share new content quickly, and the digital effect on a business that operates like this is transformative. A different employee explains each winning behaviour in a short video on the MyMO platform, the company's very own internal community network that operates very much like a social media channel. It has become so embedded in their operational practice that one of the requirements of the induction process for any new employee at Mandarin Oriental's corporate office is to read every Teamship principle and agree to them.

The **Red Flag** rules are as follows:

- We understand that there are times when colleagues need to concentrate on a piece of work and do not want to be disturbed by others.
- If you can't book a flexi-room but do not want to be disturbed, simply put the flag on your desk so other colleagues know not to disturb you.
- If you see someone's flag raised, please respect their need for privacy.
- Please make sure that you only have your flag raised when absolutely necessary, the red flag should not be the default option!

The **10@10** rules are as follows:

- Every Tuesday at 10 a.m. we host a team meeting called '10 at 10' to share the key priorities for each department and key company news that week.
- Each department will nominate a spokesperson who will have 1 minute to provide an update on their area so the meeting lasts for 10 minutes.
- We encourage attendance from 9.50 a.m. and a sound will signify the start of the meeting.
- Attendance at this meeting is mandatory for everyone who is in the office. A summary of the key points will be circulated to anyone who cannot attend.

Power of partnerships

Finally, the winning culture approach focuses on understanding the real importance of partnerships in creating success. Partnerships provide the platform to exponentially expand the capability of an organisation by focusing on the development of strong effective working relationships with both internal and external partners.

Partnerships are an essential asset in success, offering the opportunity for the synergy of different talents and expertise, often of sport and business. All too often, however, the first step in any proposed partnership is shaped by self-interest: *What can you provide for me?* To really utilise the potential of a partnership you have to invert the question: *How can we help you?*

This is more than semantics. By shifting the phrasing of the question, you are fundamentally rebalancing the relationship. Furthermore, that open question may unlock different levels of knowledge and expertise that you did not know existed. The

most progressive companies now provide athletes with 'values in kind'. In 2012, Accenture gave some of their employees a sabbatical in order to work with Team GB during the Games; O2 provided technical support with the data collection; GSK took over some of the blood-testing processes to ensure the absolute security of our samples; BMW provided gold cars to Olympic Champion athletes.

Effective partnerships start with a clear understanding of the motivations and needs of your partners, who in turn must recognise your goals. In the world of rugby, I discovered that in order to expect the sponsors, premiership clubs, wives, girlfriends and family to support the team in a world-class way, I first needed to ask a question: *How can England rugby help them?* Without exception, all of these groups delivered more than could have been asked of them because they were made to feel part of a winning culture. They were contributing to the success.

Lesson from Japan: Rugby's future

On the eve of the Japan tournament, Scotland No 8 David Denton announced his retirement from the game because of concussion, while the list of recent early retirements (Sam Warburton, Pat Lambie, Rob Horne) and players absent from the World Cup through injury (Gareth Anscombe, Wesley Fofana) brings into focus how much we need to continue to find ways to manage the future of rugby.

In Japan, the 'tier-two' countries were, in the main, better prepared than at previous tournaments – fitter, more conditioned, less tactically naive. Namibia made twice as many clean breaks against New Zealand as South Africa managed in their pool match. After thirty minutes, the lowest-ranked side in the tournament, with a team that included a dentist, a banker and a farmer, were trailing New Zealand by only a point.

But such moments flatter to deceive and there is still so much to do. Rugby is in a great place, but there are opportunities that need to be seized.

World Rugby finances must be distributed in a way that does not calcify the division in the global game between the haves and the have-nots, but instead supports the smaller nations to grow and compete.

World Cup warm-up matches should be spread in a way that ensures the likes of Fiji, Namibia and Japan get match-sharp against top opponents. Samoa's warm-up games were against Russia, Tonga, America and Fiji. That is not sufficient preparation for a sustained challenge against Ireland, Scotland and Japan. Tonga have a population of approximately 110,000, which is the size of Stockport, and the country is shifting away from union and towards rugby league as a more popular – and fairer – alternative national sport.

We have to stop talking of 'tier-one' and 'tier-two' rugby nations – the language itself only serves to entrench this false sense of hierarchy. In any case, the supposed 'tier one' title is no kitemark of excellence. Italy and Argentina have been two of the most disappointing teams in the tournament. You could make a credible case for Georgia being a better team right now.

Finally, the lack of promotion and relegation in rugby's leading competitions – the northern hemisphere's Six Nations and the southern hemisphere's Rugby Championship – is holding the game back. Meritocracy is the fairest way to run the global game. You should have to earn your seat at the top table.

The more competitive the international game, the more compelling its future will be.

CHAPTER XX

JAPAN RUGBY WORLD CUP 2019

How the World Cup was won

Every World Cup has a defining character. Each tournament has a running thread which captures the attention of the watching world, a narrative that fascinates us. This one, more than any other, was a World Cup defined by leadership. The tournament's most successful coaches established learning-based cultures long before landing in Japan, and its standout captains followed those principles with conviction and carried them into battle.

But it was also a tournament with a unique Asian flavour. The Japanese were a gracious and impassioned host nation, under-lining rugby's potential to expand beyond its traditional strongholds. This is, after all, a country with only eighty amateur rugby clubs, and even those are small organisations that can only afford to rent pitches from the local district council for training sessions. And while the 'Land of the Rising Sun' may seem to offer a foreign rugby culture in certain detailed respects – one in which opposing captains exchange gifts at full time inside a mixed circle of players – it was while spending time in Japan that I realised the country fundamentally possesses a deeply familiar rugby culture in its foundational values of respect and passion for the game.

On and off the pitch, this tournament could signal the future. Rugby really can cross new borders. The average points differential between so-called tier-one and tier-two nations was 45 points at the 2003 World Cup. It has steadily decreased at every tournament since and in Japan it was 30 points.

Perhaps even ten years ago, it would have been difficult to imagine a ramen bar in downtown Tokyo packed full of locals cheering on their national side in a World Cup quarter-final. But by late October 2019, with the country enraptured by this compelling tournament, it felt almost normal.

The pool stages were dramatic and memorable: the controversies and conflicting interpretations of the High Tackle Framework; the record number of red cards (in the pool stages alone, thirty-three tries were conceded by teams down to fourteen men); the greasy humidity of the conditions; some breathtaking performances and remarkable upsets; the first tournament with Hawk-Eye's enhanced SMART cameras (Synchronised Multi-Angle Relay Technology) available to TV viewers, which offered some astonishing perspectives on its finest tries and tackles; and – devastatingly – a typhoon of tragic ferocity which the country endured with stoicism and dignity.

But the pool stages also established the tournament's heavy hitters.

England's early signs . . .

England's early performances were measured and systematic. They were playing the long game, quietly confident, cranking up their preparation for the latter knockout stages, when they had to be at their best. There was a composure and a discernible sense of belief in the way they navigated their pool fixtures. And in flashes of power and accuracy, there were signs of what was to come.

England's opening 35–3 victory over Tonga was unspectacular but unyielding. In the face of dogged and aggressive opponents, Manu Tuilagi's two powerful tries fired a warning to all nations that he was going to be a tormentor at this tournament, and that sides would have to double up in the tackle to mitigate his gain-line momentum. Tuilagi's defensive discipline was also outstanding, both in the height of his tackles and in his decision-making when rushing up in the outside channel to prevent long passes circumventing England's defensive shape and getting behind the white wall.

Elsewhere, the so-called 'Kamikaze Kids' Curry and Underhill, aged twenty-one and twenty-three respectively, arrived in Japan with fewer than thirty caps between them. But they quickly established themselves as the leading back-row players of the tournament through an unrivalled work ethic and warrior spirit. Curry's physical preparation would go on to make him the only player to play every minute of every game at the World Cup, right up to the final. While their combined tackle numbers over the next few weeks would be eye-watering, it is all the more impressive when you consider the destructive impact of their hits: legal but lethal to an opponent's gain-line ambitions and scything an attack at source.

Four days after their opening fixture, in their tightest turnaround of the tournament, England's 45-7 win over the USA captured the strength in depth of the squad: you cannot sustain a tournament unless you can rely on your thirty-one-man squad. With the exception of Jack Nowell – who never really got the chance to establish himself back in the first team – and a late call-up for Ben Spencer ahead of the final, Jones had the rare luxury of a full squad from which to select his teams. There is inevitably an element of good fortune to that, but it is also a testament to the physical conditioning in the set-up and the discipline of their post-match rehabilitation protocols.

The competition within England's thirty-one-man playing group also ensured the quality and focus of training for the full seven weeks, especially so with a coach who backs his players to adapt to different tactical strategies and who is therefore flexible and pragmatic in selection. Nobody in a high-performing environment allows complacency to creep into their routine. England certainly didn't.

Another testament to Jones's coaching pedigree is the nurturing of talent. Jonny May is an example of the effect of his leadership in harnessing the ability of an individual. May arrived on the international scene as an exciting raw talent, selected for his dynamite speed but still with elements of his game to finesse and develop, and he has become a complete player: one of the most prolific and predatory finishers in world rugby.

The 39-10 victory over Argentina – which was ultimately England's final pool match as the France fixture was cancelled because of the typhoon – was not flawless, but there were flashes of the decisive ruthlessness we would see in the knockout stages.

Argentina tried to physically impose themselves on England – in many cases resorting to illegal means – but England remained unruffled and unflappable.

Once Argentina were reduced to fourteen men after only eighteen minutes, England scored six tries to secure their third successive bonus-point victory and qualify at the top of their group. An accomplished performance by Elliot Daly at full-back and vital Test-match minutes for Billy Vunipola aside, this was mostly useful to show that England were not interested in a dogfight at this tournament. They were here to play.

England then used their free fortnight to finalise their preparation for the three southern-hemisphere heavyweights who would await them in the knockout stages: Australia, New Zealand and South Africa.

Elsewhere in the pools . . .

New Zealand showed early promise against South Africa in one of the most anticipated pool matches of the World Cup. For the opening quarter, the Springboks won the collision and imprinted their muscle on the game – a brand of rugby which was going to take them to the final and earn them ultimate success. But, in a three-minute flash, the All Blacks showed their intelligence and flexibility, identifying that the space was around the outside of the blitz defence. In the blink of an eye, they scored two tries – the first following Richie Mo'unga's cross-field kick to Sevu Reece, the second through Scott Barrett's ruthless instincts – and they turned the game. They especially showed their precision off turnover ball on the counter-attack. It was clearly going to take a special team to stop them – and it did.

Unlike New Zealand's relatively young side, Wales showed their seasoned experience in their opening 43–14 victory over Georgia by fielding the oldest Wales starting side at a Rugby World Cup – with an average age of twenty-eight years and 331 days. Next came the defining pool match for Gatland's side: Australia. In terms of momentum and psychology, Wales's three-point victory over the Wallabies in Cardiff in November 2018 was integral to their preparation for the Japan tournament. Prior to that victory, they had lost thirteen games in a row against Australia, many by the smallest of margins and often in the most dramatic circumstances. But in Japan, in their second pool match, they went 3–0 up with a turnover from the kick-off and a drop goal after thirty-six seconds, before digging in for victory with a characteristically tenacious defensive display.

Wales had lost fly-half Gareth Anscombe in their final warm-up match but Dan Biggar stepped in as a competitive and confident No 10 who controls games well. When Wales came out and dropped that goal against Australia in the opening moments of their crunch pool game, I wondered if they were really going to pursue that strategy for the tournament: dominate the breakdown and squeeze games with drop goals and penalties.

There were already signs from Australia that their forward pack – despite boasting the strongest set piece they have possessed in a while – were not going to be able to impose or dominate physically, and that their goal-kicking was inconsistent. Furthermore, coach Michael Cheika never seemed sure of his strongest backline selection and they were a team who arrived in Japan stuck in an experimental phase of their development.

Ireland, who never managed to hit the heights of their form between World Cups, showed signs of creeping sterility even in their competent first victory over Scotland. Then, in their second game – that pulsating defeat by the host nation – their reliance on multi-phase rugby seemed tired and ineffective when it was up against the meticulous discipline of Japan at the breakdown. Ireland's go-to ball-carriers struggled to cross the gain line, let alone make clean breaks, and without that platform the side stuttered.

Meanwhile, Japan worked tirelessly to prevent their pool games from becoming a static arm-wrestle – showing the world very clearly the team they had trained so hard to become. In the dying moments of that game against Ireland, with Kenki Fukuoka's interception of Jordan Larmour's pass on the Japanese 10-metre line, it felt like the fuse had been lit on the home nation's tournament. The deafening roar in the Shizuoka Stadium, with hundreds of thousands of supporters in fan zones across the country and more than 25 million Japanese fans watching on TV, reverberated around the country. The following morning announced the arrival of Japan's rugby team to the unconverted on the front of the Sunday papers. A collective readership of 50 million woke up to pages and pages of adulation. The tournament had landed.

At the end of a week that brought a ruinous typhoon, and gave everyone a sense of perspective, the pool stages ended with the home nation's pulsating victory over Scotland, built on fault-less execution and flawless skill, in front of an understandably emotional home crowd. Given their resources and playing infra-structure, the Japan rugby team grossly over-achieved and deserved the world's praise for their style of play.

Yet aside from Japan's attention-grabbing performances, there were some other wonderfully dramatic match-ups in these opening weekends. Uruguay's emotional victory over Fiji was enthralling for its passion. Uruguay only have twenty-two profes-sional players and, despite their technical imprecision, they showed a tenacity and determination to win.

But, once the dust settles on a World Cup, the first forty matches of the tournament can always be seen as the early rounds of a game of poker, the sparring sessions before the knockouts begin . . .

The knockout stages

Quarter-final 1
England 40 – 16 Australia

Tries
England: May (2), Sinckler, Watson. Australia: Koroibete.

Conversions
England: Farrell (4). Australia: Leali'ifano.

Penalties
England: Farrell (4). Australia: Leali'ifano (3).

After their professional but measured pool-stage victories, England laid down their marker against Australia with a sustained performance of polished execution. Prior to kick-off, only four of England's entire squad had played in a knockout match before, but this consummate performance was littered with moments that captured the ethos and mentality of the group. This was a young England team unfazed by the occasion.

For starters, Jones made a sharp decision and moved fly-half George Ford, one of England's outstanding performers in the tournament, to the bench. Jones wanted Owen Farrell marshalling the No 10 channel in defence to mitigate the impact of Australia's momentous ball-carrier Samu Kerevi. It was a strong call – based on reason not emotion – to change tack on the 10-12 dual-playmaking axis that had provided the foundations for attack in the tournament up till then. The best leaders make those uncompromising decisions, even when the potential consequences are at their most severe.

The reaction to selection is a test of any culture and Ford was the very first player to run over and congratulate Jonny May on his eighteenth-minute try. Later on in the game, when Ford was brought on, he pinned Australia back deep in their territory and forced them to overplay their hand in a calm and commanding cameo. His mindset and execution showed his complete commitment to the culture, the team and the process.

For a young side, England showed maturity, too. They patiently endured an opening onslaught from Australia because they had faith in their defensive fitness and discipline. Farrell flourished in the fly-half position, running two waves of attack at each phase and orchestrating the dynamic pace in England's multi-option attack. His miss-pass to Kyle Sinckler, skipping Billy Vunipola, who was running a decoy line and distracting defenders, was sublime. It came in the forty-sixth minute, only three minutes after Australia had made it a one-point game, and it showed his calm fortitude in a period of the game in which the pressure was at its most intense.

There were other signs that England were a mentally disciplined group. Sinckler, with an old reputation as a hothead, ignored the targeted goading from the Australian tight five after an early scrum infringement and just turned around and smirked to himself. There were bigger things to worry about than a petty shoving match. Jones was a teacher before he was a full-time coach and I know how much he enjoyed teaching young players to keep calm and focused in the cauldron of a rugby match. I also hope that Sinckler, a star of the tournament who took an atypical route into professional rugby from Tooting to Tokyo, might encourage other boys and girls from different circumstances to take up the game.

During England's imperious control of the last quarter of the game, Australia's tactical naivety was exposed. Their exit strategy was hopeless. At 17–16 Australia had managed to narrow the gap, but they showed no ability to manage possession. High-risk rugby has a place, but chipping the ball out of your own 22 in a knockout match – with no team-mates plugged into that strategy or chasing to compete for the ball – was bewildering.

England's defensive statistics at the end of the quarter-final encounter were incredible, especially considering the near 30-point winning margin. No England player in World Cup history had ever made seventeen tackles in a single game. In this contest, Sam Underhill made twenty, Mako Vunipola eighteen, Jamie George seventeen and Owen Farrell seventeen (justifying Jones's selection of shifting him to work in the 10 defensive channel). Tom Curry made a record-equalling sixteen tackles and only just made it into the top five!

The game was won comfortably. One late moment captured England's clinical execution. Ford and Farrell pummelled Kurtley Beale with a powerful tackle on the hour mark and, immediately after smashing him to the deck, they each reached out a hand to help him back to his feet. They were not interested in petty niggle but in professional execution of a game plan. It was a classy touch from two best friends who had bought into the dynamic of putting the team's needs ahead of any individual preference – whether that meant starting on the bench or wearing the 12 shirt.

The most impressive thing from a coaching perspective was that this performance was earned on the training ground. The clockwork exactitude of their attacking play embodied the 'tactical periodisation' coaching technique that Jones first used with Japan and then with England. It is essentially a training method that combines skill and fitness, rather than distinguishing the two as separate entities. His training drills sharpen not only the players' physical preparation but also their tactical acuity and decision-making. Rather than doing fitness-based drills training itself is done at intense speeds, so players train at a quicker and sharper pace than during matches. Australia came up against a team who had trained better, physically and mentally, and who were able to transfer that clinical preparation to the Test match arena.

From Australia's perspective, the aftermath of this defeat brought out the fault lines in Australian rugby, and the division between the head coach and the union. A team cannot sustain high-quality performances – nor can any high-performing culture – without a collective sense of strategy and direction.

From England's perspective, it laid the foundations for the semi-final to come. Within seconds of the final whistle, Farrell's facial expression and body language changed.

He – and England – were waiting for the All Blacks.

Quarter-final 2
New Zealand 46 – 14 Ireland

Tries
New Zealand: A Smith (2), B. Barrett, Taylor, Todd, Bridge, J. Barrett. Ireland: Henshaw, penalty try.

Conversions
New Zealand: Mo'unga (4). Ireland: Carbery.

Penalties
New Zealand: Mo'unga.

This was New Zealand's most complete performance at the World Cup and arguably Ireland's worst. Watching this game established for me the importance of timing in a four-year cycle. Peaking at the right time is another requisite for winning and Ireland have not worked out how to manage that cycle in recent history.

Ireland's preparations were disrupted by the suspension of a crucial player. In the build-up, they had to fly a specialist lawyer to Japan in a desperate bid to keep centre Bundee Aki in the tournament following his red card in Ireland's last pool match for a high tackle on Samoa's UJ Seuteni. They were unsurprisingly unsuccessful and lost their primary percussive runner from their line-up.

New Zealand showed control in their ability to switch between their structured game plan and striking with an improvised attack as soon as they detected the smallest vulnerability in Ireland's defensive set-up. They were clinical in their execution, running strong dummy lines to bring hesitation to the Irish defence and then unleashing outstanding quality from the bench. On a local level, it was fascinating to watch the Japanese fans adopt their second-favourite team. The All Blacks were the only team who had to hire a full-time translator, while Mitsubishi launched an All-Black-themed SUV for the tournament.

There was a final cruel irony for Ireland in that they had found ways to beat New Zealand twice over the previous four years and, in fact, their most recent win catalysed a significant All Black rebirth in both tactics and personnel. While Ireland were reliant on a power-based game and trying to force mistakes on the All Blacks with defensive pressure, the All Blacks simply dominated proceedings.

Ireland struggled without Jonathan Sexton at full sharpness, but even so, quarter-finals of World Cups should not be 40-point victories. It was a mismatch and a sorry way for Joe Schmidt and Rory Best to end their Irish careers.

It cannot be the sole reason for the defeat, but I had a clear rule in 2003 that a successful World Cup campaign could never be a retirement party. It was notable to see so many teams with retiring coaches and captains – Ireland, New Zealand, Wales, Italy – fail to fully realise their ambitions at this tournament. Meanwhile, those teams with a sense of stability and continuity, with a very clear eye on the future – England, Japan and South Africa – excelled.

Quarter-final 3
Wales 20 – 19 France

Tries
Wales: Wainwright, Moriarty. France: Vahaamahina, Ollivon, Vakatawa.

Conversions
Wales: Biggar (2). France: Ntamack (2).

Penalties
Wales: Biggar (2).

Wales did not play their best rugby in Japan, but it is a testament to the mental fortitude that Gatland instilled in his playing group that they were still finding ways to grind out victories.

The flip side of that is that France – somehow – managed to find a way to lose.

France were playing well. In brief patches, they were scintillating. They had strung together some dazzling and beguiling play – their forwards were powerful in contact, their backs skilful in offloading – and they were consequently dominating the game. But in the forty-ninth minute, they were 19–10 up and had constructed a rumbling, driving maul pushing towards the try line. The ball was secure at the back of the maul, moving forwards, with Antoine Dupont waiting to pounce for the line. Then came an unforgivable moment of madness from Sébastien Vahaamahina, elbowing Aaron Wainwright in the chin and leaving referee Jaco Peyper no choice. It is these tiny margins that can define careers. A crystalline example of T-CUP in action. Or not.

This was an unexpected mirror image of the 2011 World Cup semi-final between these teams in which Sam Warburton was sent off for a tip-tackle: a one-point victory after a game-changing red card in a closely fought arm-wrestle. But while the circumstances of Warburton's red card were completely different – an unfortunate merging of power, weight and timing on a much smaller player – Vahaamahina's moment of blind fury was unforgivably stupid considering what was at stake.

In the second half, France failed to score a single point, nor did they convert a single penalty kick in the whole match. They were six points up and showed no ability to manage a game by kicking for territory and keeping the scoreboard ticking over. Camille Lopez tried one drop goal from too far out, but they never tried again. They remain, without question, the most under-achieving team in rugby. They need a new coaching structure and a modern, progressive and professional culture at the top of the game.

The missed-tackle count was hugely uncharacteristic of the Welsh team under Shaun Edwards and they progressed through determined will. But will could only take them so far.

Quarter-final 4

Japan 3 – 26 South Africa

Tries
South Africa: Mapimpi (2), de Klerk.

Conversions
South Africa: Pollard.

Penalties
Japan: Tamura. South Africa: Pollard (3).

This quarter-final confirmed that South Africa were contenders for the tournament simply by the might of their pack. South Africa can execute a simple game plan with devastating power. Featherweight Japan were more agile and more evasive, but their heavyweight opponents were stronger.

Japan, persisting with their unwavering ambition to force a high tempo, enjoyed an outstanding opening twenty minutes, using quick handling in close contact to shift the point of attack. Joseph's leadership meant they continued to think cleverly, recognising they might lose some collisions and employing a clear strategy in which the ball-carrier would release the ball on the ground, regather possession and steal another few yards to try to keep the attack advancing.

But slowly the Springboks tightened their muscular grip on the game and smothered the Japanese. Ultimately, South Africa were able to bully them into submission with constant carries around the fringes of the breakdown, eating gain-line yards with every drive. With their maul and their physicality in every contact, Japan lost their sense of momentum. South Africa only looked to unleash their backline as a Plan F or off turnover ball, but Plan A worked just fine.

And so the four coaches in the semi-final – Eddie Jones, Steve Hansen, Warren Gatland and Rassie Erasmus – would be the leading coaches in world rugby over the past few years.

The semi-finals were, quite rightly, billed by the world's media as the 'battle of the super coaches'.

Semi-final 1
England 19 – 7 New Zealand

Tries
England: Tuilagi. New Zealand: Savea.

Conversions
England: Farrell. New Zealand: Mo'unga.

Penalties
England: Ford (4).

It only took ninety-eight seconds to storm the citadel.

The omens were not in England's favour. New Zealand had won eighteen successive World Cup matches and, before the semi-final, had accrued per game more points (51), tries (7.3), metres (642), breaks (22), defenders beaten (39) and offloads (17) than any other side in the tournament. But after ninety-eight seconds of sublime rugby, with Tuilagi ploughing over the line to score, England made a mockery of those numbers.

Publicly, during the build-up, Jones had suggested that the myth and mystique surrounding the All Blacks was not dissimilar to that of the Japanese samurai. Privately, inside the camp,

England were using the three models of samurai culture – trust, hard work and discipline – as the values the team would embody. They were not scared of this fixture; they were excited by it. New Zealand are good, but they are not gods.

I was pitchside during the warm-up, a few metres from where Underhill, Curry and the rest of the pack were smashing tackle bags together. You could see the intensity and hunger in their eyeballs. The warm-up was charged: not overly emotional but ferocious. Something was in the air.

Then came the haka. England decided to confront the challenge. To form a 'V' around the haka was neither disrespectful nor discourteous. However, by straying across the halfway line, they breached a rule of World Rugby. More importantly, it was a team saying, in their own words, 'Bring it on.' They did not want to passively accept the challenge but to front up and accept accountability for the next eighty minutes. England even placed their captain, Farrell, at the pivot of the 'V', smiling as his team visually wrapped up the traditional dance. It was marvellous theatre. And it was Jones's idea: the perfect way to combat the cult of exceptionalism that surrounds the All Blacks. Farrell's smile was the smile of someone who could not wait to compete.

Then came kick-off.

The opposing armies were dressed in black and white but this was no game of chess. It was confrontational, imposing, whip-smart, dynamic, majestic. In fact, this was England's greatest performance of the professional era.

England's formidable runners in the midfield were destructive, but they were only one option in this multi-faceted onslaught. This victory was earned through precision and variety in attack, and ferocity and mobility in defence. New Zealand could not cope with the diversity of England's attacking arsenal. On the ball, the All Blacks were never more than two passes away from a dominant hit.

The mobility of this team has added 'wide wide' to England's playbook – an ability to stretch defences from touchline to touchline because of speed of handling and fitness around the pitch, and their confidence in recycling the ball cleanly and quickly to launch the next wave. The faith in the process and the confidence in their own execution to do this in the opening seconds of a semi-final against New Zealand was deeply impressive.

New Zealand have traditionally been dangerous off a break and clinical in converting any opportunity, so England refused to allow them clean line breaks. Similarly, when you kick to Beauden Barrett you have to make him turn behind. You cannot allow him to run on to the ball so he is already moving at pace. The chase cannot be disjointed, and if you create a mismatch in personnel (for example, an outside centre attacking a channel between a second row and a tighthead prop), he can exploit that. England swallowed him up with pressure, staying connected on the kick-chase and never slipping off that first tackle.

The variety of skill from England's tight five was dazzling – close-quarter distribution and angles of running from the likes of Kyle Sinckler, Mako Vunipola, Maro Itoje and Jamie George – while the defensive accuracy and power of England's back row, alongside Courtney Lawes, was destructive. Ten years ago it was southern-hemisphere teams whose forwards outplayed England, but this England team far surpassed the skills of New Zealand.

Itoje, especially, played one of the most commanding matches in Test history. Consider the calibre of the opposition – two of the world's great second-row players in Brodie Retallick and Sam Whitelock – and consider his dominance in contact: outstanding physicality, priceless turnovers, steals on the floor, poacher in the lineout, the orchestrator of England's rolling mauls and the destroyer of New Zealand's. Ford, the diminutive England fly-half back in the team with supposed question marks over his defensive impact, stripped the ball from New Zealand tighthead Nepo Laulala. It was one of those days.

Farrell played through an agonising dead leg with sheer strength of will, while England's scrambling defence was implacable. New Zealand are a team known for converting turnovers into points, but their breakaways were swarmed by waspish defence, followed by a lung-bursting work rate to win the ball back.

But for one error of communication and timing at the lineout, England would have 'nilled' New Zealand altogether.

From a coaching perspective, this performance was the consequence of a culture which had trained players to push beyond their own limitations. Jones does this in training. It can begin with a simple tactic. The first time you do an endurance test, you do it over fifty metres. The second time you run the test, you do it over fifty-one metres, but you don't tell the players. They think they are running the same distance, but they are all covering more mileage because they have set heightened expectations of themselves. These are the kinds of one per-centers that continually raise the aspirations of the group.

Jones outfoxed Hansen with a Test match of relentless rising standards. Just two England teams had beaten the All Blacks away from Twickenham – in 1973 and 2003 – and never before in a World Cup.

And never like this.

Semi-final 2
Wales 16 – 19 South Africa

Tries
Wales: Adams. South Africa: de Allende.

Conversions
Wales: Halfpenny. South Africa: Pollard.

Penalties
Wales: Biggar (3). South Africa: Pollard (4).

The Welsh game plan of dominating territory requires two things – pinpoint precision with box-kicking and an accuracy that ensures the opposition make more mistakes. They had eked out victories for years based on fight and fitness, but they met their match with this South African team.

Both these two sides were intent on dominating the breakdown, a punishing defensive mindset and suffocating the other into submission. It did not make for the prettiest of World Cup quarter-finals. South Africa's counter-rucking was especially successful in disrupting Wales's platform of quick, clean front-foot ball and it knocked the rhythm out of their game.

The kicking figures were extraordinarily high because the two sides were employing mirror-image tactics. The difference was that South Africa's defence held firm: Wales's average gain of 1.6 metres per carry was the lowest any side has ever recorded in a World Cup fixture. In one attacking set on the twenty-minute mark, Wales lost about thirty yards over a series of five phases.

Wales lost their authority at the breakdown, but they might have shown a more attacking mentality. Late in the second half, Alun Wyn Jones showed courage in his penalty decisions when he opted to kick to the corner and seek to launch a driving maul, and moments later opted for the scrum rather than the points under the posts. It was this aggressive decision-making that earned Wales their only try.

South Africa operated a rush defence, especially out wide. A blitz defence system is high-risk, high-reward and Wales needed to introduce an element of doubt by peppering early kicks in the space behind to force a sense of hesitation to that strategy.

As the pressure mounted, Wales created a drop-goal shot for replacement fly-half Rhys Patchell, but it was too far out and the execution was poor. They should have had more patience to work the ball upfield.

In a final ten-minute spell, Wales lost their composure, conceding a maul penalty, a scrum penalty and a turnover. It was uncharacteristic of a Gatland side and costly. Such indiscipline – giving away such 'soft penalties' – becomes incrementally more significant as the match clock ticks to full time. In this context it proved fatal.

There are some mitigating circumstances for Wales's performance in this semi-final. To some extent, Gatland over-achieved with so many of his standout players, some in world-class form, unavailable to him: Taulupe Faletau and Gareth Anscombe before the tournament, and then Josh Navidi and Liam Williams in the space of the week – arguably his most essential attacking threats in the pack and in the backs. By the second half, he had also lost George North, while Jonathan Davies was clearly doing the best he could with one leg taped together.

From the culture of belief and loyalty he nurtured behind the scenes, to innovations such as using portable cryotherapy chambers in the Twickenham car park, Gatland revolutionised and modernised Welsh rugby. It is because of his coaching that, despite a poor regional game, Wales have performed consistently well over the past decade. He selected Sam Warburton as captain before the flanker had even secured his starting place in the Cardiff side because he identified potential. He has been excellent at spotting talent; players in the Welsh squad know that if they impress in training then they really will get a chance. And you could see that in how much they wanted to beat New Zealand in their third-place play-off.

Bronze medal match

New Zealand 40 – 17 Wales

Tries

New Zealand: Moody, B. Barrett, B. Smith (2), Crotty, Mo'unga.
Wales: Amos, Adams.

Conversions

New Zealand: Mo'unga (5). Wales: Patchell, Biggar.

Penalties

Wales: Patchell.

The sky was red over Mount Fuji at kick-off as Wales said goodbye and thank you to Warren Gatland. It was not the game he would have coveted for his final match in charge, but it was a madcap eighty minutes of entertainment, with all the pace and flavour of a Barbarians exhibition.

With only a five-day turnaround, Gatland had been forced to make nine changes, while New Zealand named one of their strongest line-ups. It was therefore not surprising when the Wales squad, already heavily bandaged for the semi-final defeat, began to strain under intense waves of All Black pressure.

But more than a pursuit of a bronze medal, this was a game of World Cup goodbyes. In the red corner, Gatland and Alun Wyn Jones had their befitting ovations as the highest-profile tournament farewells in the Welsh camp. In the black corner, the likes of Kieran Read and Sonny Bill Williams, alongside Steve Hansen himself, were saying goodbye to the jersey for good.

The difference on the pitch was one of penetration and execution. Every time an All Black forward carried the ball, they made yards over the gain line and often managed to shift the ball in an offload behind the tackle. Wales could not cope with the tempo. New Zealand's clinical execution was remarkable, too. In their first seven visits to the Wales 22, they scored five tries and had another disallowed by the TMO.

Read's running lines and close-contact handling were sublime. Williams was playing something between basketball and water polo. Before the World Cup, he had only played thirty-seven games in four years because of injuries, but here he showed his world-class ability to keep the ball free in any contact situation, even with two tacklers wrapped around him, and seek out visionary offloading options. There were patches of enterprising attack from both sides, and Welsh winger Josh Adams deserved his seventh try of the tournament as one of his team's most potent players.

For Wales, there was nothing dishonourable about this farewell, nor does it taint Gatland's legacy.

CHAPTER XXI

JAPAN RUGBY WORLD CUP 2019

The story of the World Cup final

The build-up: Assume nothing

It is difficult to play the best game of your life two weekends in a row. England prepared for the final as they had for every other game in the tournament. They were focused, calm, professional. Eddie Jones, ever meticulous and obsessive, ensured there was no complacency in the camp. They understood all too well the task of replicating a complete Test match performance on two successive Saturdays.

There was also a sense of continuity and stability. Jones named an unchanged line-up for the first time in three and a half years. Compared with teams from World Cup history, the side possessed a promising blend of youth and experience. The England players who started against Australia in 2003 had a total of 638 caps between them, while in Japan the starting team against South Africa shared a total of 731. And yet, with an average age of twenty-seven years and sixty days, they were also the youngest team in a World Cup final in the professional era.

That is an exciting and compelling prospect for the future.

Jones's ambition had been to build such a strong leadership group in the camp that he would make himself 'redundant' (his own word) by the time of the final and, true to form, it was Farrell who led the final team meeting on the Friday night before the match. His message, a simple one, had been the mantra of England's training for the best part of four months: *Make good decisions constantly and control the physicality*.

For South Africa, Rassie Erasmus showed his hand early, declaring his playbook to make clear that there would be no tactical ambush in the final, but instead that he backed his team to win the contest by a well-known method: combat. It was an ominous sign and the words of a coach confident in the physical superiority of his team.

The head-to-head match-ups only built the sense of expectation for the final. The headlines wrote themselves: the Springbok 'Bomb Squad' taking on England's 'Kamikaze Kids'; the humble, brave captain from an impoverished township who idolised the England-beating 2007 champions; the Springbok head coach who only took the job to find a quick fix for a frail Test team.

Then there were the statistics. Itoje had won more turnovers than any other player at the World Cup, an extraordinary achievement for a second row. Underhill had made the most sack tackles (impact tackles sending the ball carrier backwards). But the Springboks had only lost one lineout in the entire tournament, while the six forwards waiting on their bench – world-class talent to a man and very much 'finishers' in the Eddie Jones mould – made crystal clear that South Africa's combative game plan would be defined by their physical threat.

Both teams were chasing history, too. From England's perspective, no team had beaten Australia, New Zealand and South Africa in the same edition of the World Cup. From South Africa's, no team had lost in the pool stages and gone on to win the final.

On Friday afternoon, after England's captain's run (the final training session held at the stadium the day before a Test match), Jones took a training session for some local Japanese schoolchildren, while the players were given space to rest up and spend important down time with family and friends.

By that stage of your preparation, there is nothing left to do but wait.

The final

England 12 – 32 South Africa

Tries
South Africa: Mapimpi, Kolbe.
Conversions
South Africa: Pollard (2).
Penalties
England: Farrell (4). South Africa: Pollard (6).

The first half: Basics and Dislocated Expectations

Even on the biggest stage of all, and even for the best players in the world, rugby relies on a simple idea: basics. The scrum, the lineout and the restart. Those three basics are the foundation upon which any team wins a game and it was these basics that would ultimately cost England the greatest prize of all.

You cannot fire a gun without bullets. You cannot fire a cannon from a canoe. You will not win a Test match if you cannot secure a platform of possession at the scrum, and you certainly will not beat one of the strongest teams in the world. I was reminded of my time with Yehuda exploring the concept of basics, and his insistence that every field of activity is comprised of several 'obligatory' steps: the methods, tactics or techniques that you have to follow 'to the letter' if you are to have any chance of success. The World Cup final became a cruel example of the fundamental necessity of these basics.

In Test match rugby the scrum is not just a restart button. It is a competition for possession and an opportunity to wrestle control of proceedings. England's ambition to pick up the tempo and keep the South African forwards on the move was suffocated under the strangling pressure of South Africa's style, both at the set piece and in contact.

The Springboks' plan was to be pragmatic and bullish – but if anyone was deceived by its seeming simplicity, they were quickly corrected. The forward pack were not only physically superior but, crucially, more imposing in their technical precision. The execution was flawless. South Africa's threat was that, if there was any indiscipline from an opponent, they had one of two options: take the three points with one of the most consistent kickers in world rugby in fly-half Handré Pollard, or kick to the corner and score a try off their driving maul. For England's tight five, the final became a cascade of punishing penalties at the scrum, and Pollard alone kicked 22 points.

The game began with all the tentative characteristics of a World Cup final and some ominous errors from England. The opening kick-off receipt was slightly disjointed. After forty-three seconds, Courtney Lawes was caught on the wrong side of the breakdown and, in the eyes of referee Jérôme Garcès, failed to make sufficient effort to roll away. Pollard missed a relatively easy penalty and the nerves from both teams were evident. It was to England's cost that he would not miss again.

England were forced to cope with a number of dislocated expectations and the pressure seemed to tell. The team bus was late to the stadium, something for which Jones had rehearsed in the summer but still an inconvenience that curtailed the warm-up routine, and worse was to come in the third minute. Kyle Sinckler, one of the tournament's few consistently outstanding performers, was knocked out while wrapping up Makazole Mapimpi in the tackle.

The clock was paused at two minutes fifty-three seconds for more than five minutes. These are precisely the kinds of scenario for which you plan a process, a way to manage the unforeseen. It was an unanticipated early injury to a fulcrum of England's attack – at the set piece and in the loose – and a sudden change to key personnel. Sinckler's link play at first receiver off front-foot ball had been a huge asset in the quarter-final and semi-final, never mind his strength and technique as England's superior tighthead.

Tightheads have become a priceless commodity in the professional era, often the highest earners in any club side. It is the tighthead who can do most to disrupt the opposition's scrum on their put-in and it is the tighthead who can do most to establish a solid platform on his own side's put-in. Dan Cole, intended to be a finisher on England's bench but heralded as the stronger scrummager, was brought on to play seventy-seven minutes, perhaps the longest stint of his Test match career.

Meanwhile, England's backline were making nervy decisions under pressure and fumbling the ball in crucial areas of the pitch. They made two sweeping, hopeful passes inside their own dead-ball area. It was an ambitious, perhaps courageous tactic – running the ball back might force the South African backs to stay up in defence and to commit fewer players in the back field – but the threat lacked incisiveness and South Africa continued to look comfortable without the ball.

The errors continued. There were some poor loose passes to ground. When Farrell had to pick up a ball from Billy Vunipola off the base of the scrum, England were penalised at the breakdown and Pollard did not make the same mistake again. The Springboks took a 3-0 lead.

Referee Garcès is known for his patient leniency at the breakdown and for allowing a fierce contest on the floor, and here it prevented England from matching the ferocious tempo of their semi-final as the Springboks were able to ensnare English forwards in a breakdown grapple. England tried to get things moving. There was a planned two-phase move off the lineout and Youngs forced the play, passing straight into touch after Faf de Klerk had read the blindside switch and rushed up to block the move.

England were not clicking but they needed field position. Ford tried to take command of proceedings. He pumped the ball towards the South Africa 22. May chased well and suddenly provided a platform to attack. But England were not able to capitalise and it was then that the lineout stuttered, costing them a vital shot at managing both territory and possession.

As predicted, it was a physically abrasive game in the contact, and South Africa lost Mbongeni Mbonambi to a head-injury assessment and Lodewyk de Jager to a shoulder injury. More alarmingly for England, more errors were creeping into the game: uncharacteristic knock-ons, passes missing their intended target, spills under the high ball, mistimed running lines and – worst of all – a set piece creaking under the pressure.

In the twenty-second minute, after a more solid passage of play, England drew level with a Farrell penalty. Yet, just as they were finding their rhythm, South Africa were allowed to respond. There was an England error from the kick-off, with Itoje knocking back to Curry, who knocked on. These tiny mistakes after scoring are the crucial moments of high-stakes Test match rugby. For the first time in Japan, England's basics were not providing a platform. The scrum following the knock-on saw England concede another penalty and South Africa pulled three points ahead again.

Scrummaging deficiencies aside, the other strongest statement of the first half was an extended period of consecutive-phase defence from South Africa. England played twenty-five phases in South Africa's 22 – an extraordinary statistic – but the Springboks held out through courageous defence and street-smart infringements. England simply could not cross the try line, but they drew level through a penalty. It was 6–6.

But again, mistakes were repeated. South Africa pulled ahead within minutes after a breakdown infringement. England were simply not able to manage the breakdown as decisively as they had the week before. For the first time in Japan, Curry, Underhill and Vunipola looked like a back-row unit who had only played together for the first time three months previously, rather than being born at the hip.

It was 6–9, but what might have been a flattering half-time scoreline was compounded by another unlikely England mistake, this time a handling error when Daly, already targeted by South Africa under the high ball, fumbled while trying to regather possession on his 10-metre line.

Yet the story of the first half was one of the set piece. Six scrums, three South Africa penalties, 6–12.

No side had ever come back from a half-time deficit to win the World Cup.

The second half: T-CUP

At half-time Jones had to act. He had to be decisive to give England a chance to earn parity at the set piece, to try to fix the basics, so he sacrificed Lawes's exceptional breakdown and defensive work for George Kruis, a set-piece expert. It brought fluency to the lineout but sadly made little difference to the scrum. South Africa won a penalty with the first of the second half. Pollard made it 6-15 from only just inside England's half, the exact spot from which he had practised during his warm-up.

England tried another change. Bringing on Joe Marler for Mako Vunipola was the last roll of the dice in the front row, but by the forty-eighth minute, England had conceded five penalties in eight scrums. More punishingly still, seven of the ten penalties England conceded in the game were within their own half and well within the range of Pollard's right boot.

The Springboks continued to smother England at the tackle. Their pragmatic plan was working, supported by the heavyweight artillery that was stopping England gaining any momentum and forcing more errors.

There was one last stand. On the fiftieth minute there was a dominant scrum from England. Garcès might have played a longer advantage, but he blew his whistle and Farrell made it 9-15. Minutes later, Watson made a tap tackle on Pollard and Curry was in a perfect jackal position over the ball to earn another penalty, but Farrell's kick crept just to the right of the post. South Africa then put together their most clinical series of phases: recovering the 22 drop out, taking a clever lineout, setting up a superb maul. A huge hit from Manu Tuilagi on Duane Vermeulen gave Farrell one last desperate chance to take the game within a try, and it was 12-18 with twenty minutes on the clock.

Extra time did not look impossible. England's football team needed extra time in 1966, the 2003 rugby team needed extra time in Sydney, the 2019 cricket team needed a super over at

Lord's, and there were millions of TV viewers hoping that if England could match the Springboks on the penalty count, then they might just draw level and maybe, just maybe . . .

Jones took off Underhill and George to back his finishers to work a late miracle. But instead, No 8 Vermeulen continued to make relentless carries into traffic, making ground, recycling possession and controlling the scoreboard. Assistant referee Romain Poite saw Watson change his line of running to impede fair competition on Daly's gathering of a kick, and it was another shot for Pollard to keep the scoreboard ticking.

By then the Springboks had started to gallop. They strung together a much quicker series of phases – from power to panache – executing a more expansive style of play. The ambition of South Africa's box-kicking strategy had been to compete and win possession, counter-ruck and turn over the ball or, at the very least, sacrifice possession for better field possession and disrupt at the breakdown. In the final quarter, they added to that repertoire by spraying the ball wide off quick possession and posing problems out wide.

Then came the killer blow. Some quick, slick handling, a delicate chip on from Makazole Mapimpi and a perfect one-two with Lukhanyo Am as he passed the ball immediately back to Mapimpi with the line in front of him. It was 12–25 and England were out of touch.

It was a sign of how desperate England were to make something happen that by the seventieth minute, the backline was an almost complete change from the starting line-up: Farrell had moved from centre to fly-half, Tuilagi to inside centre, Daly from full-back to wing; Joseph had been brought on at outside centre, Slade at centre, before moving to full-back.

South Africa had previous in shoring up their defence in finals – in 1995 they even prevented Jonah Lomu's prolific New Zealand team from scoring a try, and in 2007 they had done the same to England. Here they shut out England again, becoming the first team to win the Rugby Championship and the World Cup in the same year.

In the final ten minutes, South Africa had the opportunity to end with a finishing flourish and to really demonstrate they were more than a side built on brawn. It was telling of their more open play that it was the wingers on either flank who scored the two tries. The second was created by a moment of magic from Cheslin Kolbe down the right flank – firework feet and a mighty fend – and the game was gone: 12-32.

At the start of this book, I mentioned how sport can throw up some unexpected symmetries. During the 2007 final, future England captain Owen Farrell was sitting in the stands, then aged sixteen, looking after Lawrence Dallaglio's children. Meanwhile, on a different continent, South Africa captain Siya Kolisi was watching the game in a local township tavern in Zwide because he had no TV at home.

Twelve years later, the two men were locked in combat in Tokyo, and if the England captain was going to lose to anyone, it is hard to think of a worthier opponent. The young scholar, a boy who first saw the ocean aged fourteen and burst into tears, who dreamed of wearing the green jersey against all the odds, became the first black captain to lead the Springboks to victory in the World Cup final.

Kolisi, still breathless at the final whistle, had the wherewithal to recognise their remarkable achievement. 'I have never seen South Africa like this,' he said. 'We were playing for the people back home. We can achieve anything if we work together as one.'

The aftermath: Teamship

England's huddle said it all. In the face of the most heartbreaking scenario a professional rugby player can know on the pitch, they stuck together.

Soon after the final whistle, Ben Youngs was sitting on an advertising hoarding, reflecting on what might have been, Billy Vunipola's shirt was bloodied, Sinckler's shirt was still a crisp white after his match had been so cruelly cut short. The England players were magnanimous in defeat, but they are competitive beasts and the memories will rankle because they landed in Japan with a different intention. Farrell gathered his troops together for one final talk. He was looking to the future.

Behind them, smiling in green jerseys, was the other side of the coin.

For South Africa, these were glorious scenes. Rassie Erasmus had done an outstanding leadership job with South Africa, taking on the director of rugby role in 2017 and realising his biggest priority was to rehabilitate the struggling Springboks, down to eighth in the world rankings and flailing in the Rugby Championship, losing to the All Blacks by nearly 60 points. He decided to delegate his wider organisational responsibilities concerning the running of the national game and focus instead on its top team.

Notably, he had only two years to prepare for the tournament, while almost every other coach had a four-year run-up. He took on coaching the national side as an interim fix and quietly but consistently built belief and harmony in the set-up. It was impressive leadership in underlining the value of simplicity: doing the basics of the game better than anybody else in the world.

It was a wonderful sight to see South Africa president Cyril Ramaphosa back in the No 6 shirt that Mandela had worn twenty-four years previously to play a part in the presentation ceremony and to mark this significant chapter in his country's history. The Springboks became the second team to emulate New Zealand and win three World Cups. England have now suffered the sting of three World Cup final defeats.

The future: Success from setbacks

The leadership group in England's team was the engine of their success in Japan and their disciplined culture will not erode away because of eighty minutes of rugby.

Take the captain: putting aside his competitive hunger, Farrell studied leadership at university and chose to write his thesis on reflective learning. He spent more hours poring over team footage than any other player in the camp. He made his first professional start, aged seventeen, the year after watching the 2007 final. Ask him about his debut for England in 2012 and all he can remember are his mistakes. He will learn so much from this tournament.

Take a future England captain in the making: Itoje has also

long been fascinated by business and military leadership, speaking before the tournament about how true leadership is magnifying your role in a way that most benefits the team. Within two hours of the final whistle, and with a nod to his heritage, Itoje tweeted the following Nigerian proverb: 'When a Ram goes backwards it is not retreating, it moves back to gather more strength.' Just like Farrell, he was already thinking about the next step.

Take the team: with their deep history and bonds, there is a genuine sense of unity and cohesion. Four of them played at the same school; nine of them play for the same club.

For Jones, there should be no recriminations, just heartfelt commiserations. Professional sport can be a fickle business and the successes of his team should not be airbrushed from history. He painstakingly put together a brilliant, innovative rugby programme to give England every chance of winning. And he was dignified in defeat.

The outcome was not what he desired, but that does not destroy what he has built.

England's sweet chariot will ride again.

ACKNOWLEDGEMENTS

A huge thank you and love to Jayne, Jess, Joe and Freddie for their patience, advice and support. It's not always easy living with a self-confessed obsessive.

It has been wonderful to work with my publisher, Roddy Bloomfield, and the talented team at Hodder. Thank you, Roddy, once again, for encouraging me to follow *Winning!* with *How to Win*.

Furthermore, it has been an absolute joy to team up with Luke Benedict again in writing this book. We produced a lot of column inches together during his years as a sports journalist for the *Daily Mail*, and I am indebted to Luke for his talent and huge contribution.

As always, Matt Moore and Angela Russell have kept me ticking over, reaching deadlines and managing the process. Thank you both.

Finally, without having had the opportunity to work with the most talented players, athletes and coaches that the United Kingdom can produce, I would not be in a position to share what I have learned with you.

I will always be deeply grateful for my time spent with them – and for what they have taught me.

PICTURE ACKNOWLEDGEMENTS

The author and publisher would like to thank the following for permission to reproduce photographs:

Section One

Russell Cheyne/Allsport/Getty Images, David Rogers/Getty Images, Bob Thomas Sports Photography/Getty Images, Mike Hewitt/Allsport/ Getty Images, David Rogers/Allsport/Getty Images, David Rogers/Getty Images, Bob Thomas Sports Photography/Getty Images, Tom Jenkins/Getty Images, Dean Lewins/EPA/Shutterstock, Clive Mason/Getty Images, David Davies/PA Archive/PA Images, Dita Alangkara/AP/Shutterstock, Ryan Pierse/Getty Images, Charlie Crowhurst/Getty Images, David Davies/PA Wire/PA Images, Cameron Spencer/Getty Images, William West/AFP via Getty Images, Mike Hewitt/Getty Images, Michael Steele/Getty Images.

Section Two